# CDC'S COMPLETE GUIDE TO HEALTHY TRAVEL

## THE CENTERS FOR DISEASE CONTROL AND PREVENTION'S RECOMMENDATIONS FOR INTERNATIONAL TRAVELERS

> ## YOUR PASSPORT TO GREAT TRAVEL!

*From the Foreword by Charles D. Ericsson, M.D.,*
*Editor-in-Chief, Journal of Travel Medicine:*

"This practical guide enables travelers to read a chapter about the region to which they are traveling and learn what is important for them to do to remain healthy. The text is clearly written and refreshingly jargon-free...

Travel medicine has become specialized enough that many primary care physicians simply have not been adequately trained in specific details...

...a well-informed traveler is an important deterrent against illness during travel. Using this book will enable any person to be a strong advocate for their own preventative health care."

## ABOUT THE AUTHOR

Kent C. Davis is a health consultant who makes his home in Alpharetta, Georgia. He designed both the CDC's automated telephone system and their fax information system to provide travel health recommendations to the general public. This book is the next step in Kent's efforts to bring the most up-to-date and jargon-free travel health information to travelers everywhere.

## HIT THE OPEN ROAD -
## WITH OPEN ROAD PUBLISHING!

Open Road Publishing now has guide books to exciting, fun destinations on four continents. As veteran travelers, our goal is to bring you the best travel guides available anywhere!

No small task, but here's what we offer:

• All Open Road travel guides are written by authors with a distinct, opinionated point of view – not some sterile committee or team of writers. Our authors are experts in the areas covered and are polished writers.

• Our guides are geared to people who want great vacations, great value, and great tips for both standard tourist sights *and* fun, unique alternatives.

• We're strong on the basics, but we also provide terrific choices for those looking to get off the beaten path and *experience* the country or city – not just *see* it or pass through it.

• We give you the best, but we also tell you about the worst and what to avoid. Nobody should waste their time and money on their hard-earned vacation because of bad or inadequate travel advice.

• Our guides assume nothing. We tell you everything you need to know to have the trip of a lifetime – presented in a fun, literate, no-nonsense style.

• And, above all, we welcome your input, ideas, and suggestions to help us put out the best travel guides possible.

# CDC'S COMPLETE GUIDE TO HEALTHY TRAVEL

## THE CENTERS FOR DISEASE CONTROL AND PREVENTION'S RECOMMENDATIONS FOR INTERNATIONAL TRAVELERS

**YOUR PASSPORT TO GREAT TRAVEL!**

## KENT C. DAVIS

## OPEN ROAD PUBLISHING

1st Edition

# TABLE OF CONTENTS

# FOREWORD

As we near the 21st century, a new focus in American medicine is emerging. Regardless of whether our health care system is managed, regulated, insurance-based or fee-for-service, the new focus is prevention. As we have become more sophisticated about costs of medical care in one area of medicine after another, it is clear that it is much less expensive to prevent disease than it is to intervene acutely with evaluation and treatment of active disease. A corollary of the ascendent role of prevention in medicine has been the development, just in the last two decades, of the field of travel medicine.

The academic discipline of travel medicine has rapidly developed recognition as a full-fledged specialty. An International Society of Travel Medicine now draws together expert nurses, physicians, and others from around the world every two years to share results of research and the latest approaches to disease prevention. This society now even publishes its own journal for the dissemination of knowledge. Regional societies and associations are also springing up.

The clinical discipline has evolved well beyond the immunization clinic that focused on what shots were necessary for entry into a country. Exemplary travel medicine clinics now pride themselves on educating travelers about how to avoid risky behavior that might lead to disease. For instance, malaria can be nearly completely prevented in most parts of malaria-infested tropical countries simply by taking one pill a week. Yet pills are not 100% protective and there really is no substitute for: "Don't get bit by the mosquito in the first place!" This requires understanding the proper use of DEET-containing insect repellents and bug killing sprays. Additionally, mosquito netting might be advisable, but recommendations depend on the nature of the traveler's sleeping arrangements.

Likewise, traveler's diarrhea can now be very effectively treated by medications that travelers can carry with them, just in case. The best approach, however, is common sense avoidance of risky food and water and adherence to simple rules of thumb like "Heat kills germs."

The only immunization mandated for travel (and only in some countries) is yellow fever. The modern travel clinic, however, will want to bring routine immunizations up-to-date. Specialized immunizations such as typhoid, polio, hepatitis A or B, meningococcal, rabies or Japanese B encephalitis will be considered based on the traveler's itinerary.

One problem is that travel clinics and travel specialists are not always equivalently trained. Some clinics are run entirely by nurses who are often very knowledgeable. Physicians can be primarily trained in disciplines such as family practice, emergency medicine, or infectious diseases, but there is currently no certification process for calling oneself a travel medicine expert.

For many years the **Centers for Disease Control and Prevention** (CDC) has published a technical reference book titled *Health Information for International Travel* for health care providers. In 1988, due to increased public awareness, CDC contracted with Kent Davis to help develop an automated telephone system to provide travel health recommendations in a simplified format to the general public. Then, in 1992, Mr. Davis was again contracted to develop a fax information system to furnish concise health recommendations to most travelers in written form. These CDC recommendations were developed to help travelers cope with uncertainties and to empower travelers to assume responsibility for their own preventative medicine in a medical system that often will not insist on or pay for prevention.

Now Kent Davis has adapted the CDC materials into the handy text that follows. This practical guide enables travelers to read a chapter about the region to which they are traveling and learn what is important for them to do to remain healthy. The text is clearly written and refreshingly jargon-free. Especially if travelers do not have access to a travel clinic, they can feel confident that they are reminding, if not educating, their personal physicians about the most important issues.

Travel medicine has become specialized enough that many primary care physicians simply have not been adequately trained in specific details. This book is especially useful for the frequent traveler with multiple destinations. Likewise, it should be an invaluable resource for corporations, even if they have their own travel medicine facility, because the recommendations carry the authoritative endorsement of CDC experts. Extensive use of this book by travelers should help to bring about consistent and reliable practice among all physicians and nurses, regardless of whether they are travel experts.

The bottom line is that a well-informed traveler is an important deterrent against illness during travel. Using this book will enable any person to be a strong advocate for their own preventative health care.

Bon voyage and travel healthy!

**– Charles D. Ericsson, M.D.**
*Professor and Head, Clinical Infectious Diseases, University of Texas– Houston Medical School; Director, Travel Medicine Clinic at Hermann Hospital, Houston, Texas; and Editor-in-Chief, Journal of Travel Medicine.*

# ACKNOWLEDGMENTS

This project began in 1988 with a phone call from Jack Brantley. It was earlier that year when Judith Aguilar and Debbie Jones of The Centers for Disease Control and Prevention (CDC) had approached Jacks's voice services company seeking help for their overloaded staff. The public, it seemed, had just discovered CDC as a source of health information, and the CDC's researchers were now being inundated with phone calls. An automated health information system accessed via the telephone seemed to be the answer to all concerned. Jack asked me if I wanted the consulting assignment and I jumped at the chance.

With a team of telecommunication specialists, Bob Nacon, Warren Smay, Georgia Morrow, Paul Humphries, a young and budding voice talent Liz Storch, and an excellent voice studio and engineer Brandon Wade, we established CDC's Voice Information System (VIS).

One of the biggest successes for the CDC VIS was the Traveler's Health Hotline. Roz Dewart, program chief for Health Information for International Travel, allowed me the opportunity of developing this massive system and worked patiently with me for almost a year during its creation. After Betsy Wade mentioned it in her *New York Times* column, it became an overnight success.

From the early days, we knew that delivering health information by phone was not the best means of transmission - it was just too slow. For example, the original Travelers Health Hotline required 40 minutes of telephone time to deliver the complete script to a caller. So in 1989, I began experimenting with fax transmission.

Mike Clark programmed a test fax system and I wrote some information for malaria. I then approached Dr. Hans Lobel of the malaria section with the concept. He encouraged me to use the information as a test and allowed me to speak and demonstrate the concept at the International Medical Society meeting. We received an overwhelming response.

When Judith Aguilar was promoted, Diane Wylie became the CDC Project Officer. She further encouraged me to expand and develop the VIS. Then in 1991, Diane handed me and the VIS off to Dottie Knight, who became a zealot for the system.

By this time, the test fax system had accumulated a wealth of knowledge which I used to develop the concepts in this book. Working with Roz Dewart, I wrote a set of documents which demonstrated the power of the fax system to CDC management. The idea was so intuitive and impressive that in 1992 CDC's FAX information system was born. I'm grateful to CDC's management: Dr. Alan Hinman, Dr. Howard Ory, Jim Seligman, Dr. Charles McCance and Tony Perez for allowing us to produce this information and create CDC's VIS/FAX system.

The content of this book was developed based on statistical results from the VIS, continued feedback from travelers, and the research efforts of many at CDC. The list of professionals at CDC who contributed to these documents in one way or another is impressive. These men and women are, in many respects, at the head of the class in their chosen specialities, and I am deeply indebted to their efforts and their patience as we tried to make this text readable and yet informative: Dr. Miriam Alter, Dr. William Atkinson, Ann Barber, Dr. Robert Craven, Dr. David Dennis, Brenda Garza, Dr. Barbara Herwaldt, Dr. Duane Gubler, Dr. Hans Lobel, Linda Moyer, Dr. Jose Rigau, Dr. Lawrence Schonberger, Dr. John Stewart, Dr. Robert Tauxe, Dr. Theodore Tsai, Dr. Jay Wenger, and Skip Wolf.

Finally, I am grateful to my family: Mom and Dad, who encouraged me; my wife, Becky, and my children, Micah, Seth, and Amber, who gave me love, understanding, and the time to participate in this project.

# 1. INTRODUCTION

Staying healthy abroad remains an overriding concern for the traveling public. In 1996, nearly one million travelers sought health recommendations from **The Centers for Disease Control & Prevention** (CDC), the federal agency based in Atlanta responsible for researching infectious diseases and making recommendations to the public. Designed for the traveling layman, and arranged in a region-by-region user-friendly format, Open Road Publishing presents CDC's original and authoritative information.

This book is written for today's busy and well-informed traveler. The unique format of the book contains 16 short, specific geographic chapters, along with 16 appendices. In clear and jargon-free language, each chapter categorizes diseases by their mode of transmission: insect-borne, food and water, and person to person contact.

Each disease is described by general information, risk to the traveler, travel requirements, and prevention information. Every region of the world is covered, and the information is designed the same way throughout, so that each chapter presents the same kind of information – but tailored to each destination. The material in this book can help provide the basic information required for traveling anywhere outside the United States, and it was designed for the 1990s lifestyle. Based on CDC's information, this book is authoritative, concise, informative, and easily understood, and it covers the information needed for most travelers. Our goal is not to provide an encyclopedia on all aspects of travel, but instead to provide usable information in a consolidated format.

In the end, the more a traveler knows about diseases, risks of infection, and prevention, the better the chances for a pleasant and fun experience while traveling. It will enable you to go to your doctor's office and confidently discuss the shots and medications you may need to take for your trip abroad. In this respect, this one-of-a-kind book can empower you to assume responsibility for your own preventative medicine.

# 2. OVERVIEW

This book has been designed to be extremely easy to use!

In the pages that follow you'll find a collection of up-to-date, accurate, and above all *authoritative* information that provides the basic health recommendations for international travelers as determined by the **Centers for Disease Control and Prevention – CDC** for short.

The information is arranged to give you the necessary important advice easily and quickly. It is not a medical reference book, where you must examine all the content for relevancy to your situation and know a lot of technical jargon. Instead, the information has been researched, organized, and presented in self-contained chapters. More than two million people have received the regional fax information and in every survey they have expressed gratitude and appreciation – and an overwhelming number of people have asked for this information in book form.

Many readers have commented that the best way to use the information is to read it thoroughly and then discuss it with their doctor. This methodology allows you to formulate your questions and also provides your health care provider with the opportunity of adjusting recommendations to your specific needs.

There are two major sections - Geographical Recommendations and the Appendices.

## GEOGRAPHICAL RECOMMENDATIONS

This is where all travelers should start, for the chapters in this section compose the heart of the book. You should begin by reading the chapter covering the region to which you will be traveling. Each chapter lists the most important health advice for travelers destined for that specific region. Although additional diseases and risks could have been included, through years of experience and analysis, CDC and I concluded these were the more important health risks.

Knowing that most travelers have limited preparation time, we chose to format and limit the information to those facts that would most increase your ability to prevent an infection. Therefore, each chapter is divided into disease categories - insect borne, food and water borne, and diseases transmitted through contact. Within the chapters, the information has been arranged in order of priority - malaria to rabies. For each of these diseases, general information, risk of infection, and prevention recommendations have been listed.

I've also included a summary of information for review. The benefit of this book is that you will only have to read the chapters for the regions to which you are traveling in order to have an understanding of your health risks. For those travelers who want to learn more about a topic, additional information has been included in the appendices.

## THE APPENDICES
Although these documents are more detailed and technical, the information is understandable by most readers (all except the Comprehensive Yellow Fever Vaccination Requirements were authored by the CDC). They were designed to add depth and to more fully explain a subject introduced in the geographical section.

Two of the more important appendices are Food and Water Precautions and Vaccine Recommendations:

• **Food and Water Precautions**: Remember food and water borne infections are the number one health problem associated with international travel. You will find additional simple and practical guidelines that will help you stay healthy abroad while enjoying the local cuisine. Remember, the cause of Traveler's Diarrhea is varied and there is no magic vaccine or pill for universal prevention, so day-to-day precautions must be observed.

• **Vaccine Recommendations**: Universal vaccine information and recommendations are listed by age groups - travelers less than two years of age and travelers over two years of age.

Other appendices provide additional information concerning malaria and the drugs used for malaria, yellow fever vaccination requirements, insect diseases, dengue fever, Japanese encephalitis, hepatitis A and B, cholera, HIV/AIDS, and rabies.

The idea behind this guide is to give you the necessary information as quickly as possible so that you will have time to plan your itinerary and safely enjoy your travel abroad.

## HOW TO USE THIS BOOK

Follow these three easy steps:

1. In the table of contents find the world region to which you are traveling. Turn to that chapter in the book and read the chapter. If you have any questions, list them on paper.

2. If required, refer to the appropriate appendix for additional information.

3. After reading the information, consult with your health care provider and adapt any of the recommendations to your specific needs.

## THE CDC & STAYING HEALTHY ABROAD

Staying healthy abroad has a lot to do with understanding the risks involved, taking reasonable precautions to protect oneself, and using common sense. The big questions are: (1) What are the risks? and (2) How can I protect myself? Specific authoritative information addressing these two questions is in great demand.

Although there are other books written on the subject of travel health, one of the most authoritative and popular sources of information is The Centers for Disease Control and Prevention (CDC). This book culminates eight years of formulating and providing health information to the general public by CDC professionals and myself.

In the middle to late 1980's (CDC) was facing a new problem - too many telephone calls from an increasingly inquisitive public. Since its inception, CDC was designed and organized to provide information to the public health community and to health care providers. However, with the HIV epidemic, CDC became a household name and was viewed as a health resource to the American public.

Consequently, CDC's disease experts, the researchers, epidemiologists, and health specialists, were overloaded with new informational demands from the general public. CDC needed an easy way to handle the increasing number of telephone calls and provide service to the American public.

In 1988, I became a consultant to CDC for the expressed purpose of developing an information dissemination system. Since CDC is really a collection of "Centers," for example, The National Center for Infectious Disesaes, each containing multiple divisions, spread out over multiple sites in a number of different states, the project encompassed working with many project teams, each team with expertise in specific diseases. The first project was designed for the Influenza Branch to provide weekly updates for flu activity throughout the United States and was highly successful. During the last eight years, over 100 other projects were designed and implemented.

The **Center for Prevention Services** had for years published a book entitled *Health Information for International Travel*, which was a technical reference guide for health care providers. This branch of the CDC was staffing a "telephone help desk," but unfortunately the budgets could not keep up with the needs. An analysis of CDC's public inquiries provided a number of facts, the two most important of which were "most travelers were ignorant of the situations they were going to face," and "a vast discrepancy existed between the questions asked by travelers and the important information required to stay healthy."

It took almost six months and the help of scores of CDC experts to write and produce an automated voice travel service. It had hundreds of messages, covering potential diseases in a regional format. Although the telephone service was extremely popular, we all knew it took 20 to 40 minutes of listening to receive the required information. Our analysis of this new service showed that many callers were not receiving all the information they needed to stay healthy abroad because of the time and cost of a long distance call.

In 1990, I began investigating other technologies and decided to test a fax information service. The positive public comments received from this test were so powerful, it convinced CDC to allow me to develop new information for the "fax system." By 1991, I had written a new group of concise documents for international travelers, and this information became the heart of CDC's health and travel recommendations to the general public. The popularity of this information went far beyond our wildest expectations. In 1995, the voice and fax systems at CDC were handling over 700,000 calls, delivering over 2,250,000 voice messages, and faxing over 1,250,000 pages of prevention information.

However, the number one public request was that this information be made available in bookstores – and this book is the response.

# 3. NORTH AFRICA

## COUNTRIES IN THIS REGION
Algeria
Canary Islands
Egypt
Libyan Arab Jamahiriya (Libya)
Morocco
Tunisia

**NORTH AFRICA TRAVELER'S OVERVIEW**

*Travelers to North Africa may be exposed to potential diseases from a number of sources. **The most frequently reported illness is traveler's diarrhea**, but North Africa contains a variety of diseases transmitted by:*
- *insects,*
- *contaminated food and water, or*
- *close contact with infected people.*

*In this chapter, specific diseases, their causes, symptoms, geographic areas of risk, and prevention recommendations or requirement information are discussed under their topical headings. As a general guideline, in order to reduce the risk of infection, travelers must:*
- *protect themselves from insects,*
- *ensure the quality of their food and drinking water,*
- *be knowledgeable about potential diseases in the region to be visited,*
- *receive all recommended vaccines and preventive medications.*

*In addition, travelers should note that diseases are not restricted to cleanly defined geographical areas. For example, mosquitoes can fly over city or country borders, so all travelers should protect themselves by taking the basic preventive precautions as described under each section and disease. Where appropriate, more detailed information is referenced in the Appendices.*

## DISEASES TRANSMITTED BY INSECTS

Many diseases are transmitted through the bite of infected insects such as mosquitoes, flies, fleas, ticks and lice. In general, **travelers must protect themselves from insect bites**. Travelers are at a higher risk for insect bites if they participate in outdoor activities during night time hours from dusk to dawn when mosquitoes bite, or if their living accommodations are unscreened. If a mosquito net is unlikely to be available, consider buying a portable mosquito net.

## PREVENTING INSECT BITES

To reduce the risk of mosquito bites, travelers should remain in well-screened areas, use mosquito nets, and wear clothes that cover most of the body. Travelers should also take insect repellent with them to use on any exposed areas of the skin. The most effective compound in a repellent is **DEET**, which may be listed as an ingredient on repellant labels as "**N,N-diethyl meta-toluamide**." Check the repellent label to ensure DEET is an ingredient.

Travelers should note, however, that insect repellents containing DEET should always be used according to label directions and sparingly on children. **Avoid applying high-concentration (greater than 35%) products to the skin, particularly on children, and refrain from applying repellent to portions of the hands that are likely to come in contact with the eyes and mouth**. Pediatric insect repellents with 6-10% DEET are available without prescription in many drug stores. In rare instances, toxic reactions or other problems have developed after contact with DEET.

Travelers should also purchase a flying insect-killing spray to use in living and sleeping areas during the evening and night. For greater protection, clothing and bednets can be soaked in or sprayed with **permethrin**, which is an insect repellent licensed for use on clothing. If applied according to the directions, permethrin will repel insects from clothing for several weeks. Portable mosquito bednets, repellents containing DEET, and permethrin can be purchased in hardware, backpacking, and military surplus stores.

## MALARIA

Malaria is a serious parasitic infection transmitted to humans by an Anopheles mosquito. These mosquitoes bite at night, from dusk to dawn. Symptoms of malaria range from flu-like symptoms with fever, general achiness, headache, and fatigue, to a cycle of shaking chills, high fever, and sweating. If left untreated, malaria can cause anemia, kidney failure, coma, and death. Drugs are available to help prevent a malaria infection.

However, in spite of all protective measures, travelers occasionally develop malaria. Therefore, while traveling and up to one year after returning home, travelers should seek medical evaluation for any flu-like illness.

### Risk to Traveler
*Limited Risk*
Only travelers to **Egypt** who will spend the night in rural areas of the Nile Delta, the El Faiyum area, the oases, and southern Egypt near the Sudan border need to take a weekly **chloroquine tablet**. Persons taking cruises on the Nile do not need preventive medication. The dominant form of malaria is *P. vivax*, which has not been reported to be resistant to the drug chloroquine (see below).

*Minor Risk*
In **Algeria**, **Egypt**, **Libya**, **Western Sahara** and **Morocco**, there is a very limited risk of malaria. However, travelers following the usual tourist itineraries do not need drugs for malaria prevention.

*No Risk*
The Canary Islands and Tunisia.

## Prevention & Recommendations
Travelers at risk for malaria should take the prescription drug **chloroquine** to prevent malaria. The weekly dosage for an adult is 500 mg (salt) once a week. This drug should be taken one week before entering a malarious area, weekly while there, and weekly for 4 weeks after leaving the malarious area. No other anti-malarial drugs are needed.

In addition to using drugs to prevent malaria and treat a possible malaria attack, travelers should use measures to reduce exposure to malaria-carrying mosquitoes and protect themselves from mosquito bites. Remember, these mosquitoes bite mainly during the evening and night, from dusk to dawn.

Additional general malaria information, as well as specific information for women who are pregnant or children, is found in *Appendix 1, Malaria Information.*

## YELLOW FEVER
Yellow fever is a viral disease transmitted to humans by a mosquito bite. The mosquitoes are most active during the evening hours. Symptoms range from fever, chills, headache, and vomiting to jaundice, internal bleeding, and kidney failure. Death occurs in about 5% of those infected. There is no specific drug to treat an infection of yellow fever, therefore prevention of infection is important.

## Risk to Traveler
There is little or no risk of yellow fever infection in North Africa. However, if you are traveling to **Algeria**, **Egypt**, **Libya**, and **Tunisia** a yellow fever vaccination and certificate for entry may be required. Read the following requirements carefully.

## Prevention
Yellow fever vaccination, a one-dose shot, is effective for up to 10 years for the prevention of yellow fever and may be administered to adults and

children over 9 months of age. This vaccine is only administered at designated yellow fever centers, usually your local health department. **The vaccine and the official certificate become effective 10 days after vaccination**. Travelers at continued risk need a booster and a new certificate every 10 years.

*Travelers who should not be immunized include:*
- Infants under 4 months.
- Persons severely allergic to eggs.
- Pregnant women or people whose immune systems are not functioning normally.

In addition to the vaccine, travelers should use measures to reduce exposure to mosquitoes and protect themselves from mosquito bites. Remember, these mosquitoes bite mainly during the evening hours.

## Yellow Fever Certificate
After immunization, an International Certificate of Vaccination is issued and is valid 10 days after vaccination to meet entry and exit requirements for all countries. The Certificate is good for 10 years. **You must take the Certificate with you**.

## Medical Waiver
Travelers who have a medical reason not to receive the yellow fever vaccine should obtain a medical waiver. Most countries will accept a medical waiver for persons with a medical reason not to receive the vaccine (e.g. infants less than 4 months old, pregnant women, persons hypersensitive to eggs, or those with an immunosuppressed condition.) When required, CDC recommends obtaining written waivers from consular or embassy officials before departure. Follow these guidelines:
- A physician's letter clearly stating the medical reason not to receive the vaccine might be acceptable to some governments.
- It should be written on letterhead stationery and bear the stamp used by a health department or official immunization center to validate the International Certificate of Vaccination.
- Check embassies or consulates for specific waiver requirements.

## Recommendations & Requirements
*Special Note: Some countries in North Africa require yellow fever vaccination for entry*. In general, CDC does not recommend a yellow fever vaccination when traveling to a North African country from countries not infected with yellow fever. However, some countries require a yellow fever

**TRAVELING FROM ANY OF THE FOLLOWING "ENDEMIC" YELLOW FEVER INFECTED COUNTRIES**

**Africa:**

Angola
Benin
Burundi
Burkina Faso
Cameroon
Central African Republic
Chad
Congo
Cote d'Ivoire, (Ivory Coast)
Equatorial Guinea
Ethiopia
Gabon
Gambia
Ghana
Guinea
Guinea Bissau
Kenya
Liberia
Mali
Mauritania
Niger
Nigeria
Rwanda
Sao Tome and Principe
Senegal
Sierra Leone
Somalia
Sudan
Tanzania
Togo
Uganda
Zaire

**South America:**

Bolivia
Brazil
Colombia
Ecuador
French Guiana
Guyana
Panama
Peru
Suriname
Venezuela

**TRAVELING TO THESE NORTH AFRICAN COUNTRIES**

Algeria
Egypt
(In addition, if you are traveling to Egypt from
- Botswana,
- Malawi, or
- Zambia,
you will need a yellow fever vaccination.)
Libya
Tunisia

**Yellow Fever Certificate Required**

vaccination when travelers arrive from certain African and South American countries. Therefore, sometimes the easiest and safest thing to do is to get a yellow fever vaccination and a signed certificate to take with you.

The Canary Islands and Morocco have no yellow fever vaccination entry requirements. Algeria, Egypt, Libya, and Tunisia have the following conditional requirements: If you are traveling from a country listed in the left two columns of the table on the preceding page to a North African country in the right hand column, **you are required to have a yellow fever vaccination and to take the certificate with you**.

For comprehensive country-by-country yellow fever vaccine requirements, see *Appendix 2, Yellow Fever Requirements*.

## DENGUE FEVER

Dengue fever is a viral infection transmitted to humans by mosquito bites. These mosquitoes are most active during the day, especially around dawn and dusk, and are frequently found in or around residential areas. The illness is flu-like and characterized by sudden onset, high fever, severe headaches, joint and muscle pain, and rash. Severe cases of dengue hemorrhagic fever produce shock, internal bleeding, and death. The rash appears 3-4 days after the onset of fever. Since there is no vaccine or specific treatment available, prevention is important.

### Risk to Traveler

Dengue fever occurs sporadically in **Egypt**. The risk of infection is small for most travelers except during periods of epidemic transmission.

### Prevention

There is no vaccine for dengue fever, therefore, the traveler should avoid mosquito bites. These mosquitoes may bite anytime during the day, especially in shady areas, indoors, or when the sky is overcast, but prefer feeding around dawn and dusk. For additional information on dengue fever, refer to *Appendix 12, Dengue Fever*.

## OTHER INSECT DISEASES
### Risks to Traveler

Other diseases spread by mosquitoes, sand flies, black flies, or other insects are prevalent, especially in rural areas. These diseases include: *filariasis* and *Chikungunya* (mosquito), *leishmaniasis* (sandfly), *onchocerciasis* (black flies), *African trypanosomiasis* (flies), *typhus* (lice), and *plague* (fleas).

## Prevention

For most of these diseases, a vaccine is not available and treatment is limited. Therefore, travelers must follow the guidelines at the beginning of this chapter under "Preventing Insect Bites." For additional detailed information on these and other insect diseases, please read *Appendix 3, Other Insect Diseases.*

## DISEASES TRANSMITTED THROUGH FOOD & WATER

Food and waterborne diseases are the number one cause of illness to travelers and are very common in North Africa. **Traveler's diarrhea is the most frequent health problem for travelers**. It can be caused by viruses, bacteria, or parasites that are found universally throughout the region. Transmission is most often through contaminated food or water. Infections may cause diarrhea and vomiting (typhoid fever, cholera, and parasites), liver damage (hepatitis), or muscle paralysis (polio).

## GENERAL PRECAUTIONS

**Water**: The following beverages are safe to drink: boiled water or beverages made with boiled water, canned or carbonated beverages, beer, or wine. Impure water often contaminates drinking containers, ice, and tap water.

**Food**: Food that has been cooked to 165° F (74° C) is generally safe. As a reference, food at this temperature cannot be put directly into your mouth, but must cool a bit. Foods of concern are salads, uncooked vegetables and fruit, unpasteurized milk and milk products, raw meat, and shellfish. If you peel fruit yourself, it is generally safe. A simple rule of thumb is: "Boil it, cook it, peel it, or forget it."

For additional detailed precautions, be sure to read *Appendix 4, Traveler's Diarrhea & Food and Water Precautions.*

## TYPHOID FEVER

Typhoid fever is a bacterial infection transmitted to humans through contaminated food and/or water, or directly between people. Symptoms of typhoid fever include fever, headaches, fatigue, loss of appetite, and constipation. Typhoid fever can be treated effectively with antibiotics.

## Risk to Traveler

Travelers to North Africa are at risk for typhoid fever, especially when traveling to smaller cities, villages, or rural areas.

## Prevention

By drinking only bottled or boiled beverages and eating only thoroughly cooked food, a traveler lowers the risk of infection. Currently available vaccines have been shown to protect 70-90% of the recipients. Therefore, even vaccinated travelers should be cautious in selecting their food and water.

Two vaccines are recommended for protection against typhoid fever. An oral vaccine, **TY21a**, consists of a total of 4 capsules taken (one per day, every other day) over a seven day period, and requires a booster every five years. Reactions to the TY21a vaccine are rare but include nausea, vomiting, abdominal cramps, and skin rash.

A new single-dose injectable vaccine, **Typhim Vi** or **ViCPS**, is equally effective, and requires a booster dose every two years. Reactions to Typhim Vi are also rare, but include discomfort at the site of injection and headaches. An earlier typhoid vaccine developed years ago, which uses killed typhoid organisms and is administered in a two dose series, had more reported side effect and is currently not preferred. Instead, use one of the newer vaccines. Based on the vaccine chosen, booster doses are required every two to five years.

## Recommendations

CDC recommends a typhoid vaccination for those travelers who are going off the usual tourist itineraries, traveling to smaller cities and rural areas, or staying long term, that is, for six weeks or more. Vaccination should be completed at least two weeks before travel. Typhoid vaccination is not required for international travel.

## CHOLERA

Cholera is an acute diarrheal illness caused by an infection of the intestine with the bacterium *Vibrio cholerae*. Infection is acquired by ingesting contaminated water or food. The infection is often mild without symptoms, but sometimes can be severe. Approximately one in 20 infected persons has severe disease characterized by an abrupt onset of profuse watery diarrhea, vomiting, dehydration, and leg cramps.

## Risk to Traveler

Cholera cases have been reported from most of the countries of North Africa. The risk of infection to the US traveler is low, especially those who are following the usual tourist itineraries and staying in standard accommodations. Travelers should consider the vaccine if they have stomach ulcers, use anti-acid therapy, or if they will be living in less than sanitary conditions in areas of high cholera activity. A list of cholera-infected countries is given in *Appendix 10, CDC's Blue Sheet.*

## Prevention

Travelers to cholera infected areas should:
- avoid eating high risk foods, especially fish and shellfish, and
- follow the standard food and water precautions of eating only thoroughly cooked food that is served hot, peeling their own fruit, and drinking beverages and ice made from boiled or chlorinated water, bottled carbonated water, or bottled carbonated soft drinks.

Persons with severe cases of cholera respond well to simple fluid and electrolyte-replacement therapy, but medical attention must be sought quickly when cholera is suspected.

The cholera vaccine licensed for use in the United States confers only brief and incomplete immunity (50% effective in reducing the illness). The risk of cholera to US travelers is so low that it is questionable whether the vaccine is of benefit, and therefore it is not recommended routinely for travelers. The primary series for this cholera vaccine is normally two injections with booster doses given every 6 months for persons who remain at high risk. **Cholera vaccine is not recommended for infants under 6 months old or for pregnant women.**

For additional information about cholera, read *Appendix 4, Traveler's Diarrhea & Food and Water Precautions,* and *Appendix 8, Cholera Information.*

## HEPATITIS A

Hepatitis A is a viral infection of the liver transmitted to humans by the fecal-oral route; through direct person-to-person contact; from contaminated water, ice, or shellfish; or from fruits or uncooked vegetables contaminated through handling. Symptoms include fatigue, fever, loss of appetite, nausea, dark urine, jaundice, vomiting, aches and pains, and light stools. No specific therapy, only supportive care, is available.

## Risk to Traveler

Travelers are at high risk for hepatitis A, especially if travel plans include visiting rural areas and extensive travel in the countryside, frequent close contact with local persons, or eating in settings of poor sanitation. Be aware that a study has shown that many cases of travel-related hepatitis A occur in travelers to developing countries with "standard" itineraries, accommodations, and food consumption behaviors.

## Prevention

The virus is inactivated by boiling or cooking to 185° F (85° C) for one minute. Therefore, eating thoroughly cooked foods and drinking only treated water serve as general precautions. In addition, **Immune globulin (IG)** *or* **hepatitis A vaccine** is recommended before travel. Two hepatitis A vaccines, **Havrix®** and **VAQTA®**, are currently licensed in the US.

Immune globulin and the hepatitis A vaccine marketed in the United States (US) are safe. American travelers should note that IG manufactured in foreign countries may or may not meet these requirements. Therefore, American travelers who will need to receive additional doses of IG in other countries should use products that meet US standards and license requirements. For reference, the method of manufacturing IG in the US is called the **Cohn-Oncley procedure**.

## Recommendations

CDC recommends Immune globulin (IG) or hepatitis A vaccine before travel for protection against hepatitis A.

**Immune globulin** is recommended for persons of all ages who:
- desire only short term protection (one dose is effective for three months)
- need immediate protection, and
- are too young for the vaccine (less than 2 years of age).

**Hepatitis A vaccine** is preferred for persons two years of age and older who plan to travel repeatedly or reside for long periods of time in intermediate or high risk areas. Bear in mind:
- The complete hepatitis A vaccine series requires a minimum of six months to complete.
- For these travelers over 18 years of age, hepatitis A vaccine should be given in a two-dose series with the second dose administered 6-12 months after the first.
- For children and adolescents between ages 2 through 18, a two or three dose series of hepatitis A vaccine is recommended depending on the vaccine chosen.

Travelers can be considered to be protected four weeks after receiving the initial vaccine dose. If the vaccine is administered less than four weeks

before travel, then IG should also be given. The vaccine series must be completed for long-term protection. Hepatitis A vaccination is not required for travel to any country.

In addition to receiving IG or the vaccine, all travelers should follow the food and water precautions as described in *Appendix 4, Traveler's Diarrhea & Food and Water Precautions.*

Additional IG and hepatitis A information covering the vaccine and its safety are found in *Appendix 9, Hepatitis A Vaccine & Immune Globulin (IG) - Disease and Vaccine Information.*

## PARASITES

Parasitic infections are acquired by eating or drinking contaminated food or water, through direct contact with soil or water containing parasites or their larva, or by contact with biting insects. Symptoms and evidence of infection may include, but are not limited to: fever, swollen lymph nodes, rashes or itchy skin, digestive problems such as abdominal pain or diarrhea, eye problems, and anemia.

### Risk to Traveler

Travelers to North Africa are at risk of parasitic infections. There are many types of parasites and infection may occur in several ways: by eating undercooked meats infected with parasites or their larva; by eating food or drinking water contaminated with parasites or their eggs; by contact with soil or water infected with parasites; or through insect bites. Several types of parasites, for example schistosomiasis, can penetrate intact human skin and travelers are advised to wear shoes and avoid swimming, wading, or washing in fresh water.

### Prevention

Travelers should eat only thoroughly cooked food, drink safe water, wear shoes, refrain from swimming in fresh water, and avoid contact with insects, particularly mosquitoes, biting flies, gnats, and midges.

## DISEASES TRANSMITTED THROUGH INTIMATE CONTACT WITH PEOPLE

### HIV/AIDS

Human immunodeficiency virus, or HIV, which causes acquired immunodeficiency syndrome or AIDS, is found primarily in blood, semen, and vaginal secretions of an infected person. HIV is spread by sexual contact with an infected person, by needle-sharing among injecting drug users, and through transfusions of infected blood and blood clotting factors. Babies born to HIV-infected women may become infected before, during, or shortly after birth.

In the United States, blood is screened for HIV antibodies, but this screening may not take place in all countries. Scientific studies have revealed no evidence that HIV is transmitted by air, food, water, insects, inanimate objects or casual contact. Even though HIV antibodies are normally detected on a test within 6 months after infection, the period between infection and development of disease symptoms (incubation period) may be 10 years or longer. Treatment has prolonged the survival of some HIV infected persons but there is no known cure or vaccine available. For additional information, see *Appendix 7, HIV/AIDS Information.*

### Risk to Traveler

AIDS is found throughout the region. However, little information is available regarding the rates of infection or the extent of risk behaviors. The risk to a traveler depends on whether the traveler will be involved in sexual or needle-sharing contact with a person who is infected with HIV. Receipt of unscreened blood for transfusion poses a risk for HIV infection.

### Prevention

No effective vaccine has been developed for HIV. Travelers should avoid sexual or needle-sharing contact with a person who is infected with HIV. If a blood transfusion is necessary, screened blood should come from an HIV-negative blood donor.

### Recommendations

Travelers should avoid activities known to carry risks for infection with HIV.

### HEPATITIS B

Hepatitis B is a viral infection of the liver. Hepatitis B is transmitted to humans primarily through behavior that result in the exchange of blood or fluids containing blood. Risky behavior includes heterosexual or homosexual contact or sharing needles or drug paraphernalia with a person infected with the hepatitis B virus. Any unscreened or improperly screened blood or blood product, as well as unsterilized needles, or contact with potentially infected people who have open skin sores due to impetigo, scabies, and scratched insect bites, heightens the potential for infection to the traveler. An effective vaccine for prevention of hepatitis B is available.

## Risk to Traveler

The risk of hepatitis B virus infection is high for Africa. The risk to the individual international traveler is greater if the traveler:

- has direct contact with blood or fluids containing blood;
- has intimate sexual contact with an infected person;
- remains in the country for longer than six months or has close contact with the local population.

## Prevention

**Hepatitis B vaccine** should be considered for those traveling to countries with high to intermediate rates of hepatitis B infection. For those travelers expecting to reside in countries of high risk, as well as all health workers, vaccination is strongly recommended.

Vaccination should ideally begin 6 months before travel, in order to complete the full series, which is needed for optimal protection. The three intramuscular doses of vaccine should be spaced so that the second dose is given one month after the first. The final dose is given 6 months after the first. The vaccination schedule should be initiated even if it will not be completed before travel begins. There is an alternative four-dose schedule that may provide protection if the first three doses can be delivered before departure. After completing the primary series, booster doses of the vaccine are not necessary.

## Recommendations

CDC recommends vaccination for any of the following people:

- any health care worker (medical, dental, or laboratory) whose activities might result in blood exposure;
- any traveler who may have intimate sexual contact with the local population;
- any long-term (6 months or more) traveler, e.g. teachers, who will reside in rural areas or have daily physical contact with the local population; or
- any traveler who is likely to seek either medical, dental, or other treatment in local facilities during their stay.

Hepatitis B vaccination is not required for travel to any country. Additional hepatitis B information is found in *Appendix 15, Hepatitis B.*

## OTHER DISEASES

## SCHISTOSOMIASIS

Schistosomiasis is a parasitic infection that develops after the larvae of a flatworm have penetrated the human skin. These larvae live in fresh water lakes, ponds, and streams and can penetrate unbroken skin. Water treated with chlorine or iodine is virtually safe, and salt water poses no risk.

### Risk to Traveler

The main risk of schistosomiasis is in the Nile River delta and valley region of **Egypt**. Schistosomiasis is also a risk in the North African countries of **Algeria** and **Libya**. The risk is a function of the frequency and degree of contact with contaminated fresh water for bathing, wading, or swimming.

### Prevention

The traveler cannot distinguish between infested and non-infested water. Therefore, swimming in fresh water in rural areas should be avoided. Bath water should either be heated to 50° (122° F) for five minutes or treated with chlorine or iodine as done for drinking water. If exposed, immediate and vigorous towel drying or application of rubbing alcohol to the exposed areas may reduce the risk of infection. Screening procedures are available for those who suspect infection, and schistosomiasis is treatable with drugs.

### Recommendations

Avoid contact with potentially contaminated water, such as swimming in lakes, ponds, rivers, etc.

## RABIES

Rabies is a viral infection that affects the central nervous system. It is transmitted to humans by warm-blooded animal (mammal) bites that introduce the virus into the wound. Although dogs are the main reservoir of the disease, all warm-blooded animal bites should be suspect.

### Risk to Traveler

For countries in North Africa, there is a risk of rabies infection, particularly in rural areas or in areas where large numbers of dogs are found.

### Prevention

Do not handle animals! Any animal bite should receive prompt medical attention. When wounds are thoroughly cleaned with large amounts of soap and water, the risk of rabies infection is reduced. Exposed individuals should receive prompt medical attention and advice on post-exposure preventive treatment.

## Recommendations

There are no requirements for vaccination, but pre-exposure vaccination is recommended for:
- travelers visiting foreign areas where dog rabies is known to exist and whose activities may place them at high risk of exposure;
- veterinarians and animal handlers;
- spelunkers; and
- certain rabies laboratory workers.

Pre-exposure vaccination does not nullify the need for post-exposure vaccine, but reduces the number of injections and may provide protection under circumstances in which rabies exposure is unrecognized. For additional rabies information, refer to *Appendix 11, Rabies Information.*

---

### SUMMARY OF RECOMMENDATIONS FOR NORTH AFRICA

*Travelers should:*
- *take the appropriate country-specific malaria prevention measures, (chloroquine, Egypt only)*
- *follow precautions to prevent insect bites*
- *pay attention to the quality of their drinking water and food*
- *have a dose of Immune Globulin (IG) or the hepatitis A vaccine, and consider booster doses of tetanus (Td) and polio (eIPV) vaccines.*
- *Depending on the locations to be visited, planned activities, and health of the traveler, the following vaccines should be considered: Hepatitis B, Yellow Fever, Typhoid, Rabies (pre-exposure), and Cholera.*
- *Finally, the normal "childhood" vaccines should be up-to-date: Measles, Mumps, Rubella (MMR Vaccine); Diphtheria, Tetanus, Pertussis (DTP Vaccine if traveler is less than 7 years of age, or Td if older than 7 years of age), and Polio vaccine. For additional information on these "childhood" vaccines, refer to Appendix 5, Vaccine Recommendations.*

# 4. WEST AFRICA

## COUNTRIES IN THIS REGION
Benin
Burkina Faso
Cape Verde Islands
Cote d'Ivoire
Gambia
Ghana
Guinea
Guinea-Bissau
Liberia
Mali
Mauritania
Niger
Nigeria
Sao Tome & Principe
Senegal
Sierra Leone
Togo

## WEST AFRICA TRAVELER'S OVERVIEW

*Travelers to West Africa may be exposed to potential diseases from a number of sources. The most frequently reported illness is traveler's diarrhea, but West Africa contains a variety of diseases transmitted by:*

- *insects,*
- *contaminated food and water, or*
- *close contact with infected people.*

*In this chapter, specific diseases, their causes, symptoms, geographic areas of risk, and prevention recommendations or requirement information are discussed under their topical headings. As a general guideline, in order to reduce the risk of infection, travelers must:*

- *protect themselves from insects*
- *ensure the quality of their food and drinking water*
- *be knowledgeable about potential diseases in the region to be visited*
- *receive all recommended vaccines and preventive medications.*

*In addition, travelers should note that diseases are not restricted to cleanly defined geographical areas. For example, mosquitoes can fly over city or country borders, so all travelers should protect themselves by taking the basic preventive precautions as described under each section and disease. Where appropriate, more detailed information is referenced in the Appendices.*

## DISEASES TRANSMITTED BY INSECTS

Many diseases are transmitted through the bite of infected insects such as mosquitoes, flies, fleas, ticks and lice. In general, **travelers must protect themselves from insect bites**. Travelers are at a higher risk for insect bites if they participate in outdoor activities during night time hours from dusk to dawn when mosquitoes bite, or if their living accommodations are unscreened. If a mosquito net is unlikely to be available, consider buying a portable mosquito net.

## PREVENTING INSECT BITES

To reduce the risk of mosquito bites, travelers should remain in well-screened areas, use mosquito nets, and wear clothes that cover most of the body. Travelers should also take insect repellent with them to use on any exposed areas of the skin. The most effective compound in a repellent is **DEET**, which may be listed as an ingredient on repellant labels as "**N,N-diethyl meta-toluamide.**" Check the repellent label to ensure DEET is an ingredient.

Travelers should note, however, that insect repellents containing DEET should always be used according to label directions and sparingly on children. **Avoid applying high-concentration (greater than 35%) products to the skin, particularly on children, and refrain from applying repellent to portions of the hands that are likely to come in contact with the eyes and mouth.** Pediatric insect repellents with 6-10% DEET are available without prescription in many drug stores. In rare instances, toxic reactions or other problems have developed after contact with DEET.

Travelers should also purchase a flying insect-killing spray to use in living and sleeping areas during the evening and night. For greater protection, clothing and bednets can be soaked in or sprayed with **permethrin**, which is an insect repellent licensed for use on clothing. If applied according to the directions, permethrin will repel insects from clothing for several weeks. Portable mosquito bednets, repellents containing DEET, and permethrin can be purchased in hardware, backpacking, and military surplus stores.

## MALARIA

Malaria is a serious parasitic infection transmitted to humans by an Anopheles mosquito. These mosquitoes bite at night, from dusk to dawn. Symptoms of malaria range from flu-like symptoms with fever, general achiness, headache, and fatigue, to a cycle of shaking chills, high fever, and sweating. If left untreated, malaria can cause anemia, kidney failure, coma, and death. Drugs are available to help prevent a malaria infection.

However, in spite of all protective measures, travelers occasionally develop malaria. Therefore, while traveling and up to one year after returning home, travelers should seek medical evaluation for any flu-like illness.

### Risk to Traveler

*High Risk*
In **Benin, Burkina Faso, Cote d'Ivoire, Gambia, Ghana, Guinea, Guinea-Bissau, Liberia, Mali, Mauritania, Niger, Nigeria, Sao Tome & Principe, Senegal, Sierra Leone**, and **Togo**, a high risk for malaria exists throughout the year in all parts of these countries including the urban areas. The dominant form is *P. falciparum* (the most dangerous type), which has been reported to be resistant to the drug chloroquine.

*Minor Risk*
**Cape Verde Islands** – the island of Sáo Tiago only; no preventive drug therapy is recommended.

*No Risk*
Cape Verde Islands – all islands except Sáo Tiago.

## Prevention & Recommendations

Travelers at risk for malaria should take **mefloquine** to prevent this strain of malaria. This drug is marketed in the United States under the name **Lariam™**. The adult dosage is 250 mg (one tablet) once a week. Mefloquine should be taken one week before leaving, weekly while in the malarious area, and weekly for 4 weeks after leaving the malarious area.

Minor side effects one may experience while taking mefloquine include gastrointestinal disturbances and dizziness. More serious side effects at the recommended dosage have rarely occurred. Consult a physician for other precautions.

Mefloquine should not be used by travelers with a:
- history of epilepsy or psychiatric disorder,
- known hypersensitivity to mefloquine.

In consultation with a physician, mefloquine may be used by pregnant women and children weighing less than 30 pounds, when travel to an area with chloroquine-resistant malaria is unavoidable. Travelers who cannot take mefloquine should read the section "Prescription Drugs for Malaria" found in *Appendix 1, Malaria Information*.

In addition to using drugs to prevent malaria and treat a possible malaria attack, travelers should use measures to reduce exposure to malaria-carrying mosquitoes and protect themselves from mosquito bites. Remember, these mosquitoes bite mainly during the evening and night, from dusk to dawn.

Additional general malaria information, as well as specific information for women who are pregnant or children, is found in *Appendix 1, Malaria Information*.

## YELLOW FEVER

Yellow fever is a viral disease transmitted to humans by a mosquito bite. The mosquitoes are most active during the evening hours. Symptoms range from fever, chills, headache, and vomiting to jaundice, internal bleeding, and kidney failure. Death occurs in about 5% of those infected. There is no specific drug to treat an infection of yellow fever, therefore prevention of infection is important.

## Risk to Traveler

Outbreaks of yellow fever have occurred in **Burkina Faso, Cote d'Ivoire, Gambia, Ghana, Mali, Mauritania, Nigeria, Senegal, Sierra Leone**, and **Togo**. Yellow fever is not always active in all countries of this region, but there is a significant risk to all travelers throughout the year, especially in travel or visits to rural settings.

## Prevention

Yellow fever vaccination, a one-dose shot, is effective for up to 10 years for the prevention of yellow fever and may be administered to adults and children over 9 months of age. This vaccine is only administered at designated yellow fever centers, usually your local health department. **The vaccine and the official certificate become effective 10 days after vaccination.** Travelers at continued risk need a booster and a new certificate every 10 years.

*Travelers who should not be immunized include:*
- Infants under 4 months.
- Persons severely allergic to eggs.
- Pregnant women or people whose immune systems are not functioning normally.

In addition to the vaccine, travelers should use measures to reduce exposure to mosquitoes and protect themselves from mosquito bites. Remember, these mosquitoes bite mainly during the evening hours.

## Yellow Fever Certificate

After immunization, an International Certificate of Vaccination is issued and is valid 10 days after vaccination to meet entry and exit requirements for all countries. The Certificate is good for 10 years. **You must take the Certificate with you**.

## Medical Waiver

Travelers who have a medical reason not to receive the yellow fever vaccine should obtain a medical waiver. Most countries will accept a medical waiver for persons with a medical reason not to receive the vaccine (e.g. infants less than 4 months old, pregnant women, persons hypersensitive to eggs, or those with an immunosuppressed condition.) When required, CDC recommends obtaining written waivers from consular or embassy officials before departure. Follow these guidelines:
- A physician's letter clearly stating the medical reason not to receive the vaccine might be acceptable to some governments.

- It should be written on letterhead stationery and bear the stamp used by a health department or official immunization center to validate the International Certificate of Vaccination.
- Check embassies or consulates for specific waiver requirements.

## Recommendations & Requirements

If you are traveling to any country in West Africa, CDC recommends and many countries require a yellow fever vaccination.

The majority of countries in West Africa **require** yellow fever vaccination for entry for any traveler. The remaining countries require a vaccination if travel plans include travel from specific countries.

The following 10 West African countries **absolutely require** a Yellow Fever Vaccination Certificate:
- **Benin**
- **Burkina Faso**
- **Cote d'Ivoire, (Ivory Coast)**
- **Ghana**
- **Liberia**
- **Mali**
- **Mauritania**
- **Niger**
- **Sao Tome and Principe**
- **Togo**

In addition to the 10 countries listed above, if you are traveling from a country listed in the left two columns of the following table to a West African country in the right hand column, **you are required to have a yellow fever vaccination and to take the certificate with you.**

For comprehensive country-by-country yellow fever vaccine requirements, see *Appendix 2, Yellow Fever Requirements*.

Note: Due to potential origin and destination combinations in travel plans, some countries may appear in both columns.

**TRAVELING FROM ANY OF THE FOLLOWING "ENDEMIC" YELLOW FEVER INFECTED COUNTRIES**

### Africa:

Angola
Benin
Burundi
Burkina Faso
Cameroon
Central African Republic
Chad
Congo
Cote d'Ivoire, (Ivory Coast)
Equatorial Guinea
Ethiopia
Gabon
Gambia
Ghana
Guinea
Guinea Bissau
Kenya
Liberia
Mali
Mauritania
Niger
Nigeria
Rwanda
Sao Tome and Principe
Senegal
Sierra Leone
Somalia
Sudan
Tanzania
Togo
Uganda
Zaire

### South America:

Bolivia
Brazil
Colombia
Ecuador
French Guiana
Guyana
Panama
Peru
Suriname
Venezuela

**TRAVELING TO THESE WEST AFRICAN COUNTRIES**

Cape Verde Islands
Equatorial Guinea
Gambia
Guinea
Guinea-Bissau
Nigeria
Senegal
Sierra Leone

**Yellow Fever Certificate Required**

## DENGUE FEVER

Dengue fever is a viral infection transmitted to humans by mosquito bites. These mosquitoes are most active during the day, especially around dawn and dusk, and are frequently found in or around residential areas. The illness is flu-like and characterized by sudden onset, high fever, severe headaches, joint and muscle pain, and rash. Severe cases of dengue hemorrhagic fever produce shock, internal bleeding, and death. The rash appears 3-4 days after the onset of fever. Since there is no vaccine or specific treatment available, prevention is important.

### Risk to Traveler

Dengue fever occurs sporadically in epidemics. The risk of infection is small for most travelers except during periods of epidemic transmission.

*Recent Epidemics*
**Burkina Faso**, **Cote d'Ivoire** (Ivory Coast), **Guinea**, **Nigeria** and **Senegal**.

### Prevention

There is no vaccine for dengue fever, therefore, the traveler should avoid mosquito bites. These mosquitoes may bite anytime during the day, especially in shady areas, indoors, or when the sky is overcast, but prefer feeding around dawn and dusk. For additional information on dengue fever, refer to *Appendix 12, Dengue Fever*.

## OTHER INSECT DISEASES

### Risks to Traveler

Other diseases spread by mosquitoes, sand flies, black flies, or other insects are prevalent, especially in rural areas. These diseases include: *filariasis* and *Chikungunya* (mosquito), *leishmaniasis* (sand fly), *onchocerciasis* (black flies), *African trypanosomiasis* (flies), *Congo-Crimean hemorrhagic fever* (ticks), *typhus* (lice), and *plague* (fleas).

### Prevention

For most of these diseases, a vaccine is not available and treatment is limited. Therefore, travelers must follow the guidelines at the beginning of this chapter under "Preventing Insect Bites." For additional detailed information on these and other insect diseases, please read *Appendix 3, Other Insect Diseases*.

## DISEASES TRANSMITTED THROUGH FOOD & WATER

Food and waterborne diseases are the number one cause of illness to travelers and are very common in West Africa. **Traveler's diarrhea is the**

**most frequent health problem for travelers.** It can be caused by viruses, bacteria, or parasites that are found universally throughout the region. Transmission is most often through contaminated food or water. Infections may cause diarrhea and vomiting (typhoid fever, cholera, and parasites), liver damage (hepatitis), or muscle paralysis (polio).

## GENERAL PRECAUTIONS

**Water**: The following beverages are safe to drink: boiled water or beverages made with boiled water, canned or carbonated beverages, beer, or wine. Impure water often contaminates drinking containers, ice, and tap water.

**Food**: Food that has been cooked to 165° F (74° C) is generally safe. As a reference, food at this temperature cannot be put directly into your mouth, but must cool a bit. Foods of concern are salads, uncooked vegetables and fruit, unpasteurized milk and milk products, raw meat, and shellfish. If you peel fruit yourself, it is generally safe. A simple rule of thumb is: "Boil it, cook it, peel it, or forget it."

For additional detailed precautions, be sure to read *Appendix 4, Traveler's Diarrhea & Food and Water Precautions.*

## TYPHOID FEVER

Typhoid fever is a bacterial infection transmitted to humans through contaminated food and/or water, or directly between people. Symptoms of typhoid fever include fever, headaches, fatigue, loss of appetite, and constipation. Typhoid fever can be treated effectively with antibiotics.

### Risk to Traveler

Travelers to West Africa are at risk for typhoid fever, especially when traveling to smaller cities, villages, or rural areas.

### Prevention

By drinking only bottled or boiled beverages and eating only thoroughly cooked food, a traveler lowers the risk of infection. Currently available vaccines have been shown to protect 70-90% of the recipients. Therefore, even vaccinated travelers should be cautious in selecting their food and water.

Two vaccines are recommended for protection against typhoid fever. An oral vaccine, **TY21a**, consists of a total of 4 capsules taken (one per day, every other day) over a seven day period, and requires a booster every five years. Reactions to the TY21a vaccine are rare but include nausea, vomiting, abdominal cramps, and skin rash.

A new single-dose injectable vaccine, **Typhim Vi** or **ViCPS**, is equally effective, and requires a booster dose every two years. Reactions to Typhim Vi are also rare, but include discomfort at the site of injection and headaches. An earlier typhoid vaccine developed years ago, which uses killed typhoid organisms and is administered in a two dose series, had more reported side effect and is currently not preferred. Instead, use one of the newer vaccines. Based on the vaccine chosen, booster doses are required every two to five years.

## Recommendations

CDC recommends a typhoid vaccination for those travelers who are going off the usual tourist itineraries, traveling to smaller cities and rural areas, or staying long term, that is, for six weeks or more. Vaccination should be completed at least two weeks before travel. Typhoid vaccination is not required for international travel.

## CHOLERA

Cholera is an acute diarrheal illness caused by an infection of the intestine with the bacterium *Vibrio cholerae*. Infection is acquired by ingesting contaminated water or food. The infection is often mild without symptoms, but sometimes can be severe. Approximately one in 20 infected persons has severe disease characterized by an abrupt onset of profuse watery diarrhea, vomiting, dehydration, and leg cramps.

## Risk to Traveler

Cholera cases have been reported from most of the countries of West Africa. The risk of infection to the US traveler is low, especially those who are following the usual tourist itineraries and staying in standard accommodations. A list of cholera-infected countries is given in *Appendix 10, CDC's Blue Sheet.*

## Prevention

Travelers to cholera infected areas should:
- avoid eating high risk foods, especially fish and shellfish, and
- follow the standard food and water precautions of eating only thoroughly cooked food that is served hot, peeling their own fruit, and drinking beverages and ice made from boiled or chlorinated water, bottled carbonated water, or bottled carbonated soft drinks.

Persons with severe cases of cholera respond well to simple fluid and electrolyte-replacement therapy, but medical attention must be sought quickly when cholera is suspected.

The cholera vaccine licensed for use in the United States confers only brief and incomplete immunity (50% effective in reducing the illness). The risk of cholera to US travelers is so low that it is questionable whether the vaccine is of benefit, and therefore it is not recommended routinely for travelers. The primary series for this cholera vaccine is normally two injections with booster doses given every 6 months for persons who remain at high risk. **Cholera vaccine is not recommended for infants under 6 months old or for pregnant women.**

For additional information about cholera, read *Appendix 4, Traveler's Diarrhea & Food and Water Precautions*, and *Appendix 8, Cholera Information*.

## HEPATITIS A
Hepatitis A is a viral infection of the liver transmitted to humans by the fecal-oral route; through direct person-to-person contact; from contaminated water, ice, or shellfish; or from fruits or uncooked vegetables contaminated through handling. Symptoms include fatigue, fever, loss of appetite, nausea, dark urine, jaundice, vomiting, aches and pains, and light stools. No specific therapy, only supportive care, is available.

### Risk to Traveler
Travelers are at high risk for hepatitis A, especially if travel plans include visiting rural areas and extensive travel in the countryside, frequent close contact with local persons, or eating in settings of poor sanitation. Be aware that a study has shown that many cases of travel-related hepatitis A occur in travelers to developing countries with "standard" itineraries, accommodations, and food consumption behaviors.

### Prevention
The virus is inactivated by boiling or cooking to 185° F (85° C) for one minute. Therefore, eating thoroughly cooked foods and drinking only treated water serve as general precautions. In addition, **Immune globulin (IG)** *or* **hepatitis A vaccine** is recommended before travel. Two hepatitis A vaccines, **Havrix®** and **VAQTA®**, are currently licensed in the United States.

Immune globulin and the hepatitis A vaccine marketed in the United States (US) are safe. American travelers should note that IG manufactured in foreign countries may or may not meet these requirements. Therefore, American travelers who will need to receive additional doses of IG in other countries should use products that meet US standards and license requirements. For reference, the method of manufacturing IG in the US is called the **Cohn-Oncley procedure.**

## Recommendations

CDC recommends Immune globulin (IG) or hepatitis A vaccine before travel for protection against hepatitis A.

**Immune globulin** is recommended for persons of all ages who:
- desire only short term protection (one dose is effective for three months)
- need immediate protection, and
- are too young for the vaccine (less than 2 years of age).

**Hepatitis A vaccine** is preferred for persons two years of age and older who plan to travel repeatedly or reside for long periods of time in intermediate or high risk areas. Bear in mind:
- The complete hepatitis A vaccine series requires a minimum of six months to complete.
- For these travelers over 18 years of age, hepatitis A vaccine should be given in a two-dose series with the second dose administered 6-12 months after the first.
- For children and adolescents between ages 2 through 18, a two or three dose series of hepatitis A vaccine is recommended depending on the vaccine chosen.

Travelers can be considered to be protected four weeks after receiving the initial vaccine dose. If the vaccine is administered less than four weeks before travel, then IG should also be given. The vaccine series must be completed for long-term protection. Hepatitis A vaccination is not required for travel to any country.

In addition to receiving IG or the vaccine, all travelers should follow the food and water precautions as described in *Appendix 4, Traveler's Diarrhea & Food and Water Precautions.*

Additional IG and hepatitis A information covering the vaccine and its safety are found in *Appendix 9, Hepatitis A Vaccine & Immune Globulin (IG) - Disease and Vaccine Information.*

## PARASITES

Parasitic infections are acquired by eating or drinking contaminated food or water, through direct contact with soil or water containing parasites or their larva, or by contact with biting insects. Symptoms and evidence of infection may include, but are not limited to: fever, swollen lymph nodes, rashes or itchy skin, digestive problems such as abdominal pain or diarrhea, eye problems, and anemia.

### Risk to Traveler

Travelers to West Africa are at risk of parasitic infections. There are many types of parasites and infection may occur in several ways: by eating undercooked meats infected with parasites or their larva; by eating food or drinking water contaminated with parasites or their eggs; by contact with soil or water infected with parasites; or through insect bites. Several types of parasites, for example schistosomiasis, can penetrate intact human skin and travelers are advised to wear shoes and avoid swimming, wading, or washing in fresh water.

### Prevention

Travelers should eat only thoroughly cooked food, drink safe water, wear shoes, refrain from swimming in fresh water, and avoid contact with insects, particularly mosquitoes, biting flies, gnats, and midges.

## DISEASES TRANSMITTED THROUGH INTIMATE CONTACT WITH PEOPLE

### HIV/AIDS

Human immunodeficiency virus, or HIV, which causes acquired immunodeficiency syndrome or AIDS, is found primarily in blood, semen, and vaginal secretions of an infected person. HIV is spread by sexual contact with an infected person, by needle-sharing among injecting drug users, and through transfusions of infected blood and blood clotting factors. Babies born to HIV-infected women may become infected before, during, or shortly after birth.

In the United States, blood is screened for HIV antibodies, but this screening may not take place in all countries. Scientific studies have revealed no evidence that HIV is transmitted by air, food, water, insects, inanimate objects or casual contact. Even though HIV antibodies are normally detected on a test within 6 months after infection, the period between infection and development of disease symptoms (incubation period) may be 10 years or longer. Treatment has prolonged the survival of some HIV infected persons but there is no known cure or vaccine available. For additional information, see *Appendix 7, HIV/AIDS Information.*

## Risk to Traveler

AIDS is found throughout the region. In West Africa, heterosexual transmission accounts for the majority of the cases. The risk to a traveler depends on whether the traveler will be involved in sexual or needle-sharing contact with a person who is infected with HIV. Receipt of unscreened blood for transfusion poses a risk for HIV infection.

## Prevention

No effective vaccine has been developed for HIV. Travelers should avoid sexual or needle-sharing contact with a person who is infected with HIV. If a blood transfusion is necessary, screened blood should come from an HIV-negative blood donor.

## Recommendations

Travelers should avoid activities known to carry risks for infection with HIV.

## HEPATITIS B

Hepatitis B is a viral infection of the liver. Hepatitis B is transmitted to humans primarily through behavior that result in the exchange of blood or fluids containing blood. Risky behavior includes heterosexual or homosexual contact or sharing needles or drug paraphernalia with a person infected with the hepatitis B virus. Any unscreened or improperly screened blood or blood product, as well as unsterilized needles, or contact with potentially infected people who have open skin sores due to impetigo, scabies, and scratched insect bites, heightens the potential for infection to the traveler. An effective vaccine for prevention of hepatitis B is available.

## Risk to Traveler

The risk of hepatitis B virus infection is **high** for Africa. The risk to the individual international traveler is greater if the traveler:
   •    has direct contact with blood or fluids containing blood;
   •    has intimate sexual contact with an infected person;
   •    remains in the country for longer than six months or has close contact with the local population.

## Prevention

**Hepatitis B vaccine** should be considered for those traveling to countries with high to intermediate rates of hepatitis B infection. For those travelers expecting to reside in countries of high risk, as well as all health workers, vaccination is strongly recommended.

Vaccination should ideally begin 6 months before travel, in order to complete the full series, which is needed for optimal protection. The three intramuscular doses of vaccine should be spaced so that the second dose is given one month after the first. The final dose is given 6 months after the first. The vaccination schedule should be initiated even if it will not be completed before travel begins. There is an alternative four-dose schedule that may provide protection if the first three doses can be delivered before departure. After completing the primary series, booster doses of the vaccine are not necessary.

## Recommendations

CDC recommends vaccination for any of the following people:
- any health care worker (medical, dental, or laboratory) whose activities might result in blood exposure;
- any traveler who may have intimate sexual contact with the local population;
- any long-term (6 months or more) traveler, e.g. teachers, who will reside in rural areas or have daily physical contact with the local population; or
- any traveler who is likely to seek either medical, dental, or other treatment in local facilities during their stay.

Hepatitis B vaccination is not required for travel to any country. Additional hepatitis B information is found in *Appendix 15, Hepatitis B*.

## MENINGOCOCCAL DISEASE

Meningococcal disease (bacterial meningitis) is a bacterial infection in the lining of the brain or spinal cord. Early symptoms are headache, stiff neck, a rash, and fever. The bacteria is transmitted to humans through respiratory droplets when an infected person sneezes or coughs on you.

### Risk to Traveler

There is seasonal risk of meningococcal disease in parts of West Africa, primarily in the savannah regions of **Benin**, **Burkina Faso**, **Cote d'Ivoire**, **Ghana**, **Guinea Bissau**, **Guinea**, **Mali**, **Niger**, **Nigeria** and **Togo** during the dry season from December through June. Many of the countries in

West Africa are recognized to have epidemic meningococcal disease, and to be a part of the "meningitis belt" that runs from Guinea and Mali in the west all the way across Africa to Ethiopia and Djibouti on the eastern coast. When a traveler lives and works around the local population, the risk increases.

### Prevention
A one dose meningococcal vaccine called **Menomune** is available.

### Recommendations
Vaccination is not required for entry into any country in this region. CDC recommends vaccination with meningococcal vaccine for travelers going to Mali and all countries directly eastward, including Burkina Faso, Niger, Benin, and Nigeria, when travel occurs between December and June.

## OTHER DISEASES
## SCHISTOSOMIASIS
Schistosomiasis is a parasitic infection that develops after the larvae of a flatworm have penetrated the human skin. These larvae live in fresh water lakes, ponds, and streams and can penetrate unbroken skin. Water treated with chlorine or iodine is virtually safe, and salt water poses no risk.

### Risk to Traveler
Schistosomiasis infection is widespread in West Africa, especially in the savannah regions of **Burkina Faso, Mali, Niger, and Nigeria**. The risk is a function of the frequency and degree of contact with contaminated fresh water for bathing, wading, or swimming.

### Prevention
The traveler cannot distinguish between infested and non-infested water. Therefore, swimming in fresh water in rural areas should be avoided. Bath water should either be heated to 50° (122° F) for five minutes or treated with chlorine or iodine as done for drinking water. If exposed, immediate and vigorous towel drying or application of rubbing alcohol to the exposed areas may reduce the risk of infection. Screening procedures are available for those who suspect infection, and schistosomiasis is treatable with drugs.

### Recommendations
Avoid contact with potentially contaminated water, such as swimming in lakes, ponds, rivers, etc.

## RABIES

Rabies is a viral infection that affects the central nervous system. It is transmitted to humans by warm-blooded animal (mammal) bites that introduce the virus into the wound. Although dogs are the main reservoir of the disease, all warm-blooded animal bites should be suspect.

### Risk to Traveler

For all countries in West Africa, there is a risk of rabies infection, particularly in rural areas or in urban areas where large numbers of dogs are found.

### Prevention

Do not handle animals! Any animal bite should receive prompt medical attention. When wounds are thoroughly cleaned with large amounts of soap and water, the risk of rabies infection is reduced. Exposed individuals should receive prompt medical attention and advice on post-exposure preventive treatment.

### Recommendations

There are no requirements for vaccination, but pre-exposure vaccination is recommended for:
 • travelers visiting foreign areas where dog rabies is known to exist and whose activities may place them at high risk of exposure;
 • veterinarians and animal handlers;
 • spelunkers; and
 • certain rabies laboratory workers.

Pre-exposure vaccination does not nullify the need for post-exposure vaccine, but reduces the number of injections and may provide protection under circumstances in which rabies exposure is unrecognized. For additional rabies information, refer to *Appendix 11, Rabies Information.*

## SUMMARY OF RECOMMENDATIONS FOR WEST AFRICA

*Travelers should:*

- *take mefloquine (or equivalent) for malaria prevention*
- *follow precautions to prevent insect bites*
- *pay attention to the quality of their drinking water and food*
- *have a dose of Immune Globulin (IG) or the hepatitis A vaccine, and consider booster doses of tetanus (Td) and polio (eIPV) vaccines.*
- *Depending on the locations to be visited, planned activities, and health of the traveler, the following vaccines should be considered: Hepatitis B, Yellow Fever, Typhoid, Rabies (pre-exposure), and Cholera.*
- *Finally, the normal "childhood" vaccines should be up-to-date: Measles, Mumps, Rubella (MMR Vaccine); Diphtheria, Tetanus, Pertussis (DTP Vaccine if traveler is less than 7 years of age, or Td if older than 7 years of age), and Polio vaccine. For additional information on these "childhood" vaccines, refer to Appendix 5, Vaccine Recommendations.*

# 5. CENTRAL AFRICA

## COUNTRIES IN THIS REGION
Angola
Cameroon
Central African Republic
Chad
Congo
Equatorial Guinea
Gabon
Sudan
Zaire
Zambia

## CENTRAL AFRICA TRAVELER'S OVERVIEW

*Travelers to Central Africa may be exposed to potential diseases from a number of sources. The most frequently reported illness is traveler's diarrhea, but Central Africa contains a variety of diseases transmitted by:*
- *insects,*
- *contaminated food and water, or*
- *close contact with infected people.*

*In this chapter, specific diseases, their causes, symptoms, geographic areas of risk, and prevention recommendations or requirement information are discussed under their topical headings. As a general guideline, in order to reduce the risk of infection, travelers must:*
- *protect themselves from insects*
- *ensure the quality of their food and drinking water*
- *be knowledgeable about potential diseases in the region to be visited*
- *receive all recommended vaccines and preventive medications.*

*In addition, travelers should note that diseases are not restricted to cleanly defined geographical areas. For example, mosquitoes can fly over city or country borders, so all travelers should protect themselves by taking the basic preventive precautions as described under each section and disease. Where appropriate, more detailed information is referenced in the Appendices.*

## DISEASES TRANSMITTED BY INSECTS

Many diseases are transmitted through the bite of infected insects such as mosquitoes, flies, fleas, ticks and lice. In general, **travelers must protect themselves from insect bites**. Travelers are at a higher risk for insect bites if they participate in outdoor activities during night time hours from dusk to dawn when mosquitoes bite, or if their living accommodations are unscreened. If a mosquito net is unlikely to be available, consider buying a portable mosquito net.

### PREVENTING INSECT BITES

To reduce the risk of mosquito bites, travelers should remain in well-screened areas, use mosquito nets, and wear clothes that cover most of the body. Travelers should also take insect repellent with them to use on any exposed areas of the skin. The most effective compound in a repellent is **DEET**, which may be listed as an ingredient on repellant labels as "**N,N-diethyl meta-toluamide.**" Check the repellent label to ensure DEET is an ingredient.

Travelers should note, however, that insect repellents containing DEET should always be used according to label directions and sparingly on children. **Avoid applying high-concentration (greater than 35%) products to the skin, particularly on children, and refrain from applying repellent to portions of the hands that are likely to come in contact with the eyes and mouth.** Pediatric insect repellents with 6-10% DEET are available without prescription in many drug stores. In rare instances, toxic reactions or other problems have developed after contact with DEET.

Travelers should also purchase a flying insect-killing spray to use in living and sleeping areas during the evening and night. For greater protection, clothing and bednets can be soaked in or sprayed with **permethrin**, which is an insect repellent licensed for use on clothing. If applied according to the directions, permethrin will repel insects from clothing for several weeks. Portable mosquito bednets, repellents containing DEET, and permethrin can be purchased in hardware, backpacking, and military surplus stores.

## MALARIA

Malaria is a serious parasitic infection transmitted to humans by an Anopheles mosquito. These mosquitoes bite at night, from dusk to dawn. Symptoms of malaria range from flu-like symptoms with fever, general achiness, headache, and fatigue, to a cycle of shaking chills, high fever, and sweating. If left untreated, malaria can cause anemia, kidney failure, coma, and death. Drugs are available to help prevent a malaria infection.

However, in spite of all protective measures, travelers occasionally develop malaria. Therefore, while traveling and up to one year after returning home, travelers should seek medical evaluation for any flu-like illness.

### Risk to Traveler

*High Risk*

In **Angola, Cameroon, Central African Republic, Chad, Congo, Equatorial Guinea, Gabon, Sudan, Zaire** and **Zambia** a high risk for malaria exists throughout the year in all parts of these countries, including the urban areas. The dominant form is *P. falciparum* (the most dangerous type), which has been reported to be resistant to the drug chloroquine.

### Prevention & Recommendations

Travelers at risk for malaria should take **mefloquine** to prevent this strain of malaria. This drug is marketed in the United States under the name

**Lariam™.** The adult dosage is 250 mg (one tablet) once a week. Mefloquine should be taken one week before leaving, weekly while in the malarious area, and weekly for 4 weeks after leaving the malarious area.

Minor side effects one may experience while taking mefloquine include gastrointestinal disturbances and dizziness. More serious side effects at the recommended dosage have rarely occurred. Consult a physician for other precautions.

Mefloquine should not be used by travelers with a:
- history of epilepsy or psychiatric disorder,
- known hypersensitivity to mefloquine.

In consultation with a physician, mefloquine may be used by pregnant women and children weighing less than 30 pounds, when travel to an area with chloroquine-resistant malaria is unavoidable. Travelers who cannot take mefloquine should read the section "Prescription Drugs for Malaria" found in *Appendix 1, Malaria Information.*

In addition to using drugs to prevent malaria and treat a possible malaria attack, travelers should use measures to reduce exposure to malaria-carrying mosquitoes and protect themselves from mosquito bites. Remember, these mosquitoes bite mainly during the evening and night, from dusk to dawn.

Additional general malaria information, as well as specific information for women who are pregnant or children, is found in *Appendix 1, Malaria Information.*

## YELLOW FEVER

Yellow fever is a viral disease transmitted to humans by a mosquito bite. The mosquitoes are most active during the evening hours. Symptoms range from fever, chills, headache, and vomiting to jaundice, internal bleeding, and kidney failure. Death occurs in about 5% of those infected. There is no specific drug to treat an infection of yellow fever, therefore prevention of infection is important.

### Risk to Travelers

Outbreaks of yellow fever have occurred in **Angola, Sudan,** and **Zaire.** Yellow fever is not always active in all countries of this region, but there is a significant risk to all travelers throughout the year, especially in travel or visits to rural settings.

## Prevention

Yellow fever vaccination, a one-dose shot, is effective for up to 10 years for the prevention of yellow fever and may be administered to adults and children over 9 months of age. This vaccine is only administered at designated yellow fever centers, usually your local health department. **The vaccine and the official certificate become effective 10 days after vaccination**. Travelers at continued risk need a booster and a new certificate every 10 years.

*Travelers who should not be immunized include:*
- Infants under 4 months.
- Persons severely allergic to eggs.
- Pregnant women or people whose immune systems are not functioning normally.

In addition to the vaccine, travelers should use measures to reduce exposure to mosquitoes and protect themselves from mosquito bites. Remember, these mosquitoes bite mainly during the evening hours.

## Yellow Fever Certificate

After immunization, an International Certificate of Vaccination is issued and is valid 10 days after vaccination to meet entry and exit requirements for all countries. The Certificate is good for 10 years. **You must take the Certificate with you**.

## Medical Waiver

Travelers who have a medical reason not to receive the yellow fever vaccine should obtain a medical waiver. Most countries will accept a medical waiver for persons with a medical reason not to receive the vaccine (e.g. infants less than 4 months old, pregnant women, persons hypersensitive to eggs, or those with an immunosuppressed condition.) When required, CDC recommends obtaining written waivers from consular or embassy officials before departure. Follow these guidelines:
- A physician's letter clearly stating the medical reason not to receive the vaccine might be acceptable to some governments.
- It should be written on letterhead stationery and bear the stamp used by a health department or official immunization center to validate the International Certificate of Vaccination.
- Check embassies or consulates for specific waiver requirements.

## Recommendations & Requirements

If you are traveling to any country in Central Africa, CDC recommends and many countries require a yellow fever vaccination.

Many of the countries in Central Africa require yellow fever vaccination for entry for any traveler. Several other countries require a vaccination if travel plans include travel from specific countries.

The following five Central African countries **absolutely require** a Yellow Fever Vaccination Certificate:
- **Cameroon**
- **Central African Republic**
- **Congo**
- **Gabon**
- **Zaire**

In addition:
- **Zambia** has no Yellow Fever Vaccination requirements.
- **Chad** recommends, but does not require, yellow fever vaccination.
- **Angola**, **Equatorial Guinea**, and **Sudan** have conditional requirements that are listed in the table on the next page.

In addition to Cameroon, Central African Republic, Congo, Gabon, and Zaire, if you are traveling from a country listed in the left two columns of the following table to a Central African country in the right hand column, **you are required to have a yellow fever vaccination**.

Note: Due to potential origin and destination combinations in travel plans, some countries may appear in both columns.

For comprehensive country-by-country yellow fever vaccine requirements, see *Appendix 2, Yellow Fever Requirements*.

## TRAVELING FROM ANY OF THE FOLLOWING "ENDEMIC" YELLOW FEVER INFECTED COUNTRIES

### Africa:

Angola
Benin
Burundi
Burkina Faso
Cameroon
Central African Republic
Chad
Congo
Cote d'Ivoire, (Ivory Coast)
Equatorial Guinea
Ethiopia
Gabon
Gambia
Ghana
Guinea
Guinea Bissau
Kenya
Liberia
Mali
Mauritania
Niger
Nigeria
Rwanda
Sao Tome and Principe
Senegal
Sierra Leone
Somalia
Sudan
Tanzania
Togo
Uganda
Zaire

### South America:

Bolivia
Brazil
Colombia
Ecuador
French Guiana
Guyana
Panama
Peru
Suriname
Venezuela

## TRAVELING TO CENTRAL AFRICAN COUNTRIES

Angola
Equatorial Guinea
Sudan
   (Sudan may also require a
   certificate for leaving the country.)

**Yellow Fever Certificate Required**

# DENGUE FEVER

Dengue fever is a viral infection transmitted to humans by mosquito bites. These mosquitoes are most active during the day, especially around dawn and dusk, and are frequently found in or around residential areas. The illness is flu-like and characterized by sudden onset, high fever, severe headaches, joint and muscle pain, and rash. Severe cases of dengue hemorrhagic fever produce shock, internal bleeding, and death. The rash appears 3-4 days after the onset of fever. Since there is no vaccine or specific treatment available, prevention is important.

## Risk to Traveler

Dengue fever occurs sporadically in **Cameroon**, **Congo**, **Gabon**, and **Zaire**. The risk of infection is small for most travelers except during periods of epidemic transmission.

*Recent Epidemics*
**Angola** and **Sudan**.

## Prevention

There is no vaccine for dengue fever, therefore, the traveler should avoid mosquito bites. These mosquitoes may bite anytime during the day, especially in shady areas, indoors, or when the sky is overcast, but prefer feeding around dawn and dusk. For additional information on dengue fever, refer to *Appendix 12, Dengue Fever*.

# OTHER INSECT DISEASES

## Risks to Traveler

Other diseases spread by mosquitoes, sand flies, black flies, or other insects are prevalent, especially in rural areas. These diseases include: *filariasis* and *Chikungunya* (mosquito), *leishmaniasis* (sand fly), *onchocerciasis* (black flies), *African trypanosomiasis* (flies), *Congo-Crimean hemorrhagic fever* (ticks), *typhus* (lice), and *plague* (fleas).

## Prevention

For most of these diseases, a vaccine is not available and treatment is limited. Therefore, travelers must follow the guidelines at the beginning of this chapter under "Preventing Insect Bites." For additional detailed information on these and other insect diseases, please read *Appendix 3, Other Insect Diseases*.

## DISEASES TRANSMITTED THROUGH FOOD & WATER

Food and waterborne diseases are the number one cause of illness to travelers and are very common in Central Africa. **Traveler's diarrhea is the most frequent health problem for travelers.** It can be caused by viruses, bacteria, or parasites that are found universally throughout the region. Transmission is most often through contaminated food or water. Infections may cause diarrhea and vomiting (typhoid fever, cholera, and parasites), liver damage (hepatitis), or muscle paralysis (polio).

### GENERAL PRECAUTIONS

**Water**: The following beverages are safe to drink: boiled water or beverages made with boiled water, canned or carbonated beverages, beer, or wine. Impure water often contaminates drinking containers, ice, and tap water.

**Food**: Food that has been cooked to 165° F (74° C) is generally safe. As a reference, food at this temperature cannot be put directly into your mouth, but must cool a bit. Foods of concern are salads, uncooked vegetables and fruit, unpasteurized milk and milk products, raw meat, and shellfish. If you peel fruit yourself, it is generally safe. A simple rule of thumb is: "Boil it, cook it, peel it, or forget it."

For additional detailed precautions, be sure to read *Appendix 4, Traveler's Diarrhea & Food and Water Precautions.*

### TYPHOID FEVER

Typhoid fever is a bacterial infection transmitted to humans through contaminated food and/or water, or directly between people. Symptoms of typhoid fever include fever, headaches, fatigue, loss of appetite, and constipation. Typhoid fever can be treated effectively with antibiotics.

### Risk to Traveler

Travelers to Central Africa are at risk for typhoid fever, especially when traveling to smaller cities, villages, or rural areas. Zaire recommends a typhoid vaccination.

### Prevention

By drinking only bottled or boiled beverages and eating only thoroughly cooked food, a traveler lowers the risk of infection. Currently available vaccines have been shown to protect 70-90% of the recipients. Therefore, even vaccinated travelers should be cautious in selecting their food and water.

Two vaccines are recommended for protection against typhoid fever. An oral vaccine, **TY21a**, consists of a total of 4 capsules taken (one per day, every other day) over a seven day period, and requires a booster every five years. Reactions to the TY21a vaccine are rare but include nausea, vomiting, abdominal cramps, and skin rash.

A new single-dose injectable vaccine, **Typhim Vi** or **ViCPS**, is equally effective, and requires a booster dose every two years. Reactions to Typhim Vi are also rare, but include discomfort at the site of injection and headaches. An earlier typhoid vaccine developed years ago, which uses killed typhoid organisms and is administered in a two dose series, had more reported side effect and is currently not preferred. Instead, use one of the newer vaccines. Based on the vaccine chosen, booster doses are required every two to five years.

## Recommendations

CDC recommends a typhoid vaccination for those travelers who are going off the usual tourist itineraries, traveling to smaller cities and rural areas, or staying long term, that is, for six weeks or more. Vaccination should be completed at least two weeks before travel. Typhoid vaccination is not required for international travel.

## CHOLERA

Cholera is an acute diarrheal illness caused by an infection of the intestine with the bacterium *Vibrio cholerae*. Infection is acquired by ingesting contaminated water or food. The infection is often mild without symptoms, but sometimes can be severe. Approximately one in 20 infected persons has severe disease characterized by an abrupt onset of profuse watery diarrhea, vomiting, dehydration, and leg cramps.

## Risk to Traveler

Cholera cases have been reported from most of the countries of Central Africa. The risk of infection to the US traveler is low, especially those who are following the usual tourist itineraries and staying in standard accommodations. Travelers should consider the vaccine if they have stomach ulcers, use anti-acid therapy, or if they will be living in less than sanitary conditions in areas of high cholera activity. A list of cholera infected countries is given in *Appendix 10, CDC's Blue Sheet.*

## Prevention

Travelers to cholera infected areas should:
  - avoid eating high risk foods, especially fish and shellfish, and

- follow the standard food and water precautions of eating only thoroughly cooked food that is served hot, peeling their own fruit, and drinking beverages and ice made from boiled or chlorinated water, bottled carbonated water, or bottled carbonated soft drinks.

Persons with severe cases of cholera respond well to simple fluid and electrolyte-replacement therapy, but medical attention must be sought quickly when cholera is suspected.

The cholera vaccine licensed for use in the United States confers only brief and incomplete immunity (50% effective in reducing the illness). The risk of cholera to US travelers is so low that it is questionable whether the vaccine is of benefit, and therefore it is not recommended routinely for travelers. The primary series for this cholera vaccine is normally two injections with booster doses given every 6 months for persons who remain at high risk. **Cholera vaccine is not recommended for infants under 6 months old or for pregnant women.**

For additional information about cholera, read *Appendix 4, Traveler's Diarrhea & Food and Water Precautions*, and *Appendix 8, Cholera Information*.

## HEPATITIS A

Hepatitis A is a viral infection of the liver transmitted to humans by the fecal-oral route; through direct person-to-person contact; from contaminated water, ice, or shellfish; or from fruits or uncooked vegetables contaminated through handling. Symptoms include fatigue, fever, loss of appetite, nausea, dark urine, jaundice, vomiting, aches and pains, and light stools. No specific therapy, only supportive care, is available.

### Risk to Traveler

Travelers are at high risk for hepatitis A, especially if travel plans include visiting rural areas and extensive travel in the countryside, frequent close contact with local persons, or eating in settings of poor sanitation. Be aware that a study has shown that many cases of travel-related hepatitis A occur in travelers to developing countries with "standard" itineraries, accommodations, and food consumption behaviors.

### Prevention

The virus is inactivated by boiling or cooking to 185° F (85° C) for one minute. Therefore, eating thoroughly cooked foods and drinking only treated water serve as general precautions. In addition, **Immune globulin**

(IG) *or* **hepatitis A vaccine** is recommended before travel. Two hepatitis A vaccines, **Havrix®** and **VAQTA®**, are currently licensed in the United States.

Immune globulin and the hepatitis A vaccine marketed in the United States are safe. American travelers should note that IG manufactured in foreign countries may or may not meet these requirements. Therefore, American travelers who will need to receive additional doses of IG in other countries should use products that meet US standards and license requirements. For reference, the method of manufacturing IG in the US is called the Cohn-**Oncley procedure**.

## Recommendations
CDC recommends Immune globulin (IG) or hepatitis A vaccine before travel for protection against hepatitis A.

**Immune globulin** is recommended for persons of all ages who:
• desire only short term protection (one dose is effective for three months)
• need immediate protection, and
• are too young for the vaccine (less than 2 years of age).

**Hepatitis A vaccine** is preferred for persons two years of age and older who plan to travel repeatedly or reside for long periods of time in intermediate or high risk areas. Bear in mind:
• The complete hepatitis A vaccine series requires a minimum of six months to complete.
• For these travelers over 18 years of age, hepatitis A vaccine should be given in a two-dose series with the second dose administered 6-12 months after the first.
• For children and adolescents between ages 2 through 18, a two or three dose series of hepatitis A vaccine is recommended depending on the vaccine chosen.

Travelers can be considered to be protected four weeks after receiving the initial vaccine dose. If the vaccine is administered less than four weeks before travel, then IG should also be given. The vaccine series must be completed for long-term protection. Hepatitis A vaccination is not required for travel to any country.

In addition to receiving IG or the vaccine, all travelers should follow the food and water precautions as described in *Appendix 4, Traveler's Diarrhea & Food and Water Precautions.*

Additional IG and hepatitis A information covering the vaccine and its safety are found in *Appendix 9, Hepatitis A Vaccine & Immune Globulin (IG) - Disease and Vaccine Information.*

# PARASITES

Parasitic infections are acquired by eating or drinking contaminated food or water, through direct contact with soil or water containing parasites or their larva, or by contact with biting insects. Symptoms and evidence of infection may include, but are not limited to: fever, swollen lymph nodes, rashes or itchy skin, digestive problems such as abdominal pain or diarrhea, eye problems, and anemia.

## Risk to Traveler

Travelers to Central Africa are at risk of parasitic infections. There are many types of parasites and infection may occur in several ways: by eating undercooked meats infected with parasites or their larva; by eating food or drinking water contaminated with parasites or their eggs; by contact with soil or water infected with parasites; or through insect bites. Several types of parasites, for example schistosomiasis, can penetrate intact human skin and travelers are advised to wear shoes and avoid swimming, wading, or washing in fresh water.

## Prevention

Travelers should eat only thoroughly cooked food, drink safe water, wear shoes, refrain from swimming in fresh water, and avoid contact with insects, particularly mosquitoes, biting flies, gnats, and midges.

# DISEASES TRANSMITTED THROUGH INTIMATE CONTACT WITH PEOPLE

## HIV/AIDS

Human immunodeficiency virus, or HIV, which causes acquired immunodeficiency syndrome or AIDS, is found primarily in blood, semen, and vaginal secretions of an infected person. HIV is spread by sexual contact with an infected person, by needle-sharing among injecting drug users, and through transfusions of infected blood and blood clotting factors. Babies born to HIV-infected women may become infected before, during, or shortly after birth.

In the United States, blood is screened for HIV antibodies, but this screening may not take place in all countries. Scientific studies have revealed no evidence that HIV is transmitted by air, food, water, insects, inanimate objects or casual contact. Even though HIV antibodies are normally detected on a test within 6 months after infection, the period between infection and development of disease symptoms (incubation period) may be 10 years or longer. Treatment has prolonged the survival of some HIV infected persons but there is no known cure or vaccine available. For additional information, see *Appendix 7, HIV/AIDS Information.*

## Risk to Traveler

AIDS is extensive throughout the region. In Central Africa, heterosexual transmission accounts for the majority of the cases with the number of HIV infections in men and women more or less equal. In addition, many women of child bearing age are infected, and HIV transmission from mother to infant is widespread. The risk to a traveler depends on whether the traveler will be involved in sexual or needle-sharing contact with a person who is infected with HIV. Receipt of unscreened blood for transfusion poses a risk for HIV infection.

## Prevention

No effective vaccine has been developed for HIV. Travelers should avoid sexual or needle-sharing contact with a person who is infected with HIV. If a blood transfusion is necessary, screened blood should come from an HIV-negative blood donor.

## Recommendations

Travelers should avoid activities known to carry risks for infection with HIV.

## HEPATITIS B

Hepatitis B is a viral infection of the liver. Hepatitis B is transmitted to humans primarily through behavior that result in the exchange of blood or fluids containing blood. Risky behavior includes heterosexual or homosexual contact or sharing needles or drug paraphernalia with a person infected with the hepatitis B virus. Any unscreened or improperly screened blood or blood product, as well as unsterilized needles, or contact with potentially infected people who have open skin sores due to impetigo, scabies, and scratched insect bites, heightens the potential for infection to the traveler. An effective vaccine for prevention of hepatitis B is available.

## Risk to Traveler

The risk of hepatitis B virus infection is high for Africa. The risk to the individual international traveler is greater if the traveler:

- has direct contact with blood or fluids containing blood;
- has intimate sexual contact with an infected person;
- remains in the country for longer than six months or has close contact with the local population.

## Prevention

**Hepatitis B vaccine** should be considered for those traveling to countries with high to intermediate rates of hepatitis B infection. For those travelers expecting to reside in countries of high risk, as well as all health workers, vaccination is strongly recommended.

Vaccination should ideally begin 6 months before travel, in order to complete the full series, which is needed for optimal protection. The three intramuscular doses of vaccine should be spaced so that the second dose is given one month after the first. The final dose is given 6 months after the first. The vaccination schedule should be initiated even if it will not be completed before travel begins. There is an alternative four-dose schedule that may provide protection if the first three doses can be delivered before departure. After completing the primary series, booster doses of the vaccine are not necessary.

## Recommendations

CDC recommends vaccination for any of the following people:

- any health care worker (medical, dental, or laboratory) whose activities might result in blood exposure;
- any traveler who may have intimate sexual contact with the local population;
- any long-term (6 months or more) traveler, e.g. teachers, who will reside in rural areas or have daily physical contact with the local population; or
- any traveler who is likely to seek either medical, dental, or other treatment in local facilities during their stay.

Hepatitis B vaccination is not required for travel to any country. Additional hepatitis B information is found in *Appendix 15, Hepatitis B.*

## MENINGOCOCCAL DISEASE

Meningococcal disease (bacterial meningitis) is a bacterial infection in the lining of the brain or spinal cord. Early symptoms are headache, stiff neck, a rash, and fever. The bacteria is transmitted to humans through respiratory droplets when an infected person sneezes or coughs on you.

## Risk to Traveler

There is **seasonal risk** of meningococcal disease in parts of Central Africa, primarily in the savannah regions of **Cameroon, Central African Republic, Chad,** and **Sudan** during the dry season from December through June. When a traveler lives and works around the local population, the risk increases. Some of the countries in Central Africa are recognized to have epidemic meningococcal disease, and to be a part of the "meningitis belt" that runs from Guinea and Mali in the west all the way across Africa to Ethiopia and Djibouti on the eastern coast. When a traveler lives and works around the local population, the risk increases.

## Prevention

A one dose meningococcal vaccine called **Menomune** is available.

## Recommendations

Vaccination is not required for entry into any country in this region. CDC recommends vaccination with meningococcal vaccine for travelers going to Mali and all countries directly eastward, including Cameroon, Central African Republic, Chad, and Sudan, when travel occurs between December and June.

## OTHER DISEASES
## SCHISTOSOMIASIS

Schistosomiasis is a parasitic infection that develops after the larvae of a flatworm have penetrated the human skin. These larvae live in fresh water lakes, ponds, and streams and can penetrate unbroken skin. Water treated with chlorine or iodine is virtually safe, and salt water poses no risk.

## Risk to Traveler

Schistosomiasis infection is widespread in all Central African countries: **Angola, Cameroon, Central African Republic, Chad, Congo, Equatorial Guinea, Gabon, Sudan, Zaire,** and **Zambia.** The risk is a function of the frequency and degree of contact with contaminated fresh water for bathing, wading, or swimming.

## Prevention

The traveler cannot distinguish between infested and non-infested water. Therefore, swimming in fresh water in rural areas should be avoided. Bath water should either be heated to 50° (122° F) for five minutes or treated with chlorine or iodine as done for drinking water. If exposed, immediate and vigorous towel drying or application of rubbing alcohol to the exposed areas may reduce the risk of infection. Screening procedures are available for those who suspect infection, and schistosomiasis is treatable with drugs.

### Recommendations
Avoid contact with potentially contaminated water, such as swimming in lakes, ponds, rivers, etc.

## RABIES
Rabies is a viral infection that affects the central nervous system. It is transmitted to humans by warm-blooded animal (mammal) bites that introduce the virus into the wound. Although dogs are the main reservoir of the disease, all warm-blooded animal bites should be suspect.

### Risk to Traveler
For countries in Central Africa, there is a risk of rabies infection, particularly in rural areas or in areas where large numbers of dogs are found.

### Prevention
Do not handle animals! Any animal bite should receive prompt medical attention. When wounds are thoroughly cleaned with large amounts of soap and water, the risk of rabies infection is reduced. Exposed individuals should receive prompt medical attention and advice on post-exposure preventive treatment.

### Recommendations
There are no requirements for vaccination, but pre-exposure vaccination is recommended for:
• travelers visiting foreign areas where dog rabies is known to exist and whose activities may place them at high risk of exposure;
• veterinarians and animal handlers;
• spelunkers; and
• certain rabies laboratory workers.

Pre-exposure vaccination does not nullify the need for post-exposure vaccine, but reduces the number of injections and may provide protection under circumstances in which rabies exposure is unrecognized. For additional rabies information, refer to *Appendix 11, Rabies Information*.

## SUMMARY OF RECOMMENDATIONS
## FOR CENTRAL AFRICA

*Travelers should:*

- *take mefloquine (or equivalent) for malaria prevention*
- *follow precautions to prevent insect bites*
- *pay attention to the quality of their drinking water and food*
- *have a dose of Immune Globulin (IG) or the hepatitis A vaccine, and consider booster doses of tetanus (Td) and polio (eIPV) vaccines.*
- *Depending on the locations to be visited, planned activities, and health of the traveler, the following vaccines should be considered: Hepatitis B, Yellow Fever, Typhoid, Rabies (pre-exposure), and Cholera.*
- *Finally, the normal "childhood" vaccines should be up-to-date: Measles, Mumps, Rubella (MMR Vaccine); Diphtheria, Tetanus, Pertussis (DTP Vaccine if traveler is less than 7 years of age, or Td if older than 7 years of age), and Polio vaccine. For additional information on these "childhood" vaccines, refer to Appendix 5, Vaccine Recommendations.*

# 6. EAST AFRICA

## COUNTRIES IN THIS REGION
Burundi
Comoros Island
Djibouti
Eritrea
Ethiopia
Kenya
Madagascar
Malawi
Mauritius
Mayotte
Mozambique
Reunion
Rwanda
Seychelles
Somalia
Tanzania
Uganda

---

**EAST AFRICA TRAVELER'S OVERVIEW**

*Travelers to East Africa may be exposed to potential diseases from a number of sources. **The most frequently reported illness is traveler's diarrhea**, but East Africa contains a variety of diseases transmitted by:*
- *insects,*
- *contaminated food and water, or ·*
- *close contact with infected people.*

*In this chapter, specific diseases, their causes, symptoms, geographic areas of risk, and prevention recommendations or requirement information are discussed under their topical headings. As a general guideline, in order to reduce the risk of infection, travelers must:*
- *protect themselves from insects*
- *ensure the quality of their food and drinking water*
- *be knowledgeable about potential diseases in the region to be visited*
- *receive all recommended vaccines and preventive medications.*

*In addition, travelers should note that diseases are not restricted to cleanly defined geographical areas. For example, mosquitoes can fly over city or country borders, so all travelers should protect themselves by taking the basic preventive precautions as described under each section and disease. Where appropriate, more detailed information is referenced in the Appendices.*

---

## DISEASES TRANSMITTED BY INSECTS

Many diseases are transmitted through the bite of infected insects such as mosquitoes, flies, fleas, ticks and lice. In general, **travelers must protect themselves from insect bites**. Travelers are at a higher risk for insect bites if they participate in outdoor activities during night time hours from dusk to dawn when mosquitoes bite, or if their living accommodations are unscreened. If a mosquito net is unlikely to be available, consider buying a portable mosquito net.

## PREVENTING INSECT BITES

To reduce the risk of mosquito bites, travelers should remain in well-screened areas, use mosquito nets, and wear clothes that cover most of the body. Travelers should also take insect repellent with them to use on any exposed areas of the skin. The most effective compound in a repellent is **DEET**, which may be listed as an ingredient on repellant labels as **"N,N-diethyl meta-toluamide."** Check the repellent label to ensure DEET is an ingredient.

Travelers should note, however, that insect repellents containing DEET should always be used according to label directions and sparingly on children. **Avoid applying high-concentration (greater than 35%) products to the skin, particularly on children, and refrain from applying repellent to portions of the hands that are likely to come in contact with the eyes and mouth.** Pediatric insect repellents with 6-10% DEET are available without prescription in many drug stores. In rare instances, toxic reactions or other problems have developed after contact with DEET.

Travelers should also purchase a flying insect-killing spray to use in living and sleeping areas during the evening and night. For greater protection, clothing and bednets can be soaked in or sprayed with **permethrin**, which is an insect repellent licensed for use on clothing. If applied according to the directions, permethrin will repel insects from clothing for several weeks. Portable mosquito bednets, repellents containing DEET, and permethrin can be purchased in hardware, backpacking, and military surplus stores.

## MALARIA

Malaria is a serious parasitic infection transmitted to humans by an Anopheles mosquito. These mosquitoes bite at night, from dusk to dawn. Symptoms of malaria range from flu-like symptoms with fever, general achiness, headache, and fatigue, to a cycle of shaking chills, high fever, and sweating. If left untreated, malaria can cause anemia, kidney failure, coma, and death. Drugs are available to help prevent a malaria infection.

However, in spite of all protective measures, travelers occasionally develop malaria. Therefore, while traveling and up to one year after returning home, travelers should seek medical evaluation for any flu-like illness.

### Risk to Traveler

*High Risk*

In **Burundi**, **Comoro Island**, **Djibouti**, **Madagascar** (especially coastal areas), **Malawi**, **Mayotte**, **Mozambique**, **Rwanda**, **Somalia**, **Tanzania** and **Uganda**, a high risk for malaria exists throughout the year in all parts of these countries, including the urban areas. The dominant form is *P. falciparum* (the most dangerous type), which has been reported to be resistant to the drug chloroquine.

*Other High Risk Areas*

• **Eritrea** – all areas, except no risk above 2,000 meters.

- **Ethiopia** – all areas, except no risk in Addis Ababa and above 2,000 meters.
- **Kenya** – all areas (including game parks), except no risk in Nairobi and above 2,500 meters.
- **Mauritius** – risk in the rural areas only, except no risk on Rodriguez Island (see prevention information specific to Mauritius).

*No Risk*
Reunion and Seychelles.

## Prevention & Recommendations

Travelers at risk for malaria should take **mefloquine** to prevent this strain of malaria. This drug is marketed in the United States under the name **Lariam™**. The adult dosage is 250 mg (one tablet) once a week. Mefloquine should be taken one week before leaving, weekly while in the malarious area, and weekly for 4 weeks after leaving the malarious area.

Minor side effects one may experience while taking mefloquine include gastrointestinal disturbances and dizziness. More serious side effects at the recommended dosage have rarely occurred. Consult a physician for other precautions.

Mefloquine should not be used by travelers with a:
- history of epilepsy or psychiatric disorder,
- known hypersensitivity to mefloquine.

In consultation with a physician, mefloquine may be used by pregnant women and children weighing less than 30 pounds, when travel to an area with chloroquine-resistant malaria is unavoidable. Travelers who cannot take mefloquine should read the section "Prescription Drugs for Malaria" found in *Appendix 1, Malaria Information.*

**Travelers to Mauritius** should take **chloroquine** to prevent malaria. The weekly dosage for an adult is 500 mg (salt) once a week. This drug should be taken one week before entering a malarious area, weekly while there, and weekly for 4 weeks after leaving the malarious area. No other anti-malarial drugs are needed.

In addition to using drugs to prevent malaria and treat a possible malaria attack, travelers should use measures to reduce exposure to malaria-carrying mosquitoes and protect themselves from mosquito bites. Remember, these mosquitoes bite mainly during the evening and night, from dusk to dawn.

Additional general malaria information, as well as specific information for women who are pregnant or children, is found in *Appendix 1, Malaria Information.*

## YELLOW FEVER

Yellow fever is a viral disease transmitted to humans by a mosquito bite. The mosquitoes are most active during the evening hours. Symptoms range from fever, chills, headache, and vomiting to jaundice, internal bleeding, and kidney failure. Death occurs in about 5% of those infected. There is no specific drug to treat an infection of yellow fever, therefore prevention of infection is important.

### Risk to Traveler

Outbreaks of yellow fever have occurred in **Ethiopia** and **Kenya**. Yellow fever is not always active in all countries of this region, but there is a significant risk to all travelers throughout the year, especially in travel or visits to rural settings. No risk on the islands of Comoros and Seychelles.

### Prevention

Yellow fever vaccination, a one-dose shot, is effective for up to 10 years for the prevention of yellow fever and may be administered to adults and children over 9 months of age. This vaccine is only administered at designated yellow fever centers, usually your local health department. **The vaccine and the official certificate become effective 10 days after vaccination**. Travelers at continued risk need a booster and a new certificate every 10 years.

*Travelers who should not be immunized include:*
- Infants under 4 months.
- Persons severely allergic to eggs.
- Pregnant women or people whose immune systems are not functioning normally.

In addition to the vaccine, travelers should use measures to reduce exposure to mosquitoes and protect themselves from mosquito bites. Remember, these mosquitoes bite mainly during the evening hours.

### Yellow Fever Certificate

After immunization, an International Certificate of Vaccination is issued and is valid 10 days after vaccination to meet entry and exit requirements for all countries. The Certificate is good for 10 years. **You must take the Certificate with you.**

## Medical Waiver

Travelers who have a medical reason not to receive the yellow fever vaccine should obtain a medical waiver. Most countries will accept a medical waiver for persons with a medical reason not to receive the vaccine (e.g. infants less than 4 months old, pregnant women, persons hypersensitive to eggs, or those with an immunosuppressed condition.) When required, CDC recommends obtaining written waivers from consular or embassy officials before departure. Follow these guidelines:

•   A physician's letter clearly stating the medical reason not to receive the vaccine might be acceptable to some governments.

•   It should be written on letterhead stationery and bear the stamp used by a health department or official immunization center to validate the International Certificate of Vaccination.

•   Check embassies or consulates for specific waiver requirements.

## Recommendations & Requirements

If you are traveling to most countries in East Africa, CDC recommends and many countries require a yellow fever vaccination. For travel toComoros and Mayotte, CDC does not recommend a yellow fever vaccination.

In East Africa, only Rwanda requires a yellow fever vaccination for entry for any traveler. Most of the remaining countries require a vaccination if travel plans include travel from specific countries.

The following East African country absolutely requires a Yellow Fever Vaccination Certificate:
**Rwanda**

Comoros and Mayotte do not require a yellow fever vaccination.

In addition to Rwanda, if you are traveling from a country listed in the left two columns of the following table to an East African country in the right hand column, **you are required to have a yellow fever vaccination.**

Note: Due to potential origin and destination combinations in travel plans, some countries may appear in both columns.

For comprehensive country-by-country yellow fever vaccine requirements, see *Appendix 2, Yellow Fever Requirements.*

**TRAVELING FROM ANY OF THE FOLLOWING "ENDEMIC" YELLOW FEVER INFECTED COUNTRIES**

### Africa:

Angola
Benin
Burundi
Burkina Faso
Cameroon
Central African Republic
Chad
Congo
Cote d'Ivoire, (Ivory Coast)
Equatorial Guinea
Ethiopia
Gabon
Gambia
Ghana
Guinea
Guinea Bissau
Kenya
Liberia
Mali
Mauritania
Niger
Nigeria
Rwanda
Sao Tome and Principe
Senegal
Sierra Leone
Somalia
Sudan
Tanzania
Togo
Uganda
Zaire

### South America:

Bolivia
Brazil
Colombia
Ecuador
French Guiana
Guyana
Panama
Peru
Suriname
Venezuela

**TRAVELING TO EAST AFRICAN COUNTRIES**

Burundi
Djibouti
Eritrea
Ethiopia
Kenya
Madagascar
Malawi
Mauritius
Mozambique
Reunion
Seychelles
Somalia
Tanzania
Uganda

**Yellow Fever Certificate Required**

## DENGUE FEVER

Dengue fever is a viral infection transmitted to humans by mosquito bites. These mosquitoes are most active during the day, especially around dawn and dusk, and are frequently found in or around residential areas. The illness is flu-like and characterized by sudden onset, high fever, severe headaches, joint and muscle pain, and rash. Severe cases of dengue hemorrhagic fever produce shock, internal bleeding, and death. The rash appears 3-4 days after the onset of fever. Since there is no vaccine or specific treatment available, prevention is important.

### Risk to Traveler

Most recently, epidemics of dengue fever have occurred in **Djibouti, Kenya, Mozambique**, and **Somalia**. In addition, dengue fever occurs sporadically in **Cameroon, Congo, Gabon**, and **Zaire**. The risk of infection is small for most travelers except during periods of epidemic transmission.

There is no vaccine for dengue fever, therefore, the traveler should avoid mosquito bites. These mosquitoes may bite anytime during the day, especially in shady areas, indoors, or when the sky is overcast, but prefer feeding around dawn and dusk. For additional information on dengue fever, refer to *Appendix 12, Dengue Fever.*

## OTHER INSECT DISEASES
### Risks to Traveler

Other diseases spread by mosquitoes, sand flies, black flies, or other insects are prevalent, especially in rural areas. These diseases include: *filariasis* and *Chikungunya* (mosquito), *leishmaniasis* (sand fly), *onchocerciasis* (black flies), *African trypanosomiasis* (flies), *Congo-Crimean hemorrhagic fever* (ticks), *typhus* (lice), and *plague* (fleas).

### Prevention

For most of these diseases, a vaccine is not available and treatment is limited. Therefore, travelers must follow the guidelines at the beginning of this chapter under "Preventing Insect Bites." For additional detailed information on these and other insect diseases, please read *Appendix 3, Other Insect Diseases.*

## DISEASES TRANSMITTED THROUGH FOOD & WATER

Food and waterborne diseases are the number one cause of illness to travelers and are very common in Central Africa. **Traveler's diarrhea is**

**the most frequent health problem for travelers.** It can be caused by viruses, bacteria, or parasites that are found universally throughout the region. Transmission is most often through contaminated food or water. Infections may cause diarrhea and vomiting (typhoid fever, cholera, and parasites), liver damage (hepatitis), or muscle paralysis (polio).

## GENERAL PRECAUTIONS

**Water:** The following beverages are safe to drink: boiled water or beverages made with boiled water, canned or carbonated beverages, beer, or wine. Impure water often contaminates drinking containers, ice, and tap water.

**Food:** Food that has been cooked to 165° F (74° C) is generally safe. As a reference, food at this temperature cannot be put directly into your mouth, but must cool a bit. Foods of concern are salads, uncooked vegetables and fruit, unpasteurized milk and milk products, raw meat, and shellfish. If you peel fruit yourself, it is generally safe. A simple rule of thumb is: "Boil it, cook it, peel it, or forget it."

For additional detailed precautions, be sure to read *Appendix 4, Traveler's Diarrhea & Food and Water Precautions.*

## TYPHOID FEVER

Typhoid fever is a bacterial infection transmitted to humans through contaminated food and/or water, or directly between people. Symptoms of typhoid fever include fever, headaches, fatigue, loss of appetite, and constipation. Typhoid fever can be treated effectively with antibiotics.

### Risk to Traveler

Travelers to East Africa are at risk for typhoid fever, especially when traveling to smaller cities, villages, or rural areas.

### Prevention

By drinking only bottled or boiled beverages and eating only thoroughly cooked food, a traveler lowers the risk of infection. Currently available vaccines have been shown to protect 70-90% of the recipients. Therefore, even vaccinated travelers should be cautious in selecting their food and water.

Two vaccines are recommended for protection against typhoid fever. An oral vaccine, **TY21a**, consists of a total of 4 capsules taken (one per day, every other day) over a seven day period, and requires a booster every five years. Reactions to the TY21a vaccine are rare but include nausea, vomiting, abdominal cramps, and skin rash.

A new single-dose injectable vaccine, **Typhim Vi** or **ViCPS**, is equally effective, and requires a booster dose every two years. Reactions to Typhim Vi are also rare, but include discomfort at the site of injection and headaches. An earlier typhoid vaccine developed years ago, which uses killed typhoid organisms and is administered in a two dose series, had more reported side effect and is currently not preferred. Instead, use one of the newer vaccines. Based on the vaccine chosen, booster doses are required every two to five years.

## Recommendations

CDC recommends a typhoid vaccination for those travelers who are going off the usual tourist itineraries, traveling to smaller cities and rural areas, or staying long term, that is, for six weeks or more. Vaccination should be completed at least two weeks before travel. Typhoid vaccination is not required for international travel.

## CHOLERA

Cholera is an acute diarrheal illness caused by an infection of the intestine with the bacterium *Vibrio cholerae*. Infection is acquired by ingesting contaminated water or food. The infection is often mild without symptoms, but sometimes can be severe. Approximately one in 20 infected persons has severe disease characterized by an abrupt onset of profuse watery diarrhea, vomiting, dehydration, and leg cramps.

## Risk to Traveler

Cholera cases have been reported from most of the countries of East Africa. The risk of infection to the US traveler is low, especially those who are following the usual tourist itineraries and staying in standard accommodations. Travelers should consider the vaccine if they have stomach ulcers, use anti-acid therapy, or if they will be living in less than sanitary conditions in areas of high cholera activity. A list of cholera infected countries is given in *Appendix 10, CDC's Blue Sheet*.

## Prevention

Travelers to cholera infected areas should:
- avoid eating high risk foods, especially fish and shellfish, and
- follow the standard food and water precautions of eating only thoroughly cooked food that is served hot, peeling their own fruit, and

drinking beverages and ice made from boiled or chlorinated water, bottled carbonated water, or bottled carbonated soft drinks.

Persons with severe cases of cholera respond well to simple fluid and electrolyte-replacement therapy, but medical attention must be sought quickly when cholera is suspected.

The cholera vaccine licensed for use in the United States confers only brief and incomplete immunity (50% effective in reducing the illness). The risk of cholera to US travelers is so low that it is questionable whether the vaccine is of benefit, and therefore it is not recommended routinely for travelers. The primary series for this cholera vaccine is normally two injections with booster doses given every 6 months for persons who remain at high risk. **Cholera vaccine is not recommended for infants under 6 months old or for pregnant women.**

For additional information about cholera, read *Appendix 4, Traveler's Diarrhea & Food and Water Precautions*, and *Appendix 8, Cholera Information*.

## HEPATITIS A

Hepatitis A is a viral infection of the liver transmitted to humans by the fecal-oral route; through direct person-to-person contact; from contaminated water, ice, or shellfish; or from fruits or uncooked vegetables contaminated through handling. Symptoms include fatigue, fever, loss of appetite, nausea, dark urine, jaundice, vomiting, aches and pains, and light stools. No specific therapy, only supportive care, is available.

### Risk to Traveler

Travelers are at high risk for hepatitis A, especially if travel plans include visiting rural areas and extensive travel in the countryside, frequent close contact with local persons, or eating in settings of poor sanitation. Be aware that a study has shown that many cases of travel-related hepatitis A occur in travelers to developing countries with "standard" itineraries, accommodations, and food consumption behaviors.

### Prevention

The virus is inactivated by boiling or cooking to 185° F (85° C) for one minute. Therefore, eating thoroughly cooked foods and drinking only treated water serve as general precautions. In addition, **Immune globulin (IG)** *or* **hepatitis A vaccine** is recommended before travel. Two hepatitis A vaccines, **Havrix®** and **VAQTA®**, are currently licensed in the US.

Immune globulin and the hepatitis A vaccine marketed in the United States (US) are safe. American travelers should note that IG manufactured in foreign countries may or may not meet these requirements. Therefore, American travelers who will need to receive additional doses of IG in other countries should use products that meet US standards and license requirements. For reference, the method of manufacturing IG in the US is called the **Cohn-Oncley procedure.**

## Recommendations

CDC recommends Immune globulin (IG) or hepatitis A vaccine before travel for protection against hepatitis A.

**Immune globulin** is recommended for persons of all ages who:
· desire only short term protection (one dose is effective for three months)
· need immediate protection, and
· are too young for the vaccine (less than 2 years of age).

**Hepatitis A vaccine** is preferred for persons two years of age and older who plan to travel repeatedly or reside for long periods of time in intermediate or high risk areas. Bear in mind:
· The complete hepatitis A vaccine series requires a minimum of six months to complete.
· For these travelers over 18 years of age, hepatitis A vaccine should be given in a two-dose series with the second dose administered 6-12 months after the first.
· For children and adolescents between ages 2 through 18, a two or three dose series of hepatitis A vaccine is recommended depending on the vaccine chosen.

Travelers can be considered to be protected four weeks after receiving the initial vaccine dose. If the vaccine is administered less than four weeks before travel, then IG should also be given. The vaccine series must be completed for long-term protection. Hepatitis A vaccination is not required for travel to any country.

In addition to receiving IG or the vaccine, all travelers should follow the food and water precautions as described in *Appendix 4, Traveler's Diarrhea & Food and Water Precautions.*

Additional IG and hepatitis A information covering the vaccine and its safety are found in *Appendix 9, Hepatitis A Vaccine & Immune Globulin (IG) - Disease and Vaccine Information.*

## PARASITES

Parasitic infections are acquired by eating or drinking contaminated food or water, through direct contact with soil or water containing parasites or their larva, or by contact with biting insects. Symptoms and evidence of infection may include, but are not limited to: fever, swollen lymph nodes, rashes or itchy skin, digestive problems such as abdominal pain or diarrhea, eye problems, and anemia.

### Risk to Traveler

Travelers to East Africa are at risk of parasitic infections. There are many types of parasites and infection may occur in several ways: by eating undercooked meats infected with parasites or their larva; by eating food or drinking water contaminated with parasites or their eggs; by contact with soil or water infected with parasites; or through insect bites. Several types of parasites, for example schistosomiasis, can penetrate intact human skin and travelers are advised to wear shoes and avoid swimming, wading, or washing in fresh water.

### Prevention

Travelers should eat only thoroughly cooked food, drink safe water, wear shoes, refrain from swimming in fresh water, and avoid contact with insects, particularly mosquitoes, biting flies, gnats, and midges.

## DISEASES TRANSMITTED THROUGH INTIMATE CONTACT WITH PEOPLE

### HIV/AIDS

Human immunodeficiency virus, or HIV, which causes acquired immunodeficiency syndrome or AIDS, is found primarily in blood, semen, and vaginal secretions of an infected person. HIV is spread by sexual contact with an infected person, by needle-sharing among injecting drug users, and through transfusions of infected blood and blood clotting factors. Babies born to HIV-infected women may become infected before, during, or shortly after birth.

In the United States, blood is screened for HIV antibodies, but this screening may not take place in all countries. Scientific studies have revealed no evidence that HIV is transmitted by air, food, water, insects, inanimate objects or casual contact. Even though HIV antibodies are normally detected on a test within 6 months after infection, the period between infection and development of disease symptoms (incubation period) may be 10 years or longer. Treatment has prolonged the survival of some HIV infected persons but there is no known cure or vaccine available. For additional information, see *Appendix 7, HIV/AIDS Information.*

## Risk to Traveler

AIDS is extensive throughout the region. In East Africa, heterosexual transmission accounts for the majority of the cases with the number of HIV infections in men and women more or less equal. In addition, many women of child bearing age are infected, and HIV transmission from mother to infant is widespread. The risk to a traveler depends on whether the traveler will be involved in sexual or needle-sharing contact with a person who is infected with HIV. Receipt of unscreened blood for transfusion poses a risk for HIV infection.

## Prevention

No effective vaccine has been developed for HIV. Travelers should avoid sexual or needle-sharing contact with a person who is infected with HIV. If a blood transfusion is necessary, screened blood should come from an HIV-negative blood donor.

## Recommendations

Travelers should avoid activities known to carry risks for infection with HIV.

## HEPATITIS B

Hepatitis B is a viral infection of the liver. Hepatitis B is transmitted to humans primarily through behavior that result in the exchange of blood or fluids containing blood. Risky behavior includes heterosexual or homosexual contact or sharing needles or drug paraphernalia with a person infected with the hepatitis B virus. Any unscreened or improperly screened blood or blood product, as well as unsterilized needles, or contact with potentially infected people who have open skin sores due to impetigo, scabies, and scratched insect bites, heightens the potential for infection to the traveler. An effective vaccine for prevention of hepatitis B is available.

## Risk to Traveler

The risk of hepatitis B virus infection is high for Africa. The risk to the individual international traveler is greater if the traveler:
- has direct contact with blood or fluids containing blood;
- has intimate sexual contact with an infected person;

- remains in the country for longer than six months or has close contact with the local population.

## Prevention

**Hepatitis B vaccine** should be considered for those traveling to countries with high to intermediate rates of hepatitis B infection. For those travelers expecting to reside in countries of high risk, as well as all health workers, vaccination is strongly recommended.

Vaccination should ideally begin 6 months before travel, in order to complete the full series, which is needed for optimal protection. The three intramuscular doses of vaccine should be spaced so that the second dose is given one month after the first. The final dose is given 6 months after the first. The vaccination schedule should be initiated even if it will not be completed before travel begins. There is an alternative four-dose schedule that may provide protection if the first three doses can be delivered before departure. After completing the primary series, booster doses of the vaccine are not necessary.

## Recommendations

CDC recommends vaccination for any of the following people:
- any health care worker (medical, dental, or laboratory) whose activities might result in blood exposure;
- any traveler who may have intimate sexual contact with the local population;
- any long-term (6 months or more) traveler, e.g. teachers, who will reside in rural areas or have daily physical contact with the local population; or
- any traveler who is likely to seek either medical, dental, or other treatment in local facilities during their stay.

Hepatitis B vaccination is not required for travel to any country. Additional hepatitis B information is found in *Appendix 15, Hepatitis B.*

## MENINGOCOCCAL DISEASE

Meningococcal disease (bacterial meningitis) is a bacterial infection in the lining of the brain or spinal cord. Early symptoms are headache, stiff neck, a rash, and fever. The bacteria is transmitted to humans through respiratory droplets when an infected person sneezes or coughs on you.

### Risk to Traveler

There is seasonal risk of meningococcal disease in parts of East Africa, primarily in the savannah regions of **Ethiopia** and **Djibouti** during the dry season from December through June. Many of the countries in East Africa are recognized to have epidemic meningococcal disease, and to be a part of the "meningitis belt" that runs from Guinea and Mali in the west all the way across Africa to Ethiopia and Djibouti on the eastern coast. Recently, **epidemics** have occurred in **Burundi, Kenya,** and **Tanzania**. When a traveler lives and works around the local population, the risk increases.

### Prevention
A one dose meningococcal vaccine called **Menomune** is available.

### Recommendations
Vaccination is not required for entry into any country in this region. CDC recommends vaccination with meningococcal vaccine for travelers going to Mali and all countries directly eastward, including Cameroon, Central African Republic, Chad, and Sudan, when travel occurs between December and June.

## OTHER DISEASES
## SCHISTOSOMIASIS
Schistosomiasis is a parasitic infection that develops after the larvae of a flatworm have penetrated the human skin. These larvae live in fresh water lakes, ponds, and streams and can penetrate unbroken skin. Water treated with chlorine or iodine is virtually safe, and salt water poses no risk.

### Risk to Traveler
Schistosomiasis infection is widespread in all East African countries: **Burundi, Eritrea, Ethiopia, Kenya, Madagascar, Malawi, Mauritius, Mozambique, Rwanda, Somalia, Tanzania** (including the islands), **and Uganda**. Little or no information is available for Comoros Island, Djibouti, Mayotte, Reunion, and Seychelles. The risk is a function of the frequency and degree of contact with contaminated fresh water for bathing, wading, or swimming.

### Prevention
The traveler cannot distinguish between infested and non-infested water. Therefore, swimming in fresh water in rural areas should be avoided. Bath water should either be heated to 50° (122° F) for five minutes or treated with chlorine or iodine as done for drinking water. If exposed, immediate and vigorous towel drying or application of rubbing alcohol to the exposed areas may reduce the risk of infection. Screening proce-

dures are available for those who suspect infection, and schistosomiasis is treatable with drugs.

## Recommendations
Avoid contact with potentially contaminated water, such as swimming in lakes, ponds, rivers, etc.

## RABIES
Rabies is a viral infection that affects the central nervous system. It is transmitted to humans by warm-blooded animal (mammal) bites that introduce the virus into the wound. Although dogs are the main reservoir of the disease, all warm-blooded animal bites should be suspect.

### Risk to Traveler
For countries in East Africa, there is a risk of rabies infection, particularly in rural areas or in areas where large numbers of dogs are found. Mauritius and the Seychelles have reported no rabies cases for at least the past two years.

### Prevention
Do not handle animals! Any animal bite should receive prompt medical attention. When wounds are thoroughly cleaned with large amounts of soap and water, the risk of rabies infection is reduced. Exposed individuals should receive prompt medical attention and advice on post-exposure preventive treatment.

### Recommendations
There are no requirements for vaccination, but pre-exposure vaccination is recommended for:
- travelers visiting foreign areas where dog rabies is known to exist and whose activities may place them at high risk of exposure;
- veterinarians and animal handlers;
- spelunkers; and
- certain rabies laboratory workers.

Pre-exposure vaccination does not nullify the need for post-exposure vaccine, but reduces the number of injections and may provide protection under circumstances in which rabies exposure is unrecognized. For additional rabies information, refer to *Appendix 11, Rabies Information*.

## SUMMARY OF RECOMMENDATIONS
## FOR EAST AFRICA

*Travelers should:*

- *take mefloquine (or equivalent) for malaria prevention*
- *follow precautions to prevent insect bites*
- *pay attention to the quality of their drinking water and food*
- *have a dose of Immune Globulin (IG) or the hepatitis A vaccine, and consider booster doses of tetanus (Td) and polio (eIPV) vaccines.*
- *Depending on the locations to be visited, planned activities, and health of the traveler, the following vaccines should be considered: Hepatitis B, Yellow Fever, Typhoid, Rabies (pre-exposure), and Cholera.*
- *Finally, the normal "childhood" vaccines should be up-to-date: Measles, Mumps, Rubella (MMR Vaccine); Diphtheria, Tetanus, Pertussis (DTP Vaccine if traveler is less than 7 years of age, or Td if older than 7 years of age), and Polio vaccine. For additional information on these "childhood" vaccines, refer to Appendix 5, Vaccine Recommendations.*

# 7. SOUTHERN AFRICA

## COUNTRIES IN THIS REGION
**Botswana**
**Lesotho**
**Namibia**
**South Africa**
**St. Helena** *(an island in the South Atlantic)*
**Swaziland**
**Zimbabwe**

## SOUTHERN AFRICA TRAVELER'S OVERVIEW

*Travelers to Southern Africa may be exposed to potential diseases from a number of sources. **The most frequently reported illness is traveler's diarrhea**, but Southern Africa contains a variety of diseases transmitted by:*
- *insects,*
- *contaminated food and water, or*
- *close contact with infected people.*

*In this chapter, specific diseases, their causes, symptoms, geographic areas of risk, and prevention recommendations or requirement information are discussed under their topical headings. As a general guideline, in order to reduce the risk of infection, travelers must:*
- *protect themselves from insects*
- *ensure the quality of their food and drinking water*
- *be knowledgeable about potential diseases in the region to be visited*
- *receive all recommended vaccines and preventive medications.*

*In addition, travelers should note that diseases are not restricted to cleanly defined geographical areas. For example, mosquitoes can fly over city or country borders, so all travelers should protect themselves by taking the basic preventive precautions as described under each section and disease. Where appropriate, more detailed information is referenced in the Appendices.*

## DISEASES TRANSMITTED BY INSECTS

Many diseases are transmitted through the bite of infected insects such as mosquitoes, flies, fleas, ticks and lice. In general, **travelers must protect themselves from insect bites**. Travelers are at a higher risk for insect bites if they participate in outdoor activities during night time hours from dusk to dawn when mosquitoes bite, or if their living accommodations are unscreened. If a mosquito net is unlikely to be available, consider buying a portable mosquito net.

## PREVENTING INSECT BITES

To reduce the risk of mosquito bites, travelers should remain in well-screened areas, use mosquito nets, and wear clothes that cover most of the body. Travelers should also take insect repellent with them to use on any exposed areas of the skin. The most effective compound in a repellent is **DEET**, which may be listed as an ingredient on repellant labels as "**N,N-diethyl meta-toluamide.**" Check the repellent label to ensure DEET is an ingredient.

Travelers should note, however, that insect repellents containing DEET should always be used according to label directions and sparingly on children. **Avoid applying high-concentration (greater than 35%) products to the skin, particularly on children, and refrain from applying repellent to portions of the hands that are likely to come in contact with the eyes and mouth.** Pediatric insect repellents with 6-10% DEET are available without prescription in many drug stores. In rare instances, toxic reactions or other problems have developed after contact with DEET.

Travelers should also purchase a flying insect-killing spray to use in living and sleeping areas during the evening and night. For greater protection, clothing and bednets can be soaked in or sprayed with **permethrin**, which is an insect repellent licensed for use on clothing. If applied according to the directions, permethrin will repel insects from clothing for several weeks. Portable mosquito bednets, repellents containing DEET, and permethrin can be purchased in hardware, backpacking, and military surplus stores.

## MALARIA

Malaria is a serious parasitic infection transmitted to humans by an Anopheles mosquito. These mosquitoes bite at night, from dusk to dawn. Symptoms of malaria range from flu-like symptoms with fever, general achiness, headache, and fatigue, to a cycle of shaking chills, high fever, and sweating. If left untreated, malaria can cause anemia, kidney failure, coma, and death. Drugs are available to help prevent a malaria infection.

However, in spite of all protective measures, travelers occasionally develop malaria. Therefore, while traveling and up to one year after returning home, travelers should seek medical evaluation for any flu-like illness.

### Risk to Traveler
*High Risk*
- **Zimbabwe** – there is a high risk throughout the year in all parts of the country, including the urban areas.
- **Botswana** – northern part of the country (north of 21°S Latitude).
- **Namibia** – all areas of Ovamboland and Caprivi Strip.
- **South Africa** – rural areas (including the game parks) in the north, east, and western low altitude areas of Transvaal and in the Natal coastal areas north of 28°S Latitude.
- **Swaziland** – all lowland areas.

*No Risk*
Lesotho and St. Helena.

## Prevention & Recommendations

Travelers at risk for malaria should take **mefloquine** to prevent this strain of malaria. This drug is marketed in the United States under the name **Lariam™**. The adult dosage is 250 mg (one tablet) once a week. Mefloquine should be taken one week before leaving, weekly while in the malarious area, and weekly for 4 weeks after leaving the malarious area.

Minor side effects one may experience while taking mefloquine include gastrointestinal disturbances and dizziness. More serious side effects at the recommended dosage have rarely occurred. Consult a physician for other precautions.

Mefloquine should not be used by travelers with a:
- history of epilepsy or psychiatric disorder,
- known hypersensitivity to mefloquine.

In consultation with a physician, mefloquine may be used by pregnant women and children weighing less than 30 pounds, when travel to an area with chloroquine-resistant malaria is unavoidable. Travelers who cannot take mefloquine should read the section "Prescription Drugs for Malaria" found in *Appendix 1, Malaria Information.*

In addition to using drugs to prevent malaria and treat a possible malaria attack, travelers should use measures to reduce exposure to malaria-carrying mosquitoes and protect themselves from mosquito bites. Remember, these mosquitoes bite mainly during the evening and night, from dusk to dawn.

Additional general malaria information, as well as specific information for women who are pregnant or children, is found in *Appendix 1, Malaria Information.*

## YELLOW FEVER

Yellow fever is a viral disease transmitted to humans by a mosquito bite. The mosquitoes are most active during the evening hours. Symptoms range from fever, chills, headache, and vomiting to jaundice, internal bleeding, and kidney failure. Death occurs in about 5% of those infected. There is no specific drug to treat an infection of yellow fever, therefore prevention of infection is important.

## Risk to Traveler

There is little or no risk of yellow fever infection in Southern Africa.

## Prevention

Yellow fever vaccination, a one-dose shot, is effective for up to 10 years for the prevention of yellow fever and may be administered to adults and children over 9 months of age. This vaccine is only administered at designated yellow fever centers, usually your local health department. **The vaccine and the official certificate become effective 10 days after vaccination.** Travelers at continued risk need a booster and a new certificate every 10 years.

*Travelers who should not be immunized include:*
- Infants under 4 months.
- Persons severely allergic to eggs.
- Pregnant women or people whose immune systems are not functioning normally.

In addition to the vaccine, travelers should use measures to reduce exposure to mosquitoes and protect themselves from mosquito bites. Remember, these mosquitoes bite mainly during the evening hours.

## Yellow Fever Certificate

After immunization, an International Certificate of Vaccination is issued and is valid 10 days after vaccination to meet entry and exit requirements for all countries. The Certificate is good for 10 years. **You must take the Certificate with you.**

## Medical Waiver

Travelers who have a medical reason not to receive the yellow fever vaccine should obtain a medical waiver. Most countries will accept a medical waiver for persons with a medical reason not to receive the vaccine (e.g. infants less than 4 months old, pregnant women, persons hypersensitive to eggs, or those with an immunosuppressed condition.) When required, CDC recommends obtaining written waivers from consular or embassy officials before departure. Follow these guidelines:
- A physician's letter clearly stating the medical reason not to receive the vaccine might be acceptable to some governments.
- It should be written on letterhead stationery and bear the stamp used by a health department or official immunization center to validate the International Certificate of Vaccination.
- Check embassies or consulates for specific waiver requirements.

## Recommendations & Requirements

In general, CDC does not recommend a yellow fever vaccination when traveling to a Southern African country from countries not infected with yellow fever. However, some countries require a yellow fever vaccination when travelers arrive from certain African and South American countries (see below). Therefore, sometimes the easiest and safest thing to do is to get a yellow fever vaccination and a signed certificate to take with you.

Botswana and St. Helena have no yellow fever entry requirements.

Lesotho, Namibia, South Africa, Swaziland, and Zimbabwe have the following conditional requirements listed in the accompanying table:

If you are traveling from a country on the left side of the following table to a Southern African country in the right hand column, **you are required to have a yellow fever vaccination and certificate.**

For comprehensive country-by-country yellow fever vaccine requirements, see Appendix 2, *Yellow Fever Requirements*.

## TRAVELING FROM ANY OF THE FOLLOWING "ENDEMIC" YELLOW FEVER INFECTED COUNTRIES

**Africa:**

Angola
Benin
Burundi
Burkina Faso
Cameroon
Central African Republic
Chad
Congo
Cote d'Ivoire, (Ivory Coast)
Equatorial Guinea
Ethiopia
Gabon
Gambia
Ghana
Guinea
Guinea Bissau
Kenya
Liberia
Mali
Mauritania
Niger
Nigeria
Rwanda
Sao Tome and Principe
Senegal
Sierra Leone
Somalia
Sudan
Tanzania
Togo
Uganda
Zaire

**South America:**

Bolivia
Brazil
Colombia
Ecuador
French Guiana
Guyana
Panama
Peru
Suriname
Venezuela

## TRAVELING TO SOUTHERN AFRICAN COUNTRIES

Lesotho
Namibia
South Africa
Swaziland
Zimbabwe

**Yellow Fever Certificate Required**

## DENGUE FEVER

Dengue fever is a viral infection transmitted to humans by mosquito bites. These mosquitoes are most active during the day, especially around dawn and dusk, and are frequently found in or around residential areas. The illness is flu-like and characterized by sudden onset, high fever, severe headaches, joint and muscle pain, and rash. Severe cases of dengue hemorrhagic fever produce shock, internal bleeding, and death. The rash appears 3-4 days after the onset of fever. Since there is no vaccine or specific treatment available, prevention is important.

### Risk to Traveler

Dengue fever occurs occasionally in **South Africa**, **Swaziland**, and **Zimbabwe**. The risk of infection is small for most travelers except during periods of epidemic transmission.

### Prevention

There is no vaccine for dengue fever, therefore, the traveler should avoid mosquito bites. These mosquitoes may bite anytime during the day, especially in shady areas, indoors, or when the sky is overcast, but prefer feeding around dawn and dusk. For additional information on dengue fever, refer to *Appendix 12, Dengue Fever.*

## OTHER INSECT DISEASES

### Risks to Traveler

Other diseases spread by mosquitoes, sand flies, black flies, or other insects are prevalent, especially in rural areas. These diseases include: *filariasis* and *Chikungunya* (mosquito), *leishmaniasis* (sand fly), *onchocerciasis* (black flies), *African trypanosomiasis* (flies), *Congo-Crimean hemorrhagic fever* (ticks), *typhus* (lice), and *plague* (fleas).

### Prevention

For most of these diseases, a vaccine is not available and treatment is limited. Therefore, travelers must follow the guidelines at the beginning of this chapter under "Preventing Insect Bites." For additional detailed information on these and other insect diseases, please read *Appendix 3, Other Insect Diseases.*

## DISEASES TRANSMITTED THROUGH FOOD & WATER

Food and waterborne diseases are the number one cause of illness to travelers and are very common in Southern Africa. **Traveler's diarrhea is the most frequent health problem for travelers**. It can be caused by viruses, bacteria, or parasites that are found universally throughout the region. Transmission is most often through contaminated food or water. Infections may cause diarrhea and vomiting (typhoid fever, cholera, and parasites), liver damage (hepatitis), or muscle paralysis (polio).

## GENERAL PRECAUTIONS

**Water**: The following beverages are safe to drink: boiled water or beverages made with boiled water, canned or carbonated beverages, beer, or wine. Impure water often contaminates drinking containers, ice, and tap water.

**Food**: Food that has been cooked to 165° F (74° C) is generally safe. As a reference, food at this temperature cannot be put directly into your mouth, but must cool a bit. Foods of concern are salads, uncooked vegetables and fruit, unpasteurized milk and milk products, raw meat, and shellfish. If you peel fruit yourself, it is generally safe. A simple rule of thumb is: "Boil it, cook it, peel it, or forget it."

For additional detailed precautions, be sure to read *Appendix 4, Traveler's Diarrhea & Food and Water Precautions.*

## TYPHOID FEVER

Typhoid fever is a bacterial infection transmitted to humans through contaminated food and/or water, or directly between people. Symptoms of typhoid fever include fever, headaches, fatigue, loss of appetite, and constipation. Typhoid fever can be treated effectively with antibiotics.

### Risk to Traveler

Travelers to Southern Africa are at risk for typhoid fever, especially when traveling to smaller cities, villages, or rural areas.

### Prevention

By drinking only bottled or boiled beverages and eating only thoroughly cooked food, a traveler lowers the risk of infection. Currently available vaccines have been shown to protect 70-90% of the recipients. Therefore, even vaccinated travelers should be cautious in selecting their food and water.

Two vaccines are recommended for protection against typhoid fever. An oral vaccine, **TY21a**, consists of a total of 4 capsules taken (one per day, every other day) over a seven day period, and requires a booster every five years. Reactions to the TY21a vaccine are rare but include nausea, vomiting, abdominal cramps, and skin rash.

A new single-dose injectable vaccine, **Typhim Vi** or **ViCPS**, is equally effective, and requires a booster dose every two years. Reactions to Typhim Vi are also rare, but include discomfort at the site of injection and headaches. An earlier typhoid vaccine developed years ago, which uses killed typhoid organisms and is administered in a two dose series, had more reported side effect and is currently not preferred. Instead, use one of the newer vaccines. Based on the vaccine chosen, booster doses are required every two to five years.

## Recommendations

CDC recommends a typhoid vaccination for those travelers who are going off the usual tourist itineraries, traveling to smaller cities and rural areas, or staying long term, that is, for six weeks or more. Vaccination should be completed at least two weeks before travel. Typhoid vaccination is not required for international travel.

## CHOLERA

Cholera is an acute diarrheal illness caused by an infection of the intestine with the bacterium *Vibrio cholerae*. Infection is acquired by ingesting contaminated water or food. The infection is often mild without symptoms, but sometimes can be severe. Approximately one in 20 infected persons has severe disease characterized by an abrupt onset of profuse watery diarrhea, vomiting, dehydration, and leg cramps.

## Risk to Traveler

Cholera cases have been reported from most of the countries of Southern Africa. The risk of infection to the US traveler is low, especially those who are following the usual tourist itineraries and staying in standard accommodations. Travelers should consider the vaccine if they have stomach ulcers, use anti-acid therapy, or if they will be living in less than sanitary conditions in areas of high cholera activity. A list of cholera infected countries is given in *Appendix 10, CDC's Blue Sheet*.

## Prevention

Travelers to cholera infected areas should:
- avoid eating high risk foods, especially fish and shellfish, and
- follow the standard food and water precautions of eating only thoroughly cooked food that is served hot, peeling their own fruit, and drinking beverages and ice made from boiled or chlorinated water, bottled carbonated water, or bottled carbonated soft drinks.

Persons with severe cases of cholera respond well to simple fluid and electrolyte-replacement therapy, but medical attention must be sought quickly when cholera is suspected.

The cholera vaccine licensed for use in the United States confers only brief and incomplete immunity (50% effective in reducing the illness). The risk of cholera to US travelers is so low that it is questionable whether the vaccine is of benefit, and therefore it is not recommended routinely for travelers. The primary series for this cholera vaccine is normally two injections with booster doses given every 6 months for persons who remain at high risk. **Cholera vaccine is not recommended for infants under 6 months old or for pregnant women.**

For additional information about cholera, read *Appendix 4, Traveler's Diarrhea & Food and Water Precautions*, and *Appendix 8, Cholera Information*.

## HEPATITIS A
Hepatitis A is a viral infection of the liver transmitted to humans by the fecal-oral route; through direct person-to-person contact; from contaminated water, ice, or shellfish; or from fruits or uncooked vegetables contaminated through handling. Symptoms include fatigue, fever, loss of appetite, nausea, dark urine, jaundice, vomiting, aches and pains, and light stools. No specific therapy, only supportive care, is available.

### Risk to Traveler
Travelers are at high risk for hepatitis A, especially if travel plans include visiting rural areas and extensive travel in the countryside, frequent close contact with local persons, or eating in settings of poor sanitation. Be aware that a study has shown that many cases of travel-related hepatitis A occur in travelers to developing countries with "standard" itineraries, accommodations, and food consumption behaviors.

### Prevention
The virus is inactivated by boiling or cooking to 185° F (85° C) for one minute. Therefore, eating thoroughly cooked foods and drinking only treated water serve as general precautions. In addition, **Immune globulin (IG)** *or* **hepatitis A vaccine** is recommended before travel. Two hepatitis A vaccines, **Havrix®** and **VAQTA®**, are currently licensed in the US.

Immune globulin and the hepatitis A vaccine marketed in the United States are safe. American travelers should note that IG manufactured in foreign countries may or may not meet these requirements. Therefore, American travelers who will need to receive additional doses of IG in other countries should use products that meet US standards and license requirements. For reference, the method of manufacturing IG in the US is called the **Cohn-Oncley procedure.**

## Recommendations

CDC recommends Immune globulin (IG) or hepatitis A vaccine before travel for protection against hepatitis A.

**Immune globulin** is recommended for persons of all ages who:
- desire only short term protection (one dose is effective for three months)
- need immediate protection, and
- are too young for the vaccine (less than 2 years of age).

**Hepatitis A vaccine** is preferred for persons two years of age and older who plan to travel repeatedly or reside for long periods of time in intermediate or high risk areas. Bear in mind:
- The complete hepatitis A vaccine series requires a minimum of six months to complete.
- For these travelers over 18 years of age, hepatitis A vaccine should be given in a two-dose series with the second dose administered 6-12 months after the first.
- For children and adolescents between ages 2 through 18, a two or three dose series of hepatitis A vaccine is recommended depending on the vaccine chosen.

Travelers can be considered to be protected four weeks after receiving the initial vaccine dose. If the vaccine is administered less than four weeks before travel, then IG should also be given. The vaccine series must be completed for long-term protection. Hepatitis A vaccination is not required for travel to any country.

In addition to receiving IG or the vaccine, all travelers should follow the food and water precautions as described in *Appendix 4, Traveler's Diarrhea & Food and Water Precautions.*

Additional IG and hepatitis A information covering the vaccine and its safety are found in *Appendix 9, Hepatitis A Vaccine & Immune Globulin (IG) - Disease and Vaccine Information.*

## PARASITES

Parasitic infections are acquired by eating or drinking contaminated food or water, through direct contact with soil or water containing parasites or their larva, or by contact with biting insects. Symptoms and evidence of infection may include, but are not limited to: fever, swollen lymph nodes, rashes or itchy skin, digestive problems such as abdominal pain or diarrhea, eye problems, and anemia.

Travelers to Southern Africa are at risk of parasitic infections. There are many types of parasites and infection may occur in several ways: by eating undercooked meats infected with parasites or their larva; by eating food or drinking water contaminated with parasites or their eggs; by contact with soil or water infected with parasites; or through insect bites. Several types of parasites, for example schistosomiasis, can penetrate intact human skin and travelers are advised to wear shoes and avoid swimming, wading, or washing in fresh water.

### Prevention

Travelers should eat only thoroughly cooked food, drink safe water, wear shoes, refrain from swimming in fresh water, and avoid contact with insects, particularly mosquitoes, biting flies, gnats, and midges.

## DISEASES TRANSMITTED THROUGH INTIMATE CONTACT WITH PEOPLE

### HIV/AIDS

Human immunodeficiency virus, or HIV, which causes acquired immunodeficiency syndrome or AIDS, is found primarily in blood, semen, and vaginal secretions of an infected person. HIV is spread by sexual contact with an infected person, by needle-sharing among injecting drug users, and through transfusions of infected blood and blood clotting factors. Babies born to HIV-infected women may become infected before, during, or shortly after birth.

In the US, blood is screened for HIV antibodies, but this screening may not take place in all countries. Scientific studies have revealed no evidence that HIV is transmitted by air, food, water, insects, inanimate objects or casual contact. Even though HIV antibodies are normally detected on a test within 6 months after infection, the period between infection and development of disease symptoms (incubation period) may be 10 years or longer. Treatment has prolonged the survival of some HIV infected persons but there is no known cure or vaccine available. For additional information, see *Appendix 7, HIV/AIDS Information.*

## Risk to Traveler

AIDS is extensive throughout the region. In Southern Africa, hetero-sexual transmission accounts for the majority of the cases with the number of HIV infections in men and women more or less equal. In addition, many women of child bearing age are infected, and HIV transmission from mother to infant is widespread. The risk to a traveler depends on whether the traveler will be involved in sexual or needle-sharing contact with a person who is infected with HIV. Receipt of unscreened blood for transfusion poses a risk for HIV infection.

## Prevention

No effective vaccine has been developed for HIV. Travelers should avoid sexual or needle-sharing contact with a person who is infected with HIV. If a blood transfusion is necessary, screened blood should come from an HIV-negative blood donor.

## Recommendations

Travelers should avoid activities known to carry risks for infection with HIV.

## HEPATITIS B

Hepatitis B is a viral infection of the liver. Hepatitis B is transmitted to humans primarily through behavior that result in the exchange of blood or fluids containing blood. Risky behavior includes heterosexual or homosexual contact or sharing needles or drug paraphernalia with a person infected with the hepatitis B virus. Any unscreened or improperly screened blood or blood product, as well as unsterilized needles, or contact with potentially infected people who have open skin sores due to impetigo, scabies, and scratched insect bites, heightens the potential for infection to the traveler. An effective vaccine for prevention of hepatitis B is available.

## Risk to Traveler

The risk of hepatitis B virus infection is high for Africa. The risk to the individual international traveler is greater if the traveler:
- has direct contact with blood or fluids containing blood;
- has intimate sexual contact with an infected person;
- remains in the country for longer than six months or has close contact with the local population.

## Prevention

**Hepatitis B vaccine** should be considered for those traveling to countries with high to intermediate rates of hepatitis B infection. For those travelers expecting to reside in countries of high risk, as well as all health workers, vaccination is strongly recommended.

Vaccination should ideally begin 6 months before travel, in order to complete the full series, which is needed for optimal protection. The three intramuscular doses of vaccine should be spaced so that the second dose is given one month after the first. The final dose is given 6 months after the first. The vaccination schedule should be initiated even if it will not be completed before travel begins. There is an alternative four-dose schedule that may provide protection if the first three doses can be delivered before departure. After completing the primary series, booster doses of the vaccine are not necessary.

## Recommendations

CDC recommends vaccination for any of the following people:
- any health care worker (medical, dental, or laboratory) whose activities might result in blood exposure;
- any traveler who may have intimate sexual contact with the local population;
- any long-term (6 months or more) traveler, e.g. teachers, who will reside in rural areas or have daily physical contact with the local population; or
- any traveler who is likely to seek either medical, dental, or other treatment in local facilities during their stay.

Hepatitis B vaccination is not required for travel to any country. Additional hepatitis B information is found in *Appendix 15, Hepatitis B*.

## OTHER DISEASES
## SCHISTOSOMIASIS

Schistosomiasis is a parasitic infection that develops after the larvae of a flatworm have penetrated the human skin. These larvae live in fresh water lakes, ponds, and streams and can penetrate unbroken skin. Water treated with chlorine or iodine is virtually safe, and salt water poses no risk.

### Risk to Traveler

Schistosomiasis infection can be found in the Southern African countries of **Botswana**, **Namibia**, **South Africa**, **Swaziland**, and **Zimbabwe**. The risk is a function of the frequency and degree of contact with contaminated fresh water for bathing, wading, or swimming.

## Prevention
The traveler cannot distinguish between infested and non-infested water. Therefore, swimming in fresh water in rural areas should be avoided. Bath water should either be heated to 50° (122° F) for five minutes or treated with chlorine or iodine as done for drinking water. If exposed, immediate and vigorous towel drying or application of rubbing alcohol to the exposed areas may reduce the risk of infection. Screening procedures are available for those who suspect infection, and schistosomiasis is treatable with drugs.

## Recommendations
Avoid contact with potentially contaminated water, such as swimming in lakes, ponds, rivers, etc.

## RABIES
Rabies is a viral infection that affects the central nervous system. It is transmitted to humans by warm-blooded animal (mammal) bites that introduce the virus into the wound. Although dogs are the main reservoir of the disease, all warm-blooded animal bites should be suspect.

## Risk to Traveler
For countries in Southern Africa, there is a risk of rabies infection, particularly in rural areas or in areas where large numbers of dogs are found.

## Prevention
Do not handle animals! Any animal bite should receive prompt medical attention. When wounds are thoroughly cleaned with large amounts of soap and water, the risk of rabies infection is reduced. Exposed individuals should receive prompt medical attention and advice on post-exposure preventive treatment.

## Recommendations
There are no requirements for vaccination, but pre-exposure vaccination is recommended for:
- travelers visiting foreign areas where dog rabies is known to exist and whose activities may place them at high risk of exposure;
- veterinarians and animal handlers;

- spelunkers; and
- certain rabies laboratory workers.

Pre-exposure vaccination does not nullify the need for post-exposure vaccine, but reduces the number of injections and may provide protection under circumstances in which rabies exposure is unrecognized. For additional rabies information, refer to *Appendix 11, Rabies Information.*

---

### SUMMARY OF RECOMMENDATIONS
### FOR SOUTHERN AFRICA

*Travelers should:*
- *take mefloquine (or equivalent) for malaria prevention*
- *follow precautions to prevent insect bites*
- *pay attention to the quality of their drinking water and food*
- *have a dose of Immune Globulin (IG) or the hepatitis A vaccine, and consider booster doses of tetanus (Td) and polio (eIPV) vaccines.*
- *Depending on the locations to be visited, planned activities, and health of the traveler, the following vaccines should be considered: Hepatitis B, Yellow Fever, Typhoid, Rabies (pre-exposure), and Cholera.*
- *Finally, the normal "childhood" vaccines should be up-to-date: Measles, Mumps, Rubella (MMR Vaccine); Diphtheria, Tetanus, Pertussis (DTP Vaccine if traveler is less than 7 years of age, or Td if older than 7 years of age), and Polio vaccine. For additional information on these "childhood" vaccines, refer to Appendix 5, Vaccine Recommendations.*

# 8. THE CARIBBEAN

## COUNTRIES IN THIS REGION
Antigua & Barbuda
Bahamas
Barbados
Bermuda (UK)
Cayman Islands (UK)
Cuba
Dominica
Dominican Republic
Grenada
Guadeloupe
Haiti
Jamaica
Martinique (France)
Montserrat (UK)
Netherlands Antilles
Puerto Rico (US)
Saint Lucia
St Vincent & the Grenadines
St Kitts & Nevis
Trinidad & Tobago
Virgin Islands (US)
Virgin Islands (UK)

## CARIBBEAN TRAVELER'S OVERVIEW

*Travelers to the Caribbean may be exposed to potential diseases from a number of sources. **The most frequently reported illness is traveler's diarrhea**, but the Caribbean contains a variety of diseases transmitted by:*
- *insects,*
- *contaminated food and water, or*
- *close contact with infected people.*

*In this chapter, specific diseases, their causes, symptoms, geographic areas of risk, and prevention recommendations or requirement information are discussed under their topical headings. As a general guideline, in order to reduce the risk of infection, travelers must:*
- *protect themselves from insects*
- *ensure the quality of their food and drinking water*
- *be knowledgeable about potential diseases in the region to be visited*
- *receive all recommended vaccines and preventive medications.*

*In addition, travelers should note that diseases are not restricted to cleanly defined geographical areas. For example, mosquitoes can fly over city or country borders, so all travelers should protect themselves by taking the basic preventive precautions as described under each section and disease. Where appropriate, more detailed information is referenced in the Appendices.*

## DISEASES TRANSMITTED BY INSECTS

Many diseases are transmitted through the bite of infected insects such as mosquitoes, flies, fleas, ticks and lice. In general, **travelers must protect themselves from insect bites**. Travelers are at a higher risk for insect bites if they participate in outdoor activities during night time hours from dusk to dawn when mosquitoes bite, or if their living accommodations are unscreened. If a mosquito net is unlikely to be available, consider buying a portable mosquito net.

## PREVENTING INSECT BITES

To reduce the risk of mosquito bites, travelers should remain in well-screened areas, use mosquito nets, and wear clothes that cover most of the body. Travelers should also take insect repellent with them to use on any exposed areas of the skin. The most effective compound in a repellent is **DEET**, which may be listed as an ingredient on repellant labels as "**N,N-diethyl meta-toluamide**." Check the repellent label to ensure DEET is an ingredient.

Travelers should note, however, that insect repellents containing DEET should always be used according to label directions and sparingly on children. **Avoid applying high-concentration (greater than 35%) products to the skin, particularly on children, and refrain from applying repellent to portions of the hands that are likely to come in contact with the eyes and mouth.** Pediatric insect repellents with 6-10% DEET are available without prescription in many drug stores. In rare instances, toxic reactions or other problems have developed after contact with DEET.

Travelers should also purchase a flying insect-killing spray to use in living and sleeping areas during the evening and night. For greater protection, clothing and bednets can be soaked in or sprayed with **permethrin**, which is an insect repellent licensed for use on clothing. If applied according to the directions, permethrin will repel insects from clothing for several weeks. Portable mosquito bednets, repellents containing DEET, and permethrin can be purchased in hardware, backpacking, and military surplus stores.

## MALARIA

Malaria is a serious parasitic infection transmitted to humans by an Anopheles mosquito. These mosquitoes bite at night, from dusk to dawn. Symptoms of malaria range from flu-like symptoms with fever, general achiness, headache, and fatigue, to a cycle of shaking chills, high fever, and sweating. If left untreated, malaria can cause anemia, kidney failure, coma, and death. Drugs are available to help prevent a malaria infection.

However, in spite of all protective measures, travelers occasionally develop malaria. Therefore, while traveling and up to one year after returning home, travelers should seek medical evaluation for any flu-like illness.

### Risk to Traveler
*Areas of Risk*
Throughout the year *P. falciparium*, the most dangerous type, has been confirmed in the following countries: **Dominican Republic** – all rural areas, except no risk in tourist resorts; the highest risk is in the provinces bordering Haiti; **Haiti** – risk in all areas.

*No Risk*
Malaria has been eradicated from the other islands.

## Prevention & Recommendations

Travelers at risk for malaria should take the prescription drug **chloroquine** to prevent malaria. The weekly dosage for an adult is 500 mg (salt) once a week. This drug should be taken one week before entering a malarious area, weekly while there, and weekly for 4 weeks after leaving the malarious area. No other anti-malarial drugs are needed.

In addition to using drugs to prevent malaria and treat a possible malaria attack, travelers should use measures to reduce exposure to malaria-carrying mosquitoes and protect themselves from mosquito bites. Remember, these mosquitoes bite mainly during the evening and night, from dusk to dawn.

Additional general malaria information, as well as specific information for women who are pregnant or children, is found in *Appendix 1, Malaria Information*.

## YELLOW FEVER

Yellow fever is a viral disease transmitted to humans by a mosquito bite. The mosquitoes are most active during the evening hours. Symptoms range from fever, chills, headache, and vomiting to jaundice, internal bleeding, and kidney failure. Death occurs in about 5% of those infected. There is no specific drug to treat an infection of yellow fever, therefore prevention of infection is important.

## Risk to Traveler

Cases of yellow fever have occurred in **Trinidad and Tobago**. However, if you are traveling to Antigua & Barbuda, Bahamas, Barbados, Dominica, Grenada, Guadeloupe, Haiti, Jamaica, Martinique (France), Netherlands Antilles , Saint Lucia, St Vincent & the Grenadines, St Kitts & Nevis, and Trinidad & Tobago, a yellow fever vaccination and certificate for entry may be required. Read the following requirements carefully.

## Prevention

Yellow fever vaccination, a one-dose shot, is effective for up to 10 years for the prevention of yellow fever and may be administered to adults and children over 9 months of age. This vaccine is only administered at designated yellow fever centers, usually your local health department. **The vaccine and the official certificate become effective 10 days after vaccination.** Travelers at continued risk need a booster and a new certificate every 10 years.

*Travelers who should not be immunized include:*
- Infants under 4 months.
- Persons severely allergic to eggs.
- Pregnant women or people whose immune systems are not functioning normally.

In addition to the vaccine, travelers should use measures to reduce exposure to mosquitoes and protect themselves from mosquito bites. Remember, these mosquitoes bite mainly during the evening hours.

## Yellow Fever Certificate

After immunization, an International Certificate of Vaccination is issued and is valid 10 days after vaccination to meet entry and exit requirements for all countries. The Certificate is good for 10 years. **You must take the Certificate with you.**

## Medical Waiver

Travelers who have a medical reason not to receive the yellow fever vaccine should obtain a medical waiver. Most countries will accept a medical waiver for persons with a medical reason not to receive the vaccine (e.g. infants less than 4 months old, pregnant women, persons hypersensitive to eggs, or those with an immunosuppressed condition.) When required, CDC recommends obtaining written waivers from consular or embassy officials before departure. Follow these guidelines:
- A physician's letter clearly stating the medical reason not to receive the vaccine might be acceptable to some governments.
- It should be written on letterhead stationery and bear the stamp used by a health department or official immunization center to validate the International Certificate of Vaccination.
- Check embassies or consulates for specific waiver requirements.

## Recommendations & Requirements

CDC recommends a yellow fever vaccination if you are traveling to areas of risk: the islands of Trinidad or Tobago (or the countries of tropical South America if you are traveling on to South America from the Caribbean).

If you are **only** traveling from the United States to a Caribbean country other than Trinidad or Tobago, CDC does not recommend and you are not required to have a yellow fever vaccination.

Some countries require a yellow fever vaccination when travelers arrive from certain South American and African countries (see table below).

Bermuda, Cayman Islands, Cuba, Dominican Republic, Montserrat (UK), Puerto Rico (US), Virgin Islands (US), and the Virgin Islands (UK) have no yellow fever vaccination requirements.

Antigua & Barbuda, Bahamas, Barbados, Dominica, Grenada, Guadeloupe, Haiti, Jamaica, Martinique (France), Netherlands Antilles (age 6 months), Saint Lucia, St Vincent & the Grenadines, St Kitts & Nevis, Trinidad & Tobago, require a yellow fever vaccination for all travelers (age greater than 1) arriving from all "Infected Countries" listed in the table below.

Countries Infected with Yellow Fever are listed on the left side below. If you are traveling from an "infected" country on the left side of the following table to a Caribbean country in the right hand column, **you are required to have a yellow fever vaccination.**

For comprehensive country-by-country yellow fever vaccine requirements, see *Appendix 2, Yellow Fever Requirements.*

| **TRAVELING FROM ANY OF THE FOLLOWING "ENDEMIC" YELLOW FEVER INFECTED COUNTRIES** | **TRAVELING TO CARIBBEAN COUNTRIES** |
|---|---|
| **Africa** | Antigua & Barbuda |
| Angola | Bahamas |
| Cameroon | Barbados |
| Gambia | Dominica |
| Guinea | Grenada |
| Kenya | Guadeloupe |
| Mali | Haiti |
| Nigeria | Jamaica |
| Sudan | Martinique (France) |
| Zaire | Netherlands Antilles |
| **South America** | Saint Lucia |
| Bolivia | St Vincent & the Grenadines |
| Brazil | St Kitts & Nevis |
| Colombia | Trinidad & Tobago |
| Ecuador | |
| Peru | **Yellow Fever Certificate Required** |

## DENGUE FEVER

Dengue fever is a viral infection transmitted to humans by mosquito bites. These mosquitoes are most active during the day, especially around dawn and dusk, and are frequently found in or around residential areas. The illness is flu-like and characterized by sudden onset, high fever, severe headaches, joint and muscle pain, and rash. Severe cases of dengue hemorrhagic fever produce shock, internal bleeding, and death. The rash appears 3-4 days after the onset of fever. Since there is no vaccine or specific treatment available, prevention is important.

### Risk to Traveler

In the Caribbean islands, low-level transmission occurs throughout the year in most tourist-oriented islands. Seasonal and sporadic epidemics with higher transmission rates also frequently occur. The risk of infection is small for most travelers except during periods of epidemic transmission. There is no dengue in Cuba or the Cayman Islands.

### Prevention

There is no vaccine for dengue fever, therefore, the traveler should avoid mosquito bites. These mosquitoes may bite anytime during the day, especially in shady areas, indoors, or when the sky is overcast, but prefer feeding around dawn and dusk. For additional information on dengue fever, refer to *Appendix 12, Dengue Fever.*

## OTHER INSECT DISEASES
### Risks to Traveler

Other diseases spread by mosquitoes, sand flies, black flies, or other insects are prevalent, especially in rural areas. These diseases include: *filariasis* and *Chikungunya* (mosquito), *leishmaniasis* (sand fly), *onchocerciasis* (black flies), *African trypanosomiasis* (flies), *Congo-Crimean hemorrhagic fever* (ticks), *typhus* (lice), and *plague* (fleas).

### Prevention

For most of these diseases, a vaccine is not available and treatment is limited. Therefore, travelers must follow the guidelines at the beginning of this chapter under "Preventing Insect Bites." For additional detailed information on these and other insect diseases, please read *Appendix 3, Other Insect Diseases.*

## DISEASES TRANSMITTED THROUGH FOOD & WATER

Food and waterborne diseases are the number one cause of illness to travelers and are very common in Caribbean countries. **Traveler's**

**diarrhea is the most frequent health problem for travelers.** It can be caused by viruses, bacteria, or parasites that are found universally throughout the region. Transmission is most often through contaminated food or water. Infections may cause diarrhea and vomiting (typhoid fever, cholera, and parasites), liver damage (hepatitis), or muscle paralysis (polio).

## GENERAL PRECAUTIONS

**Water**: The following beverages are safe to drink: boiled water or beverages made with boiled water, canned or carbonated beverages, beer, or wine. Impure water often contaminates drinking containers, ice, and tap water.

**Food**: Food that has been cooked to 165° F (74° C) is generally safe. As a reference, food at this temperature cannot be put directly into your mouth, but must cool a bit. Foods of concern are salads, uncooked vegetables and fruit, unpasteurized milk and milk products, raw meat, and shellfish. If you peel fruit yourself, it is generally safe. A simple rule of thumb is: "Boil it, cook it, peel it, or forget it."

For additional detailed precautions, be sure to read *Appendix 4, Traveler's Diarrhea & Food and Water Precautions.*

## TYPHOID FEVER

Typhoid fever is a bacterial infection transmitted to humans through contaminated food and/or water, or directly between people. Symptoms of typhoid fever include fever, headaches, fatigue, loss of appetite, and constipation. Typhoid fever can be treated effectively with antibiotics.

### Risk to Traveler

Travelers to the Caribbean are at risk for typhoid fever, especially when traveling to smaller cities, villages, or rural areas.

### Prevention

Two vaccines are recommended for protection against typhoid fever. An oral vaccine, **TY21a**, consists of a total of 4 capsules taken (one per day, every other day) over a seven day period, and requires a booster every five years. Reactions to the TY21a vaccine are rare but include nausea, vomiting, abdominal cramps, and skin rash.

A new single-dose injectable vaccine, **Typhim Vi** or **ViCPS**, is equally effective, and requires a booster dose every two years. Reactions to

Typhim Vi are also rare, but include discomfort at the site of injection and headaches. An earlier typhoid vaccine developed years ago, which uses killed typhoid organisms and is administered in a two dose series, had more reported side effect and is currently not preferred. Instead, use one of the newer vaccines. Based on the vaccine chosen, booster doses are required every two to five years.

## Recommendations

CDC recommends a typhoid vaccination for those travelers who are going off the usual tourist itineraries, traveling to smaller cities and rural areas, or staying long term, that is, for six weeks or more. Vaccination should be completed at least two weeks before travel. Typhoid vaccination is not required for international travel.

## CHOLERA

Cholera is an acute diarrheal illness caused by an infection of the intestine with the bacterium *Vibrio cholerae*. Infection is acquired by ingesting contaminated water or food. The infection is often mild without symptoms, but sometimes can be severe. Approximately one in 20 infected persons has severe disease characterized by an abrupt onset of profuse watery diarrhea, vomiting, dehydration, and leg cramps.

## Risk to Traveler

A recent epidemic of cholera has swept through the entire central and tropical South American area, but so far it has not reached the Caribbean region. The risk of infection to the US traveler is very low, especially those who are following the usual tourist itineraries, staying in standard accommodations, and following food and water safety instructions. A list of cholera infected countries is given in *Appendix 10, CDC's Blue Sheet*.

## Prevention

Travelers to cholera infected areas should:
- avoid eating high risk foods, especially fish and shellfish, and
- follow the standard food and water precautions of eating only thoroughly cooked food that is served hot, peeling their own fruit, and drinking beverages and ice made from boiled or chlorinated water, bottled carbonated water, or bottled carbonated soft drinks.

Persons with severe cases of cholera respond well to simple fluid and electrolyte-replacement therapy, but medical attention must be sought quickly when cholera is suspected.

The cholera vaccine licensed for use in the United States confers only brief and incomplete immunity (50% effective in reducing the illness). The risk of cholera to US travelers is so low that it is questionable whether the vaccine is of benefit, and therefore it is not recommended routinely for travelers. The primary series for this cholera vaccine is normally two injections with booster doses given every 6 months for persons who remain at high risk. **Cholera vaccine is not recommended for infants under 6 months old or for pregnant women.**

For additional information about cholera, read *Appendix 4, Traveler's Diarrhea & Food and Water Precautions*, and *Appendix 8, Cholera Information*.

## HEPATITIS A

Hepatitis A is a viral infection of the liver transmitted to humans by the fecal-oral route; through direct person-to-person contact; from contaminated water, ice, or shellfish; or from fruits or uncooked vegetables contaminated through handling. Symptoms include fatigue, fever, loss of appetite, nausea, dark urine, jaundice, vomiting, aches and pains, and light stools. No specific therapy, only supportive care, is available.

### Risk to Traveler

Travelers are at high risk for hepatitis A, especially if travel plans include visiting rural areas and extensive travel in the countryside, frequent close contact with local persons, or eating in settings of poor sanitation. Be aware that a study has shown that many cases of travel-related hepatitis A occur in travelers to developing countries with "standard" itineraries, accommodations, and food consumption behaviors.

### Prevention

The virus is inactivated by boiling or cooking to 185° F (85° C) for one minute. Therefore, eating thoroughly cooked foods and drinking only treated water serve as general precautions. In addition, **Immune globulin (IG) or hepatitis A vaccine** is recommended before travel. Two hepatitis A vaccines, **Havrix®** and **VAQTA®**, are currently licensed in the United States.

Immune globulin and the hepatitis A vaccine marketed in the United States are safe. American travelers should note that IG manufactured in foreign countries may or may not meet these requirements. Therefore, American travelers who will need to receive additional doses of IG in other countries should use products that meet US standards and license requirements. For reference, the method of manufacturing IG in the US is called the **Cohn-Oncley procedure.**

## Recommendations

CDC recommends Immune globulin (IG) or hepatitis A vaccine before travel for protection against hepatitis A.

**Immune globulin** is recommended for persons of all ages who:
- desire only short term protection (one dose is effective for three months)
- need immediate protection, and
- are too young for the vaccine (less than 2 years of age).

**Hepatitis A vaccine** is preferred for persons two years of age and older who plan to travel repeatedly or reside for long periods of time in intermediate or high risk areas. Bear in mind:
- The complete hepatitis A vaccine series requires a minimum of six months to complete.
- For these travelers over 18 years of age, hepatitis A vaccine should be given in a two-dose series with the second dose administered 6-12 months after the first.
- For children and adolescents between ages 2 through 18, a two or three dose series of hepatitis A vaccine is recommended depending on the vaccine chosen.

Travelers can be considered to be protected four weeks after receiving the initial vaccine dose. If the vaccine is administered less than four weeks before travel, then IG should also be given. The vaccine series must be completed for long-term protection. Hepatitis A vaccination is not required for travel to any country.

In addition to receiving IG or the vaccine, all travelers should follow the food and water precautions as described in *Appendix 4, Traveler's Diarrhea & Food and Water Precautions.*

Additional IG and hepatitis A information covering the vaccine and its safety are found in *Appendix 9, Hepatitis A Vaccine & Immune Globulin (IG) - Disease and Vaccine Information.*

## PARASITES

Parasitic infections are acquired by eating or drinking contaminated food or water, through direct contact with soil or water containing parasites or their larva, or by contact with biting insects. Symptoms and evidence of infection may include, but are not limited to: fever, swollen lymph nodes, rashes or itchy skin, digestive problems such as abdominal pain or diarrhea, eye problems, and anemia.

## Risk to Traveler

Travelers to The Caribbean are at risk of parasitic infections. There are many types of parasites and infection may occur in several ways: by eating undercooked meats infected with parasites or their larva; by eating food or drinking water contaminated with parasites or their eggs; by contact with soil or water infected with parasites; or through insect bites. Several types of parasites, for example schistosomiasis, can penetrate intact human skin and travelers are advised to wear shoes and avoid swimming, wading, or washing in fresh water.

## Prevention

Travelers should eat only thoroughly cooked food, drink safe water, wear shoes, refrain from swimming in fresh water, and avoid contact with insects, particularly mosquitoes, biting flies, gnats, and midges.

## DISEASES TRANSMITTED THROUGH INTIMATE CONTACT WITH PEOPLE

### HIV/AIDS

Human immunodeficiency virus, or HIV, which causes acquired immunodeficiency syndrome or AIDS, is found primarily in blood, semen, and vaginal secretions of an infected person. HIV is spread by sexual contact with an infected person, by needle-sharing among injecting drug users, and through transfusions of infected blood and blood clotting factors. Babies born to HIV-infected women may become infected before, during, or shortly after birth.

In the United States, blood is screened for HIV antibodies, but this screening may not take place in all countries. Scientific studies have revealed no evidence that HIV is transmitted by air, food, water, insects, inanimate objects or casual contact. Even though HIV antibodies are normally detected on a test within 6 months after infection, the period between infection and development of disease symptoms (incubation period) may be 10 years or longer. Treatment has prolonged the survival of some HIV infected persons but there is no known cure or vaccine available. For additional information, see *Appendix 7, HIV/AIDS Information.*

## Risk to Traveler

AIDS is found throughout the region. In the Caribbean, sexual transmission accounts for the majority of the cases. Heterosexual transmission is increasing. The risk to a traveler depends on whether the traveler will be involved in sexual or needle-sharing contact with a person who is infected with HIV. Receipt of unscreened blood for transfusion poses a risk for HIV infection.

## Prevention

No effective vaccine has been developed for HIV. Travelers should avoid sexual or needle-sharing contact with a person who is infected with HIV. If a blood transfusion is necessary, screened blood should come from an HIV-negative blood donor.

## Recommendations

Travelers should avoid activities known to carry risks for infection with HIV.

## HEPATITIS B

Hepatitis B is a viral infection of the liver. Hepatitis B is transmitted to humans primarily through behavior that result in the exchange of blood or fluids containing blood. Risky behavior includes heterosexual or homosexual contact or sharing needles or drug paraphernalia with a person infected with the hepatitis B virus. Any unscreened or improperly screened blood or blood product, as well as unsterilized needles, or contact with potentially infected people who have open skin sores due to impetigo, scabies, and scratched insect bites, heightens the potential for infection to the traveler. An effective vaccine for prevention of hepatitis B is available.

## Risk to Traveler

Hepatitis B rates are high in the **Dominican Republic** and **Haiti**, and moderate throughout the rest of the region. The risk to the individual international traveler is greater if the traveler:
- has direct contact with blood or fluids containing blood;
- has intimate sexual contact with an infected person;
- remains in the country for longer than six months or has close contact with the local population.

## Prevention

**Hepatitis B vaccine** should be considered for those traveling to countries with high to intermediate rates of hepatitis B infection. For those travelers expecting to reside in countries of high risk, as well as all health workers, vaccination is strongly recommended.

Vaccination should ideally begin 6 months before travel, in order to complete the full series, which is needed for optimal protection. The three intramuscular doses of vaccine should be spaced so that the second dose is given one month after the first. The final dose is given 6 months after the first. The vaccination schedule should be initiated even if it will not be completed before travel begins. There is an alternative four-dose schedule that may provide protection if the first three doses can be delivered before departure. After completing the primary series, booster doses of the vaccine are not necessary.

## Recommendations

CDC recommends vaccination for any of the following people:
- any health care worker (medical, dental, or laboratory) whose activities might result in blood exposure;
- any traveler who may have intimate sexual contact with the local population;
- any long-term (6 months or more) traveler, e.g. teachers, who will reside in rural areas or have daily physical contact with the local population; or
- any traveler who is likely to seek either medical, dental, or other treatment in local facilities during their stay.

Hepatitis B vaccination is not required for travel to any country. Additional hepatitis B information is found in *Appendix 15, Hepatitis B*.

## OTHER DISEASES
## SCHISTOSOMIASIS

Schistosomiasis is a parasitic infection that develops after the larvae of a flatworm have penetrated the human skin. These larvae live in fresh water lakes, ponds, and streams and can penetrate unbroken skin. Water treated with chlorine or iodine is virtually safe, and salt water poses no risk.

### Risk to Traveler

In the Caribbean, schistosomiasis is known to exist in **Antigua, the Dominican Republic, Guadeloupe, Martinique, Montserrat, Puerto Rico**, and **St. Lucia**. For travelers visiting these areas, the risk is a function of the frequency and degree of contact with contaminated fresh water for bathing, wading, or swimming.

## Prevention

The traveler cannot distinguish between infested and non-infested water. Therefore, swimming in fresh water in rural areas should be avoided. Bath water should either be heated to 50° (122° F) for five minutes or treated with chlorine or iodine as done for drinking water. If exposed, immediate and vigorous towel drying or application of rubbing alcohol to the exposed areas may reduce the risk of infection. Screening procedures are available for those who suspect infection, and schistosomiasis is treatable with drugs.

## Recommendations

Avoid contact with potentially contaminated water, such as swimming in lakes, ponds, rivers, etc.

## RABIES

Rabies is a viral infection that affects the central nervous system. It is transmitted to humans by warm-blooded animal (mammal) bites that introduce the virus into the wound. Although dogs are the main reservoir of the disease, all warm-blooded animal bites should be suspect.

## Risk to Traveler

There is a risk of rabies infection, particularly in rural areas or in areas where large numbers of dogs are found. Islands of risk include **Cuba, Dominican Republic, Grenada, Haiti, Puerto Rico,** and **Trinidad and Tobago**.

Many Caribbean islands have reported no rabies cases for at least the past two years including: Anguilla, Antigua & Barbuda, Bahamas, Barbados, Bermuda, Cayman Islands (UK), Dominica, Guadeloupe, Jamaica, Martinique (France), Montserrat (UK), Netherlands Antilles, Saint Lucia, St Martin, St Vincent & the Grenadines, St Kitts & Nevis, Turks and Caicos, and Virgin Islands, (US & UK). Check with consulates or local island health officials for specific up-to-date information.

## Prevention

Do not handle animals! Any animal bite should receive prompt medical attention. When wounds are thoroughly cleaned with large amounts of soap and water, the risk of rabies infection is reduced. Exposed individuals should receive prompt medical attention and advice on post-exposure preventive treatment.

## Recommendations

There are no requirements for vaccination, but pre-exposure vaccination is recommended for:
- travelers visiting foreign areas where dog rabies is known to exist and whose activities may place them at high risk of exposure;
- veterinarians and animal handlers;
- spelunkers; and
- certain rabies laboratory workers.

Pre-exposure vaccination does not nullify the need for post-exposure vaccine, but reduces the number of injections and may provide protection under circumstances in which rabies exposure is unrecognized. For additional rabies information, refer to *Appendix 11, Rabies Information.*

---

### SUMMARY OF RECOMMENDATIONS FOR THE CARIBBEAN

*Travelers should:*
- *take the appropriate country specific malaria prevention measures (chloroquine for Haiti and Dominican Republic only)*
- *follow precautions to prevent insect bites*
- *pay attention to the quality of their drinking water and food*
- *have a dose of Immune Globulin (IG) or the hepatitis A vaccine, and consider booster doses of tetanus (Td) and polio (eIPV) vaccines.*
- *Depending on the locations to be visited, planned activities, and health of the traveler, the following vaccines should be considered: Hepatitis B, Yellow Fever, Typhoid, Rabies (pre-exposure), and Cholera.*
- *Finally, the normal "childhood" vaccines should be up-to-date: Measles, Mumps, Rubella (MMR Vaccine); Diphtheria, Tetanus, Pertussis (DTP Vaccine if traveler is less than 7 years of age, or Td if older than 7 years of age), and Polio vaccine. For additional information on these "childhood" vaccines, refer to Appendix 5, Vaccine Recommendations.*

# 9. MEXICO & CENTRAL AMERICA

## COUNTRIES IN THIS REGION

Belize
Costa Rica
El Salvador
Guatemala
Honduras
Mexico
Nicaragua
Panama

## MEXICO & CENTRAL AMERICA
## TRAVELER'S OVERVIEW

*Travelers to Mexico & Central America may be exposed to potential diseases from a number of sources.* **The most frequently reported illness is traveler's diarrhea,** *but Mexico & Central America contains a variety of diseases transmitted by:*

- *insects,*
- *contaminated food and water, or*
- *close contact with infected people.*

*In this chapter, specific diseases, their causes, symptoms, geographic areas of risk, and prevention recommendations or requirement information are discussed under their topical headings. As a general guideline, in order to reduce the risk of infection, travelers must:*

- *protect themselves from insects*
- *ensure the quality of their food and drinking water*
- *be knowledgeable about potential diseases in the region to be visited*
- *receive all recommended vaccines and preventive medications.*

*In addition, travelers should note that diseases are not restricted to cleanly defined geographical areas. For example, mosquitoes can fly over city or country borders, so all travelers should protect themselves by taking the basic preventive precautions as described under each section and disease. Where appropriate, more detailed information is referenced in the Appendices.*

## DISEASES TRANSMITTED BY INSECTS

Many diseases are transmitted through the bite of infected insects such as mosquitoes, flies, fleas, ticks and lice. In general, **travelers must protect themselves from insect bites**. Travelers are at a higher risk for insect bites if they participate in outdoor activities during night time hours from dusk to dawn when mosquitoes bite, or if their living accommodations are unscreened. If a mosquito net is unlikely to be available, consider buying a portable mosquito net.

## PREVENTING INSECT BITES

To reduce the risk of mosquito bites, travelers should remain in well-screened areas, use mosquito nets, and wear clothes that cover most of the body. Travelers should also take insect repellent with them to use on any exposed areas of the skin. The most effective compound in a repellent is **DEET**, which may be listed as an ingredient on repellant labels as **"N,N-diethyl meta-toluamide."** Check the repellent label to ensure DEET is an ingredient.

Travelers should note, however, that insect repellents containing DEET should always be used according to label directions and sparingly on children. **Avoid applying high-concentration (greater than 35%) products to the skin, particularly on children, and refrain from applying repellent to portions of the hands that are likely to come in contact with the eyes and mouth.** Pediatric insect repellents with 6-10% DEET are available without prescription in many drug stores. In rare instances, toxic reactions or other problems have developed after contact with DEET.

Travelers should also purchase a flying insect-killing spray to use in living and sleeping areas during the evening and night. For greater protection, clothing and bednets can be soaked in or sprayed with **permethrin**, which is an insect repellent licensed for use on clothing. If applied according to the directions, permethrin will repel insects from clothing for several weeks. Portable mosquito bednets, repellents containing DEET, and permethrin can be purchased in hardware, backpacking, and military surplus stores.

## MALARIA

Malaria is a serious parasitic infection transmitted to humans by an Anopheles mosquito. These mosquitoes bite at night, from dusk to dawn. Symptoms of malaria range from flu-like symptoms with fever, general achiness, headache, and fatigue, to a cycle of shaking chills, high fever, and sweating. If left untreated, malaria can cause anemia, kidney failure, coma, and death. Drugs are available to help prevent a malaria infection.

However, in spite of all protective measures, travelers occasionally develop malaria. Therefore, while traveling and up to one year after returning home, travelers should seek medical evaluation for any flu-like illness.

### Risk to Traveler

Malaria exists throughout the year in many parts of Mexico and Central America, including some urban areas.

*Areas of Risk*
• **Belize** – risk in the rural areas (including forest preserves and offshore islands, including the resort areas), except no risk in the central coastal District of Belize.

- **Costa Rica** – limited risk in the rural areas, except no risk in the central highlands (Cartago and San Jose Provinces).
- **El Salvador** – risk in the rural areas only.
- **Guatemala** – risk in the rural areas only, no risk in the central highlands.
- **Honduras** – risk in rural areas only.
- **Mexico** – risk exists in some rural areas of the following states: Oaxaca, Chiapas, Guerrero, Campeche, Quintana Roo, Sinaloa, Michoacan, Nayarit, Colima, and Tabasco; travelers to the major resort areas on the Mexican Gulf and Pacific Coasts need no drugs for malaria prevention.
- **Nicaragua** – risk in rural areas only, however, risk exists in outskirts of Chinandega, Granada, Leon, Managua, Nandaime, and Tipitapa towns.
- **Panama** – risk in rural areas of the eastern provinces (Darien and San Blas) and the northwestern provinces (Boca del Toro and Veraguas), and around the Lake Boyana and Lake Gatun areas. There is no risk in the Canal Zone, Panama City, or surrounding vicinity. *P. falciparum* (the most dangerous type), resistant to the drug chloroquine, has been reported in Panama, east of the Canal Zone.

## Prevention & Recommendations

Travelers at risk for malaria should take the prescription drug **chloroquine** to prevent malaria. The weekly dosage for an adult is 500 mg (salt) once a week. This drug should be taken one week before entering a malarious area, weekly while there, and weekly for 4 weeks after leaving the malarious area. No other anti-malarial drugs are needed.

Most travelers to Central America who are at risk for malaria should take chloroquine to prevent malaria. (For travelers to Panama east of the Canal Zone, including the San Blas Islands, different recommendations apply; see below.) The weekly dosage for an adult is 500 mg (salt) once a week. This drug should be taken one week before entering a malarious area, weekly while there, and weekly for 4 weeks after leaving the malarious area. No other anti-malarial drugs are needed.

For travelers going to **Panama**:
- Travelers to Panama who will be visiting locations of malaria risk west of the Canal Zone should take the preventive drug **chloroquine**.
- Travelers to Panama east of the Canal Zone and to the San Blas Islands should take mefloquine to prevent **malaria**.

Mefloquine is marketed in the United States under the name **Lariam™**. The adult dosage is 250 mg (one tablet) once a week. Mefloquine should be taken one week before leaving, weekly while in the malarious area, and weekly for 4 weeks after leaving the malarious area.

Minor side effects one may experience while taking mefloquine include gastrointestinal disturbances and dizziness. More serious side effects at the recommended dosage have rarely occurred. Consult a physician for other precautions.

Mefloquine should not be used by travelers with a:
- history of epilepsy or psychiatric disorder,
- known hypersensitivity to mefloquine.

In consultation with a physician, mefloquine may be used by pregnant women and children weighing less than 30 pounds, when travel to an area with chloroquine-resistant malaria is unavoidable. Travelers who cannot take mefloquine should read the section "Prescription Drugs for Malaria" found in *Appendix 1, Malaria Information.*

In addition to using drugs to prevent malaria and treat a possible malaria attack, travelers should use measures to reduce exposure to malaria-carrying mosquitoes and protect themselves from mosquito bites. Remember, these mosquitoes bite mainly during the evening and night, from dusk to dawn.

Additional general malaria information, as well as specific information for women who are pregnant or children, is found in *Appendix 1, Malaria Information.*

## YELLOW FEVER

Yellow fever is a viral disease transmitted to humans by a mosquito bite. The mosquitoes are most active during the evening hours. Symptoms range from fever, chills, headache, and vomiting to jaundice, internal bleeding, and kidney failure. Death occurs in about 5% of those infected. There is no specific drug to treat an infection of yellow fever, therefore prevention of infection is important.

### Risk to Traveler

Cases of yellow fever are rare for Central American countries. **Panama** was the last to report a case.

However, if you are traveling to Belize, El Salvador, Guatemala, Honduras, Mexico, and Nicaragua, a yellow fever vaccination and certificate for entry may be required. Read the requirements below carefully.

## Prevention

Yellow fever vaccination, a one-dose shot, is effective for up to 10 years for the prevention of yellow fever and may be administered to adults and children over 9 months of age. This vaccine is only administered at designated yellow fever centers, usually your local health department. **The vaccine and the official certificate become effective 10 days after vaccination.** Travelers at continued risk need a booster and a new certificate every 10 years.

*Travelers who should not be immunized include:*
· Infants under 4 months.
· Persons severely allergic to eggs.
· Pregnant women or people whose immune systems are not functioning normally.

In addition to the vaccine, travelers should use measures to reduce exposure to mosquitoes and protect themselves from mosquito bites. Remember, these mosquitoes bite mainly during the evening hours.

## Yellow Fever Certificate

After immunization, an International Certificate of Vaccination is issued and is valid 10 days after vaccination to meet entry and exit requirements for all countries. The Certificate is good for 10 years. **You must take the Certificate with you.**

## Medical Waiver

Travelers who have a medical reason not to receive the yellow fever vaccine should obtain a medical waiver. Most countries will accept a medical waiver for persons with a medical reason not to receive the vaccine (e.g. infants less than 4 months old, pregnant women, persons hypersensitive to eggs, or those with an immunosuppressed condition.) When required, CDC recommends obtaining written waivers from consular or embassy officials before departure. Follow these guidelines:
· A physician's letter clearly stating the medical reason not to receive the vaccine might be acceptable to some governments.
· It should be written on letterhead stationery and bear the stamp used by a health department or official immunization center to validate the International Certificate of Vaccination.
· Check embassies or consulates for specific waiver requirements.

## Recommendations & Requirements

CDC recommends a yellow fever vaccination only if you are traveling to areas of risk: **Darien Province** in **Panama**, the countries of tropical South America, or many countries in Africa.

Some countries require a yellow fever vaccination when travelers arrive from certain South American and African countries (see below).

Costa Rica has no yellow fever vaccination requirements. Belize, El Salvador (age 6 months), Guatemala, Honduras, Mexico (age 6 months), and Nicaragua **require** a yellow fever vaccination for all travelers (under age 1) arriving from all "Infected Countries."

## DENGUE FEVER

Dengue fever is a viral infection transmitted to humans by mosquito bites. These mosquitoes are most active during the day, especially around dawn and dusk, and are frequently found in or around residential areas. The illness is flu-like and characterized by sudden onset, high fever, severe headaches, joint and muscle pain, and rash. Severe cases of dengue hemorrhagic fever produce shock, internal bleeding, and death. The rash appears 3-4 days after the onset of fever. Since there is no vaccine or specific treatment available, prevention is important.

### Risk to Traveler

In recent years, dengue fever has occurred in all Central American countries from Mexico to Panama. The risk of infection is small for most travelers, except during periods of epidemic transmission.

### Prevention

There is no vaccine for dengue fever, therefore, the traveler should avoid mosquito bites. These mosquitoes may bite anytime during the day, especially in shady areas, indoors, or when the sky is overcast, but prefer feeding around dawn and dusk. For additional information on dengue fever, refer to *Appendix 12, Dengue Fever.*

## OTHER INSECT DISEASES
### Risks to Traveler

Other diseases spread by mosquitoes, sand flies, black flies, or other insects are prevalent, especially in rural areas. These diseases include: *filariasis* (mosquito), *leishmaniasis* (sand fly), *onchocerciasis* (black flies), *American trypanosomiasis* or Chagas' disease ("cone nose or kissing" bug), *Oropouche Virus* (gnats or midges), *typhus* (lice), and *plague* (fleas).

## Prevention

For most of these diseases, a vaccine is not available and treatment is limited. Therefore, travelers must follow the guidelines at the beginning of this chapter under "Preventing Insect Bites." For additional detailed information on these and other insect diseases, please read *Appendix 3, Other Insect Diseases.*

## DISEASES TRANSMITTED THROUGH FOOD & WATER

Food and waterborne diseases are the number one cause of illness to travelers and are very common in Mexico and Central America. **Traveler's diarrhea is the most frequent health problem for travelers.** It can be caused by viruses, bacteria, or parasites that are found universally throughout the region. Transmission is most often through contaminated food or water. Infections may cause diarrhea and vomiting (typhoid fever, cholera, and parasites), liver damage (hepatitis), or muscle paralysis (polio).

## GENERAL PRECAUTIONS

**Water**: The following beverages are safe to drink: boiled water or beverages made with boiled water, canned or carbonated beverages, beer, or wine. Impure water often contaminates drinking containers, ice, and tap water.

**Food**: Food that has been cooked to 165° F (74° C) is generally safe. As a reference, food at this temperature cannot be put directly into your mouth, but must cool a bit. Foods of concern are salads, uncooked vegetables and fruit, unpasteurized milk and milk products, raw meat, and shellfish. If you peel fruit yourself, it is generally safe. A simple rule of thumb is: "Boil it, cook it, peel it, or forget it."

For additional detailed precautions, be sure to read *Appendix 4, Traveler's Diarrhea & Food and Water Precautions.*

## TYPHOID FEVER

Typhoid fever is a bacterial infection transmitted to humans through contaminated food and/or water, or directly between people. Symptoms of typhoid fever include fever, headaches, fatigue, loss of appetite, and constipation. Typhoid fever can be treated effectively with antibiotics.

### Risk to Traveler

Travelers to Mexico and Central America are at risk for typhoid fever, especially when traveling to smaller cities, villages, or rural areas.

## Prevention

By drinking only bottled or boiled beverages and eating only thoroughly cooked food, a traveler lowers the risk of infection. Currently available vaccines have been shown to protect 70-90% of the recipients. Therefore, even vaccinated travelers should be cautious in selecting their food and water.

Two vaccines are recommended for protection against typhoid fever. An oral vaccine, **TY21a**, consists of a total of 4 capsules taken (one per day, every other day) over a seven day period, and requires a booster every five years. Reactions to the TY21a vaccine are rare but include nausea, vomiting, abdominal cramps, and skin rash.

A new single-dose injectable vaccine, **Typhim Vi** or **ViCPS**, is equally effective, and requires a booster dose every two years. Reactions to Typhim Vi are also rare, but include discomfort at the site of injection and headaches. An earlier typhoid vaccine developed years ago, which uses killed typhoid organisms and is administered in a two dose series, had more reported side effect and is currently not preferred. Instead, use one of the newer vaccines. Based on the vaccine chosen, booster doses are required every two to five years.

## Recommendations

CDC recommends a typhoid vaccination for those travelers who are going off the usual tourist itineraries, traveling to smaller cities and rural areas, or staying long term, that is, for six weeks or more. Vaccination should be completed at least two weeks before travel. Typhoid vaccination is not required for international travel.

## CHOLERA

Cholera is an acute diarrheal illness caused by an infection of the intestine with the bacterium *Vibrio cholerae*. Infection is acquired by ingesting contaminated water or food. The infection is often mild without symptoms, but sometimes can be severe. Approximately one in 20 infected persons has severe disease characterized by an abrupt onset of profuse watery diarrhea, vomiting, dehydration, and leg cramps.

## Risk to Traveler

A recent epidemic of cholera has swept through the entire Central America and tropical South American area. The risk of infection to the US traveler is very low, especially those who are following the usual tourist itineraries, staying in standard accommodations, and following food and water safety instructions. A list of cholera infected countries is given in *Appendix 10, CDC's Blue Sheet.*

## Prevention
Travelers to cholera infected areas should:
- avoid eating high risk foods, especially fish and shellfish, and
- follow the standard food and water precautions of eating only thoroughly cooked food that is served hot, peeling their own fruit, and drinking beverages and ice made from boiled or chlorinated water, bottled carbonated water, or bottled carbonated soft drinks.

Persons with severe cases of cholera respond well to simple fluid and electrolyte-replacement therapy, but medical attention must be sought quickly when cholera is suspected.

The cholera vaccine licensed for use in the United States confers only brief and incomplete immunity (50% effective in reducing the illness). The risk of cholera to US travelers is so low that it is questionable whether the vaccine is of benefit, and therefore it is not recommended routinely for travelers. The primary series for this cholera vaccine is normally two injections with booster doses given every 6 months for persons who remain at high risk. **Cholera vaccine is not recommended for infants under 6 months old or for pregnant women.**

For additional information about cholera, read *Appendix 4, Traveler's Diarrhea & Food and Water Precautions*, and *Appendix 8, Cholera Information.*

## HEPATITIS A
Hepatitis A is a viral infection of the liver transmitted to humans by the fecal-oral route; through direct person-to-person contact; from contaminated water, ice, or shellfish; or from fruits or uncooked vegetables contaminated through handling. Symptoms include fatigue, fever, loss of appetite, nausea, dark urine, jaundice, vomiting, aches and pains, and light stools. No specific therapy, only supportive care, is available.

### Risk to Traveler
Travelers are at high risk for hepatitis A, especially if travel plans include visiting rural areas and extensive travel in the countryside, frequent close contact with local persons, or eating in settings of poor sanitation. Be aware that a study has shown that many cases of travel-related hepatitis A

occur in travelers to developing countries with "standard" itineraries, accommodations, and food consumption behaviors.

## Prevention

The virus is inactivated by boiling or cooking to 185° F (85° C) for one minute. Therefore, eating thoroughly cooked foods and drinking only treated water serve as general precautions. In addition, **Immune globulin (IG)** *or* **hepatitis A vaccine** is recommended before travel. Two hepatitis A vaccines, **Havrix®** and **VAQTA®**, are currently licensed in the United States.

Immune globulin and the hepatitis A vaccine marketed in the United States are safe. American travelers should note that IG manufactured in foreign countries may or may not meet these requirements. Therefore, American travelers who will need to receive additional doses of IG in other countries should use products that meet US standards and license requirements. For reference, the method of manufacturing IG in the US is called the **Cohn-Oncley procedure**.

## Recommendations

CDC recommends Immune globulin (IG) or hepatitis A vaccine before travel for protection against hepatitis A.

**Immune globulin** is recommended for persons of all ages who:
- desire only short term protection (one dose is effective for three months)
- need immediate protection, and
- are too young for the vaccine (less than 2 years of age).

**Hepatitis A vaccine** is preferred for persons two years of age and older who plan to travel repeatedly or reside for long periods of time in intermediate or high risk areas. Bear in mind:
- The complete hepatitis A vaccine series requires a minimum of six months to complete.
- For these travelers over 18 years of age, hepatitis A vaccine should be given in a two-dose series with the second dose administered 6-12 months after the first.
- For children and adolescents between ages 2 through 18, a two or three dose series of hepatitis A vaccine is recommended depending on the vaccine chosen.

Travelers can be considered to be protected four weeks after receiving the initial vaccine dose. If the vaccine is administered less than four weeks

before travel, then IG should also be given. The vaccine series must be completed for long-term protection. Hepatitis A vaccination is not required for travel to any country.

In addition to receiving IG or the vaccine, all travelers should follow the food and water precautions as described in *Appendix 4, Traveler's Diarrhea & Food and Water Precautions*.

Additional IG and hepatitis A information covering the vaccine and its safety are found in *Appendix 9, Hepatitis A Vaccine & Immune Globulin (IG) - Disease and Vaccine Information*.

## PARASITES

Parasitic infections are acquired by eating or drinking contaminated food or water, through direct contact with soil or water containing parasites or their larva, or by contact with biting insects. Symptoms and evidence of infection may include, but are not limited to: fever, swollen lymph nodes, rashes or itchy skin, digestive problems such as abdominal pain or diarrhea, eye problems, and anemia.

### Risk to Traveler

Travelers to Mexico and Central America are at risk of parasitic infections. There are many types of parasites and infection may occur in several ways: by eating undercooked meats infected with parasites or their larva; by eating food or drinking water contaminated with parasites or their eggs; by contact with soil or water infected with parasites; or through insect bites. Several types of parasites, for example schistosomiasis, can penetrate intact human skin and travelers are advised to wear shoes and avoid swimming, wading, or washing in fresh water.

### Prevention

Travelers should eat only thoroughly cooked food, drink safe water, wear shoes, refrain from swimming in fresh water, and avoid contact with insects, particularly mosquitoes, biting flies, gnats, and midges.

## DISEASES TRANSMITTED THROUGH INTIMATE CONTACT WITH PEOPLE

### HIV/AIDS

Human immunodeficiency virus, or HIV, which causes acquired immunodeficiency syndrome or AIDS, is found primarily in blood, semen, and vaginal secretions of an infected person. HIV is spread by sexual contact with an infected person, by needle-sharing among injecting drug users, and through transfusions of infected blood and blood clotting factors. Babies born to HIV-infected women may become infected before, during, or shortly after birth.

In the United States, blood is screened for HIV antibodies, but this screening may not take place in all countries. Scientific studies have revealed no evidence that HIV is transmitted by air, food, water, insects, inanimate objects or casual contact. Even though HIV antibodies are normally detected on a test within 6 months after infection, the period between infection and development of disease symptoms (incubation period) may be 10 years or longer. Treatment has prolonged the survival of some HIV infected persons but there is no known cure or vaccine available. For additional information, see *Appendix 7, HIV/AIDS Information.*

## Risk to Traveler

AIDS is found throughout the region. In Mexico and Central America, sexual transmission accounts for the majority of the cases. Heterosexual transmission is increasing. The risk to a traveler depends on whether the traveler will be involved in sexual or needle-sharing contact with a person who is infected with HIV. Receipt of unscreened blood for transfusion poses a risk for HIV infection.

## Prevention

No effective vaccine has been developed for HIV. Travelers should avoid sexual or needle-sharing contact with a person who is infected with HIV. If a blood transfusion is necessary, screened blood should come from an HIV-negative blood donor.

## Recommendations

Travelers should avoid activities known to carry risks for infection with HIV.

## HEPATITIS B

Hepatitis B is a viral infection of the liver. Hepatitis B is transmitted to humans primarily through behavior that result in the exchange of blood or fluids containing blood. Risky behavior includes heterosexual or homosexual contact or sharing needles or drug paraphernalia with a person infected with the hepatitis B virus. Any unscreened or improperly screened blood or blood product, as well as unsterilized needles, or contact with potentially infected people who have open skin sores due to impetigo, scabies, and scratched insect bites, heightens the potential for infection to the traveler. An effective vaccine for prevention of hepatitis B is available.

## Risk to Traveler

Hepatitis B rates are moderate for all of Central America, except for Mexico where the rates are low. The risk to the individual international traveler is greater if the traveler:

- has direct contact with blood or fluids containing blood;
- has intimate sexual contact with an infected person;
- remains in the country for longer than six months or has close contact with the local population.

## Prevention

**Hepatitis B vaccine** should be considered for those traveling to countries with high to intermediate rates of hepatitis B infection. For those travelers expecting to reside in countries of high risk, as well as all health workers, vaccination is strongly recommended.

Vaccination should ideally begin 6 months before travel, in order to complete the full series, which is needed for optimal protection. The three intramuscular doses of vaccine should be spaced so that the second dose is given one month after the first. The final dose is given 6 months after the first. The vaccination schedule should be initiated even if it will not be completed before travel begins. There is an alternative four-dose schedule that may provide protection if the first three doses can be delivered before departure. After completing the primary series, booster doses of the vaccine are not necessary.

## Recommendations

CDC recommends vaccination for any of the following people:

- any health care worker (medical, dental, or laboratory) whose activities might result in blood exposure;
- any traveler who may have intimate sexual contact with the local population;
- any long-term (6 months or more) traveler, e.g. teachers, who will reside in rural areas or have daily physical contact with the local population; or
- any traveler who is likely to seek either medical, dental, or other treatment in local facilities during their stay.

Hepatitis B vaccination is not required for travel to any country. Additional hepatitis B information is found in *Appendix 15, Hepatitis B*.

## OTHER DISEASES

### RABIES

Rabies is a viral infection that affects the central nervous system. It is transmitted to humans by warm-blooded animal (mammal) bites that introduce the virus into the wound. Although dogs are the main reservoir of the disease, all warm-blooded animal bites should be suspect.

### Risk to Traveler

For countries in Central America, there is a risk of rabies infection, particularly in rural areas, or in areas where large numbers of dogs are found.

### Prevention

Do not handle animals! Any animal bite should receive prompt medical attention. When wounds are thoroughly cleaned with large amounts of soap and water, the risk of rabies infection is reduced. Exposed individuals should receive prompt medical attention and advice on post-exposure preventive treatment.

### Recommendations

There are no requirements for vaccination, but pre-exposure vaccination is recommended for:
- travelers visiting foreign areas where dog rabies is known to exist and whose activities may place them at high risk of exposure;
- veterinarians and animal handlers;
- spelunkers; and
- certain rabies laboratory workers.

Pre-exposure vaccination does not nullify the need for post-exposure vaccine, but reduces the number of injections and may provide protection under circumstances in which rabies exposure is unrecognized. For additional rabies information, refer to *Appendix 11, Rabies Information.*

## SUMMARY OF RECOMMENDATIONS FOR MEXICO & CENTRAL AMERICA

*Travelers should:*

- *take the appropriate country specific malaria prevention measures (chloroquine or mefloquine or equivalent)*
- *follow precautions to prevent insect bites*
- *pay attention to the quality of their drinking water and food*
- *have a dose of Immune Globulin (IG) or the hepatitis A vaccine, and consider booster doses of tetanus (Td) and polio (eIPV) vaccines.*
- *Depending on the locations to be visited, planned activities, and health of the traveler, the following vaccines should be considered: Hepatitis B, Yellow Fever, Typhoid, Rabies (pre-exposure), and Cholera.*
- *Finally, the normal "childhood" vaccines should be up-to-date: Measles, Mumps, Rubella (MMR Vaccine); Diphtheria, Tetanus, Pertussis (DTP Vaccine if traveler is less than 7 years of age, or Td if older than 7 years of age), and Polio vaccine. For additional information on these "childhood" vaccines, refer to Appendix 5, Vaccine Recommendations.*

# 10. TROPICAL SOUTH AMERICA

## COUNTRIES IN THIS REGION
Bolivia
Brazil
Colombia
Ecuador
French Guiana
Guyana
Paraguay
Peru
Suriname
Venezuela

## TROPICAL SOUTH AMERICA TRAVELER'S OVERVIEW

*Travelers to Tropical South America may be exposed to potential diseases from a number of sources.* **The most frequently reported illness is traveler's diarrhea,** *but Tropical South America contains a variety of diseases transmitted by:*

- *insects,*
- *contaminated food and water, or*
- *close contact with infected people.*

*In this chapter, specific diseases, their causes, symptoms, geographic areas of risk, and prevention recommendations or requirement information are discussed under their topical headings. As a general guideline, in order to reduce the risk of infection, travelers must:*

- *protect themselves from insects*
- *ensure the quality of their food and drinking water*
- *be knowledgeable about potential diseases in the region to be visited*
- *receive all recommended vaccines and preventive medications.*

*In addition, travelers should note that diseases are not restricted to cleanly defined geographical areas. For example, mosquitoes can fly over city or country borders, so all travelers should protect themselves by taking the basic preventive precautions as described under each section and disease. Where appropriate, more detailed information is referenced in the Appendices.*

## DISEASES TRANSMITTED BY INSECTS

Many diseases are transmitted through the bite of infected insects such as mosquitoes, flies, fleas, ticks and lice. In general, **travelers must protect themselves from insect bites**. Travelers are at a higher risk for insect bites if they participate in outdoor activities during night time hours from dusk to dawn when mosquitoes bite, or if their living accommodations are unscreened. If a mosquito net is unlikely to be available, consider buying a portable mosquito net.

### PREVENTING INSECT BITES

To reduce the risk of mosquito bites, travelers should remain in well-screened areas, use mosquito nets, and wear clothes that cover most of the body. Travelers should also take insect repellent with them to use on any exposed areas of the skin. The most effective compound in a repellent is **DEET**, which may be listed as an ingredient on repellant labels as **"N,N-diethyl meta-toluamide."** Check the repellent label to ensure DEET is an ingredient.

Travelers should note, however, that insect repellents containing DEET should always be used according to label directions and sparingly on children. **Avoid applying high-concentration (greater than 35%) products to the skin, particularly on children, and refrain from applying repellent to portions of the hands that are likely to come in contact with the eyes and mouth.** Pediatric insect repellents with 6-10% DEET are available without prescription in many drug stores. In rare instances, toxic reactions or other problems have developed after contact with DEET.

Travelers should also purchase a flying insect-killing spray to use in living and sleeping areas during the evening and night. For greater protection, clothing and bednets can be soaked in or sprayed with **permethrin**, which is an insect repellent licensed for use on clothing. If applied according to the directions, permethrin will repel insects from clothing for several weeks. Portable mosquito bednets, repellents containing DEET, and permethrin can be purchased in hardware, backpacking, and military surplus stores.

## MALARIA

Malaria is a serious parasitic infection transmitted to humans by an Anopheles mosquito. These mosquitoes bite at night, from dusk to dawn. Symptoms of malaria range from flu-like symptoms with fever, general achiness, headache, and fatigue, to a cycle of shaking chills, high fever, and sweating. If left untreated, malaria can cause anemia, kidney failure, coma, and death. Drugs are available to help prevent a malaria infection.

However, in spite of all protective measures, travelers occasionally develop malaria. Therefore, while traveling and up to one year after returning home, travelers should seek medical evaluation for any flu-like illness.

### Risk to Traveler

Malaria exists throughout the year in many parts of the Tropical South American countries, including some urban areas. *P. falciparum* (the most dangerous type), which has been reported to be resistant to the drug chloroquine, has been confirmed in most of these countries.

*Areas of Risk:*
- **Bolivia** – Malaria risk in rural areas only, except no risk in the highland areas, i.e. Departments of Oruro, Southern and Central Potosi, La Paz, and the Provinces of Ingavi, Los Andes, Omasuyos, and Pacajes.
- **Brazil** – Malaria risk in Acre and Rondonia States, Territories of Amapá and Roraima, and in rural areas of Amazonas, Goiás, Maranahao,

Mato Grosso, and Pará States. Travelers who will only visit the coastal states from the "horn" south to the Uruguay border, including Iguassu Falls, are not at risk and need not take preventive drugs.

- **Colombia** – Malaria risk in rural areas only, except no risk in Bogota and vicinity. Malaria risk in the rural areas of Uraba (Antioquia Dept.), Bajo Cauca-Nechi (Cauca and Antioquia Dept.), Magdalena Medio, Caqueta (Caqueta Intendencia), Sarare (Arauca Intendencia), Catatumbo (Norte de Santander Dept.), Pacifico Central and Sur, Putumayo (Putumayo Intendencia), Ariari (Meta Dept.), Alto Vaupes (Vaupes Comisaria), Amazonas, and Guainia (Comisarias).
- **Ecuador** – Malaria risk in all areas in the providences along the eastern border and the Pacific coast, i.e., El Oro, Esmeraldas, Guayas (including Guayaquil), Los Rios, Manabi, Morona-Santiago, Napo, Pastaza, Pichincha, and Zamora-Chinchipe provinces. Travelers who visit only Quito and vicinity, the central highlands tourist areas, or the Galapagos Islands are not at risk and need not take preventive drugs.
- **French Guiana** – Malaria risk in all areas.
- **Guyana** – Malaria risk in rural areas in the southern interior and northwest coast, i.e., Rupununi and North West Regions.
- **Paraguay** – Malaria risk in rural areas bordering Brazil.
- **Peru** – Malaria risk exists in rural areas. Travelers who will only visit Lima and vicinity, coastal areas south of Lima, or the highland tourist areas of Cuzco, Machu Picchu, or Lake Titicaca are not at risk and need not take preventive drugs. Risk exists in rural areas of Departments of Amazonas, Cajamarca (except Hualgayoc Prov.), La Libertad (except Otuxco, Santiago de Chuco Prov.) Lambayeque, Loreto, Piura, (except Talara Prov.) San Martin and Tumbes, Provinces of Santa (Ancash Dept.); parts of La Convension (Cuzco Dept.), Tayacaja (Huancavelica Dept.), Satipo (Junin Dept.).
- **Suriname** – Malaria risk exist in rural areas, except no risk in the Paramaribo District and the coastal area north of 5°N. Lat.
- **Venezuela** – Malaria risk exists in rural areas of all border states and territories and the states of Barinas, Merida, and Portuguesa.

Travelers should note that regardless of preventive method employed, it is still possible to contract malaria. *P. falciparum* is reported in all these countries, but less so in Peru and Paraguay. *P. falciparum*, which is highly resistant to other malaria drugs (chloroquine and Fansidar), is reported.

## Prevention & Recommendations

Most travelers to Tropical South America (including travelers to Peru's eastern and northern border provinces) at risk for malaria should take

**mefloquine** to prevent malaria. Travelers to the other areas in Peru and Paraguay have other recommendations; see below.

Mefloquine is marketed in the United States under the name **Lariam™**. The adult dosage is 250 mg (one tablet) once a week. Mefloquine should be taken one week before leaving, weekly while in the malarious area, and weekly for 4 weeks after leaving the malarious area.

Minor side effects one may experience while taking mefloquine include gastrointestinal disturbances and dizziness. More serious side effects at the recommended dosage have rarely occurred. Consult a physician for other precautions.

Mefloquine should not be used by travelers with a:
- history of epilepsy or psychiatric disorder,
- known hypersensitivity to mefloquine.

In consultation with a physician, mefloquine may be used by pregnant women and children weighing less than 30 pounds, when travel to an area with chloroquine-resistant malaria is unavoidable. Travelers who cannot take mefloquine should read the section "Prescription Drugs for Malaria" found in *Appendix 1, Malaria Information.*

For travelers to **Peru** and **Paraguay**:
- Travelers to all areas of Peru, **except Peru's eastern and northern border provinces**, and Paraguay, should take **chloroquine** to prevent malaria. The weekly dosage for an adult is 500 mg (salt) once a week. This drug should be taken one week before entering a malarious area, weekly while there, and weekly for 4 weeks after leaving the malarious area. For these areas in Peru, no other anti-malarial drugs are needed.
- Travelers to Peru's eastern and northern border provinces at risk for malaria should take mefloquine to prevent malaria. (see above)

In addition to using drugs to prevent malaria and treat a possible malaria attack, travelers should use measures to reduce exposure to malaria-carrying mosquitoes and protect themselves from mosquito bites. Remember, these mosquitoes bite mainly during the evening and night, from dusk to dawn.

Additional general malaria information, as well as specific information for women who are pregnant or children, is found in *Appendix 1, Malaria Information.*

## YELLOW FEVER

Yellow fever is a viral disease transmitted to humans by a mosquito bite. The mosquitoes are most active during the evening hours. Symptoms range from fever, chills, headache, and vomiting to jaundice, internal bleeding, and kidney failure. Death occurs in about 5% of those infected. There is no specific drug to treat an infection of yellow fever, therefore prevention of infection is important.

### Risk to Traveler

Outbreaks of yellow fever have occurred in **Bolivia** and **Peru**. Yellow fever is not always active in all countries of this region, but there is a significant risk to all travelers throughout the year, especially in travel or visits to rural settings.

*Areas of Higher Risk*
- **Bolivia** – the Departments of Beni, Chuquisaca, Cochabamba, Pando, Santa Cruz, Tarija, and part of La Paz.
- **Brazil** – rural areas of Acre, Amazonas, Goias, Maranhao, Mato Grosso, Mato Grosso do Sul, Para, and Rondonia States; and the Territories of Amapa and Roraima.
- **Colombia** – middle valley of the Magdalena River, foothills of the Cordllera Oriental from border of Ecuador to Venezuela, Uraba, foothills of Sierra Nevada, Orinoquia, and Amazonia.
- **Peru** – central and northern jungle regions. Venezuela: State of Bolivar, forest around Lake Maracaibo, and San Camilo jungle.

*Lower Risk Areas*
**Ecuador**, **French Guiana**, **Guyana**, **Paraguay** and **Suriname** have reported only a few cases.

### Prevention

Yellow fever vaccination, a one-dose shot, is effective for up to 10 years for the prevention of yellow fever and may be administered to adults and children over 9 months of age. This vaccine is only administered at designated yellow fever centers, usually your local health department. **The vaccine and the official certificate become effective 10 days after vaccination.** Travelers at continued risk need a booster and a new certificate every 10 years.

*Travelers who should not be immunized include:*
- Infants under 4 months.
- Persons severely allergic to eggs.

- Pregnant women or people whose immune systems are not functioning normally.

In addition to the vaccine, travelers should use measures to reduce exposure to mosquitoes and protect themselves from mosquito bites. Remember, these mosquitoes bite mainly during the evening hours.

## Yellow Fever Certificate

After immunization, an International Certificate of Vaccination is issued and is valid 10 days after vaccination to meet entry and exit requirements for all countries. The Certificate is good for 10 years. **You must take the Certificate with you.**

## Medical Waiver

Travelers who have a medical reason not to receive the yellow fever vaccine should obtain a medical waiver. Most countries will accept a medical waiver for persons with a medical reason not to receive the vaccine (e.g. infants less than 4 months old, pregnant women, persons hypersensitive to eggs, or those with an immunosuppressed condition.) When required, CDC recommends obtaining written waivers from consular or embassy officials before departure. Follow these guidelines:

- A physician's letter clearly stating the medical reason not to receive the vaccine might be acceptable to some governments.
- It should be written on letterhead stationery and bear the stamp used by a health department or official immunization center to validate the International Certificate of Vaccination.
- Check embassies or consulates for specific waiver requirements.

## Recommendations & Requirements

If you are traveling to Tropical South America, CDC recommends and many countries require a yellow fever vaccination.

Some countries require a yellow fever vaccination when travelers arrive from certain South American and African countries (see below). Therefore, sometimes the easiest and safest thing to do is to get a yellow fever vaccination and a signed certificate to take with you.

French Guiana **requires** a yellow fever certificate for **all travelers.**

Brazil, Bolivia, Colombia and Peru, recommend a vaccination, especially if visiting rural areas.

Bolivia, Brazil, Ecuador, Guyana, Peru, and Suriname, **require** a yellow fever vaccination for all travelers arriving from all "Infected Countries."

Paraguay **requires** vaccination when leaving Paraguay and going to an "infected country."

Therefore, if you are traveling from a country listed in the left two columns of the following table to a Tropical South American country in the right hand column, **you are required to have a yellow fever vaccination.**

For comprehensive country-by-country yellow fever vaccine requirements, see *Appendix 2, Yellow Fever Requirements.*

## TRAVELING FROM ANY OF THE FOLLOWING "ENDEMIC" YELLOW FEVER INFECTED COUNTRIES

### Africa:

Angola
Benin
Burundi
Burkina Faso
Cameroon
Central African Republic
Chad
Congo
Cote d'Ivoire, (Ivory Coast)
Equatorial Guinea
Ethiopia
Gabon
Gambia
Ghana
Guinea
Guinea Bissau
Kenya
Liberia
Mali
Mauritania
Niger
Nigeria
Rwanda
Sao Tome and Principe
Senegal
Sierra Leone
Somalia
Sudan
Tanzania
Togo
Uganda
Zaire

### South America:

Bolivia
Brazil
Colombia
Ecuador
French Guiana
Guyana
Panama
Peru
Suriname
Venezuela

## TRAVELING TO TROPICAL SOUTH AMERICAN COUNTRIES

Bolivia (age 6 months)
Brazil (age 1 and older)
Ecuador (age 1 and older)
Guyana (age 1 and older)
   (In addition, if you are traveling
   to Guyana from Belize, Costa Rica,
   Guatemala, Honduras, and Nica-
   ragua, you will need a yellow fever
   vaccination.)
Peru (age 6 months)
Suriname
Paraguay

If you are traveling to an "Infected Country" from Paraguay, you will need a yellow fever vaccination.

**Yellow Fever Certificate Required**

## DENGUE FEVER

Dengue fever is a viral infection transmitted to humans by mosquito bites. These mosquitoes are most active during the day, especially around dawn and dusk, and are frequently found in or around residential areas. The illness is flu-like and characterized by sudden onset, high fever, severe headaches, joint and muscle pain, and rash. Severe cases of dengue hemorrhagic fever produce shock, internal bleeding, and death. The rash appears 3-4 days after the onset of fever. Since there is no vaccine or specific treatment available, prevention is important.

### Risk to Traveler

Dengue fever occurs throughout Tropical South America, with recent epidemics in **Brazil, Colombia, Ecuador, French Guiana, Suriname, Venezuela, and the tropical parts of Bolivia, Paraguay**, and **Peru**. The risk of infection is small for most travelers except during periods of epidemic transmission.

### Prevention

There is no vaccine for dengue fever, therefore, the traveler should avoid mosquito bites. These mosquitoes may bite anytime during the day, especially in shady areas, indoors, or when the sky is overcast, but prefer feeding around dawn and dusk. For additional information on dengue fever, refer to *Appendix 12, Dengue Fever.*

## OTHER INSECT DISEASES

### Risks to Traveler

Other diseases spread by mosquitoes, sand flies, black flies, or other insects are prevalent, especially in rural areas. These diseases include: *filariasis* (mosquito), *leishmaniasis* (sand fly), *onchocerciasis* (black flies), *American trypanosomiasis* or Chagas' disease ("cone nose or kissing" bug), *Oropouche Virus* (gnats or midges), *typhus* (lice), and *plague* (fleas).

### Prevention

For most of these diseases, a vaccine is not available and treatment is limited. Therefore, travelers must follow the guidelines at the beginning of this chapter under "Preventing Insect Bites." For additional detailed information on these and other insect diseases, please read *Appendix 3, Other Insect Diseases.*

## DISEASES TRANSMITTED THROUGH FOOD & WATER

Food and waterborne diseases are the number one cause of illness to travelers and are very common in Tropical South America. **Traveler's**

**diarrhea is the most frequent health problem for travelers.** It can be caused by viruses, bacteria, or parasites that are found universally throughout the region. Transmission is most often through contaminated food or water. Infections may cause diarrhea and vomiting (typhoid fever, cholera, and parasites), liver damage (hepatitis), or muscle paralysis (polio).

## GENERAL PRECAUTIONS

**Water**: The following beverages are safe to drink: boiled water or beverages made with boiled water, canned or carbonated beverages, beer, or wine. Impure water often contaminates drinking containers, ice, and tap water.

**Food**: Food that has been cooked to 165° F (74° C) is generally safe. As a reference, food at this temperature cannot be put directly into your mouth, but must cool a bit. Foods of concern are salads, uncooked vegetables and fruit, unpasteurized milk and milk products, raw meat, and shellfish. If you peel fruit yourself, it is generally safe. A simple rule of thumb is: "Boil it, cook it, peel it, or forget it."

For additional detailed precautions, be sure to read *Appendix 4, Traveler's Diarrhea & Food and Water Precautions.*

## TYPHOID FEVER

Typhoid fever is a bacterial infection transmitted to humans through contaminated food and/or water, or directly between people. Symptoms of typhoid fever include fever, headaches, fatigue, loss of appetite, and constipation. Typhoid fever can be treated effectively with antibiotics.

### Risk to Traveler

Travelers to Tropical South America are at risk for typhoid fever, especially when traveling to smaller cities, villages, or rural areas.

### Prevention

By drinking only bottled or boiled beverages and eating only thoroughly cooked food, a traveler lowers the risk of infection. Currently available vaccines have been shown to protect 70-90% of the recipients. Therefore, even vaccinated travelers should be cautious in selecting their food and water.

Two vaccines are recommended for protection against typhoid fever. An oral vaccine, **TY21a**, consists of a total of 4 capsules taken (one per day, every other day) over a seven day period, and requires a booster every five years. Reactions to the TY21a vaccine are rare but include nausea, vomiting, abdominal cramps, and skin rash.

A new single-dose injectable vaccine, **Typhim Vi** or **ViCPS**, is equally effective, and requires a booster dose every two years. Reactions to Typhim Vi are also rare, but include discomfort at the site of injection and headaches. An earlier typhoid vaccine developed years ago, which uses killed typhoid organisms and is administered in a two dose series, had more reported side effect and is currently not preferred. Instead, use one of the newer vaccines. Based on the vaccine chosen, booster doses are required every two to five years.

## Recommendations

CDC recommends a typhoid vaccination for those travelers who are going off the usual tourist itineraries, traveling to smaller cities and rural areas, or staying long term, that is, for six weeks or more. Vaccination should be completed at least two weeks before travel. Typhoid vaccination is not required for international travel.

## CHOLERA

Cholera is an acute diarrheal illness caused by an infection of the intestine with the bacterium *Vibrio cholerae*. Infection is acquired by ingesting contaminated water or food. The infection is often mild without symptoms, but sometimes can be severe. Approximately one in 20 infected persons has severe disease characterized by an abrupt onset of profuse watery diarrhea, vomiting, dehydration, and leg cramps.

### Risk to Traveler

A recent epidemic of cholera has swept through the entire Tropical South American Area. The risk of infection to the US traveler is very low, especially those that are following the usual tourist itineraries, staying in standard accommodations, and following food and water safety instructions. A list of cholera infected countries is given in *Appendix 10, CDC's Blue Sheet*.

### Prevention

Travelers to cholera infected areas should:
- avoid eating high risk foods, especially fish and shellfish, and
- follow the standard food and water precautions of eating only thoroughly cooked food that is served hot, peeling their own fruit, and

drinking beverages and ice made from boiled or chlorinated water, bottled carbonated water, or bottled carbonated soft drinks.

Persons with severe cases of cholera respond well to simple fluid and electrolyte-replacement therapy, but medical attention must be sought quickly when cholera is suspected.

The cholera vaccine licensed for use in the United States confers only brief and incomplete immunity (50% effective in reducing the illness). The risk of cholera to US travelers is so low that it is questionable whether the vaccine is of benefit, and therefore it is not recommended routinely for travelers. The primary series for this cholera vaccine is normally two injections with booster doses given every 6 months for persons who remain at high risk. **Cholera vaccine is not recommended for infants under 6 months old or for pregnant women.**

For additional information about cholera, read *Appendix 4, Traveler's Diarrhea & Food and Water Precautions*, and *Appendix 8, Cholera Information*.

## HEPATITIS A

Hepatitis A is a viral infection of the liver transmitted to humans by the fecal-oral route; through direct person-to-person contact; from contaminated water, ice, or shellfish; or from fruits or uncooked vegetables contaminated through handling. Symptoms include fatigue, fever, loss of appetite, nausea, dark urine, jaundice, vomiting, aches and pains, and light stools. No specific therapy, only supportive care, is available.

### Risk to Traveler

Travelers are at high risk for hepatitis A, especially if travel plans include visiting rural areas and extensive travel in the countryside, frequent close contact with local persons, or eating in settings of poor sanitation. Be aware that a study has shown that many cases of travel-related hepatitis A occur in travelers to developing countries with "standard" itineraries, accommodations, and food consumption behaviors.

### Prevention

The virus is inactivated by boiling or cooking to 185° F (85° C) for one minute. Therefore, eating thoroughly cooked foods and drinking only treated water serve as general precautions. In addition, **Immune globulin (IG)** *or* **hepatitis A vaccine** is recommended before travel. Two hepatitis A vaccines, **Havrix®** and **VAQTA®**, are currently licensed in the US.

Immune globulin and the hepatitis A vaccine marketed in the United States are safe. American travelers should note that IG manufactured in foreign countries may or may not meet these requirements. Therefore, American travelers who will need to receive additional doses of IG in other countries should use products that meet US standards and license requirements. For reference, the method of manufacturing IG in the US is called the **Cohn-Oncley procedure.**

## Recommendations

CDC recommends Immune globulin (IG) or hepatitis A vaccine before travel for protection against hepatitis A.

**Immune globulin** is recommended for persons of all ages who:
- desire only short term protection (one dose is effective for three months)
- need immediate protection, and
- are too young for the vaccine (less than 2 years of age).

**Hepatitis A vaccine** is preferred for persons two years of age and older who plan to travel repeatedly or reside for long periods of time in intermediate or high risk areas. Bear in mind:
- The complete hepatitis A vaccine series requires a minimum of six months to complete.
- For these travelers over 18 years of age, hepatitis A vaccine should be given in a two-dose series with the second dose administered 6-12 months after the first.
- For children and adolescents between ages 2 through 18, a two or three dose series of hepatitis A vaccine is recommended depending on the vaccine chosen.

Travelers can be considered to be protected four weeks after receiving the initial vaccine dose. If the vaccine is administered less than four weeks before travel, then IG should also be given. The vaccine series must be completed for long-term protection. Hepatitis A vaccination is not required for travel to any country.

In addition to receiving IG or the vaccine, all travelers should follow the food and water precautions as described in *Appendix 4, Traveler's Diarrhea & Food and Water Precautions.*

Additional IG and hepatitis A information covering the vaccine and its safety are found in *Appendix 9, Hepatitis A Vaccine & Immune Globulin (IG) - Disease and Vaccine Information.*

## PARASITES

Parasitic infections are acquired by eating or drinking contaminated food or water, through direct contact with soil or water containing parasites or their larva, or by contact with biting insects. Symptoms and evidence of infection may include, but are not limited to: fever, swollen lymph nodes, rashes or itchy skin, digestive problems such as abdominal pain or diarrhea, eye problems, and anemia.

### Risk to Traveler

Travelers to Tropical South America are at risk of parasitic infections. There are many types of parasites and infection may occur in several ways: by eating undercooked meats infected with parasites or their larva; by eating food or drinking water contaminated with parasites or their eggs; by contact with soil or water infected with parasites; or through insect bites. Several types of parasites, for example schistosomiasis, can penetrate intact human skin and travelers are advised to wear shoes and avoid swimming, wading, or washing in fresh water.

### Prevention

Travelers should eat only thoroughly cooked food, drink safe water, wear shoes, refrain from swimming in fresh water, and avoid contact with insects, particularly mosquitoes, biting flies, gnats, and midges.

## DISEASES TRANSMITTED THROUGH INTIMATE CONTACT WITH PEOPLE

### HIV/AIDS

Human immunodeficiency virus, or HIV, which causes acquired immunodeficiency syndrome or AIDS, is found primarily in blood, semen, and vaginal secretions of an infected person. HIV is spread by sexual contact with an infected person, by needle-sharing among injecting drug users, and through transfusions of infected blood and blood clotting factors. Babies born to HIV-infected women may become infected before, during, or shortly after birth.

In the United States, blood is screened for HIV antibodies, but this screening may not take place in all countries. Scientific studies have revealed no evidence that HIV is transmitted by air, food, water, insects, inanimate objects or casual contact. Even though HIV antibodies are normally detected on a test within 6 months after infection, the period between infection and development of disease symptoms (incubation period) may be 10 years or longer. Treatment has prolonged the survival of some HIV infected persons but there is no known cure or vaccine available. For additional information, see *Appendix 7, HIV/AIDS Information.*

## Risk to Traveler

AIDS is found throughout the region. In Tropical South America, sexual transmission accounts for the majority of the cases. Heterosexual transmission is increasing. The risk to a traveler depends on whether the traveler will be involved in sexual or needle-sharing contact with a person who is infected with HIV. Receipt of unscreened blood for transfusion poses a risk for HIV infection.

## Prevention

No effective vaccine has been developed for HIV. Travelers should avoid sexual or needle-sharing contact with a person who is infected with HIV. If a blood transfusion is necessary, screened blood should come from an HIV-negative blood donor.

## Recommendations

Travelers should avoid activities known to carry risks for infection with HIV.

## HEPATITIS B

Hepatitis B is a viral infection of the liver. Hepatitis B is transmitted to humans primarily through behavior that result in the exchange of blood or fluids containing blood. Risky behavior includes heterosexual or homosexual contact or sharing needles or drug paraphernalia with a person infected with the hepatitis B virus. Any unscreened or improperly screened blood or blood product, as well as unsterilized needles, or contact with potentially infected people who have open skin sores due to impetigo, scabies, and scratched insect bites, heightens the potential for infection to the traveler. An effective vaccine for prevention of hepatitis B is available.

## Risk to Traveler

The risk of hepatitis B virus infection is highest in the **interior Amazon Regions of Bolivia, Brazil, Columbia, Peru (all parts)**, and **Venezuela**, and moderate for the rest of Tropical South America. The risk to the individual international traveler is greater if the traveler:

- has direct contact with blood or fluids containing blood;
- has intimate sexual contact with an infected person;
- remains in the country for longer than six months or has close contact with the local population.

## Prevention

**Hepatitis B vaccine** should be considered for those traveling to countries with high to intermediate rates of hepatitis B infection. For those travelers expecting to reside in countries of high risk, as well as all health workers, vaccination is strongly recommended.

Vaccination should ideally begin 6 months before travel, in order to complete the full series, which is needed for optimal protection. The three intramuscular doses of vaccine should be spaced so that the second dose is given one month after the first. The final dose is given 6 months after the first. The vaccination schedule should be initiated even if it will not be completed before travel begins. There is an alternative four-dose schedule that may provide protection if the first three doses can be delivered before departure. After completing the primary series, booster doses of the vaccine are not necessary.

## Recommendations

CDC recommends vaccination for any of the following people:
- any health care worker (medical, dental, or laboratory) whose activities might result in blood exposure;
- any traveler who may have intimate sexual contact with the local population;
- any long-term (6 months or more) traveler, e.g. teachers, who will reside in rural areas or have daily physical contact with the local population; or
- any traveler who is likely to seek either medical, dental, or other treatment in local facilities during their stay.

Hepatitis B vaccination is not required for travel to any country. Additional hepatitis B information is found in *Appendix 15, Hepatitis B.*

## OTHER DISEASES
## SCHISTOSOMIASIS

Schistosomiasis is a parasitic infection that develops after the larvae of a flatworm have penetrated the human skin. These larvae live in fresh water lakes, ponds, and streams and can penetrate unbroken skin. Water treated with chlorine or iodine is virtually safe, and salt water poses no risk.

### Risk to Traveler

In Tropical South America, schistosomiasis infection may be found in parts of **Brazil**, **Suriname**, and **Venezuela**. For travelers visiting these areas, the risk is a function of the frequency and degree of contact with contaminated fresh water for bathing, wading, or swimming.

## Prevention

The traveler cannot distinguish between infested and non-infested water. Therefore, swimming in fresh water in rural areas should be avoided. Bath water should either be heated to 50° (122° F) for five minutes or treated with chlorine or iodine as done for drinking water. If exposed, immediate and vigorous towel drying or application of rubbing alcohol to the exposed areas may reduce the risk of infection. Screening procedures are available for those who suspect infection, and schistosomiasis is treatable with drugs.

## Recommendations

Avoid contact with potentially contaminated water, such as swimming in lakes, ponds, rivers, etc.

## RABIES

Rabies is a viral infection that affects the central nervous system. It is transmitted to humans by warm-blooded animal (mammal) bites that introduce the virus into the wound. Although dogs are the main reservoir of the disease, all warm-blooded animal bites should be suspect.

## Risk to Traveler

For countries in Tropical South America, there is a risk of rabies infection, particularly in rural areas or in areas where large numbers of dogs are found.

## Prevention

Do not handle animals! Any animal bite should receive prompt medical attention. When wounds are thoroughly cleaned with large amounts of soap and water, the risk of rabies infection is reduced. Exposed individuals should receive prompt medical attention and advice on post-exposure preventive treatment.

## Recommendations

There are no requirements for vaccination, but pre-exposure vaccination is recommended for:
- travelers visiting foreign areas where dog rabies is known to exist and whose activities may place them at high risk of exposure;
- veterinarians and animal handlers;

- spelunkers; and
- certain rabies laboratory workers.

Pre-exposure vaccination does not nullify the need for post-exposure vaccine, but reduces the number of injections and may provide protection under circumstances in which rabies exposure is unrecognized. For additional rabies information, refer to *Appendix 11, Rabies Information.*

## SUMMARY OF RECOMMENDATIONS FOR TROPICAL SOUTH AMERICA

*Travelers should:*

- *take the appropriate country specific malaria prevention measures (chloroquine or mefloquine or equivalent)*
- *follow precautions to prevent insect bites*
- *pay attention to the quality of their drinking water and food*
- *have a dose of Immune Globulin (IG) or the hepatitis A vaccine, and consider booster doses of tetanus (Td) and polio (eIPV) vaccines.*
- *Depending on the locations to be visited, planned activities, and health of the traveler, the following vaccines should be considered: Hepatitis B, Yellow Fever, Typhoid, Rabies (pre-exposure), and Cholera.*
- *Finally, the normal "childhood" vaccines should be up-to-date: Measles, Mumps, Rubella (MMR Vaccine); Diphtheria, Tetanus, Pertussis (DTP Vaccine if traveler is less than 7 years of age, or Td if older than 7 years of age), and Polio vaccine. For additional information on these "childhood" vaccines, refer to Appendix 5, Vaccine Recommendations.*

# 11. TEMPERATE SOUTH AMERICA

## COUNTRIES IN THIS REGION
**Argentina**
**Chile**
**Falkland Islands**
**Uruguay**

---

## TEMPERATE SOUTH AMERICA
## TRAVELER'S OVERVIEW

*Travelers to Temperate South America may be exposed to potential diseases from a number of sources.* **The most frequently reported illness is traveler's diarrhea,** *but Temperate South America contains a variety of diseases transmitted by:*

- *insects,*
- *contaminated food and water, or*
- *close contact with infected people.*

*In this chapter, specific diseases, their causes, symptoms, geographic areas of risk, and prevention recommendations or requirement information are discussed under their topical headings. As a general guideline, in order to reduce the risk of infection, travelers must:*

- *protect themselves from insects*
- *ensure the quality of their food and drinking water*
- *be knowledgeable about potential diseases in the region to be visited*
- *receive all recommended vaccines and preventive medications.*

*In addition, travelers should note that diseases are not restricted to cleanly defined geographical areas. For example, mosquitoes can fly over city or country borders, so all travelers should protect themselves by taking the basic preventive precautions as described under each section and disease. Where appropriate, more detailed information is referenced in the Appendices.*

---

## DISEASES TRANSMITTED BY INSECTS

Many diseases are transmitted through the bite of infected insects such as mosquitoes, flies, fleas, ticks and lice. In general, **travelers must protect themselves from insect bites**. Travelers are at a higher risk for insect bites if they participate in outdoor activities during night time hours from dusk to dawn when mosquitoes bite, or if their living accommodations are unscreened. If a mosquito net is unlikely to be available, consider buying a portable mosquito net.

## PREVENTING INSECT BITES

To reduce the risk of mosquito bites, travelers should remain in well-screened areas, use mosquito nets, and wear clothes that cover most of the body. Travelers should also take insect repellent with them to use on any exposed areas of the skin. The most effective compound in a repellent is **DEET**, which may be listed as an ingredient on repellant labels as "**N,N-diethyl meta-toluamide.**" Check the repellent label to ensure DEET is an ingredient.

Travelers should note, however, that insect repellents containing DEET should always be used according to label directions and sparingly on children. **Avoid applying high-concentration (greater than 35%) products to the skin, particularly on children, and refrain from applying repellent to portions of the hands that are likely to come in contact with the eyes and mouth.** Pediatric insect repellents with 6-10% DEET are available without prescription in many drug stores. In rare instances, toxic reactions or other problems have developed after contact with DEET.

Travelers should also purchase a flying insect-killing spray to use in living and sleeping areas during the evening and night. For greater protection, clothing and bednets can be soaked in or sprayed with **permethrin**, which is an insect repellent licensed for use on clothing. If applied according to the directions, permethrin will repel insects from clothing for several weeks. Portable mosquito bednets, repellents containing DEET, and permethrin can be purchased in hardware, backpacking, and military surplus stores.

## MALARIA

Malaria is a serious parasitic infection transmitted to humans by an Anopheles mosquito. These mosquitoes bite at night, from dusk to dawn. Symptoms of malaria range from flu-like symptoms with fever, general achiness, headache, and fatigue, to a cycle of shaking chills, high fever, and sweating. If left untreated, malaria can cause anemia, kidney failure, coma, and death. Drugs are available to help prevent a malaria infection.

However, in spite of all protective measures, travelers occasionally develop malaria. Therefore, while traveling and up to one year after returning home, travelers should seek medical evaluation for any flu-like illness.

### Risk to Traveler
*Areas of Risk*
• **Argentina** – the risk for malaria infection occurs only in rural areas of northern Argentina that border Bolivia (Salta and Jujuy Provinces).

*No Risk*
Chile, Falkland Islands, and Uruguay.

### Prevention & Recommendations
Travelers at risk for malaria should take the prescription drug **chloroquine** to prevent malaria. The weekly dosage for an adult is 500 mg (salt) once

a week. This drug should be taken one week before entering a malarious area, weekly while there, and weekly for 4 weeks after leaving the malarious area. No other anti-malarial drugs are needed.

In addition to using drugs to prevent malaria and treat a possible malaria attack, travelers should use measures to reduce exposure to malaria-carrying mosquitoes and protect themselves from mosquito bites. These mosquitoes bite mainly during the evening and night, from dusk to dawn.

Additional general malaria information, as well as specific information for women who are pregnant or children, is found in *Appendix 1, Malaria Information.*

## YELLOW FEVER
Yellow fever is a viral disease transmitted to humans by a mosquito bite. The mosquitoes are most active during the evening hours. Symptoms range from fever, chills, headache, and vomiting to jaundice, internal bleeding, and kidney failure. Death occurs in about 5% of those infected. There is no specific drug to treat an infection of yellow fever, therefore prevention of infection is important.

### Risk to Traveler
*Low Risk*
Only in the **northeastern forest areas of Argentina**.

*No Risk*
Chile, Falkland Islands, and Uruguay.

### Prevention
Yellow fever vaccination, a one-dose shot, is effective for up to 10 years for the prevention of yellow fever and may be administered to adults and children over 9 months of age. This vaccine is only administered at designated yellow fever centers, usually your local health department. **The vaccine and the official certificate become effective 10 days after vaccination**. Travelers at continued risk need a booster and a new certificate every 10 years.

*Travelers who should not be immunized include:*
- Infants under 4 months.
- Persons severely allergic to eggs.
- Pregnant women or people whose immune systems are not functioning normally.

In addition to the vaccine, travelers should use measures to reduce exposure to mosquitoes and protect themselves from mosquito bites. Remember, these mosquitoes bite mainly during the evening hours.

## Yellow Fever Certificate

After immunization, an International Certificate of Vaccination is issued and is valid 10 days after vaccination to meet entry and exit requirements for all countries. The Certificate is good for 10 years. **You must take the Certificate with you.**

## Medical Waiver

Travelers who have a medical reason not to receive the yellow fever vaccine should obtain a medical waiver. Most countries will accept a medical waiver for persons with a medical reason not to receive the vaccine (e.g. infants less than 4 months old, pregnant women, persons hypersensitive to eggs, or those with an immunosuppressed condition.) When required, CDC recommends obtaining written waivers from consular or embassy officials before departure. Follow these guidelines:

- A physician's letter clearly stating the medical reason not to receive the vaccine might be acceptable to some governments.
- It should be written on letterhead stationery and bear the stamp used by a health department or official immunization center to validate the International Certificate of Vaccination.
- Check embassies or consulates for specific waiver requirements.

## Recommendations & Requirements

CDC recommends a yellow fever vaccination only if you are traveling to areas of risk in northeastern Argentina, or other countries in Tropical South America, or Africa.

Argentina, Chile, Falkland Islands, and Uruguay have no yellow fever vaccination requirements.

If your travel plans include traveling to or from other countries in South America or Africa, then you should review the comprehensive country-by-country yellow fever vaccine requirements in *Appendix 2, Yellow Fever Requirements*. Many countries in South America and Africa require yellow fever vaccination for entry.

## OTHER INSECT DISEASES
### Risks to Traveler

Other diseases spread by mosquitoes, sand flies, black flies, or other insects are prevalent, especially in rural areas. These diseases include: *leishmaniasis* (sand fly), *American trypanosomiasis* or Chagas' disease ("cone nose or kissing" bug), *typhus* (lice), and *plague* (fleas).

## Prevention

For most of these diseases, a vaccine is not available and treatment is limited. Therefore, travelers must follow the guidelines under "Preventing Insect Bites." For additional detailed information of these and other insect diseases, please read *Appendix 3, Other Insect Diseases*.

## DISEASES TRANSMITTED THROUGH FOOD & WATER

Food and waterborne diseases are the number one cause of illness to travelers and are very common in Temperate South America. **Traveler's diarrhea is the most frequent health problem for travelers.** It can be caused by viruses, bacteria, or parasites that are found universally throughout the region. Transmission is most often through contaminated food or water. Infections may cause diarrhea and vomiting (typhoid fever, cholera, and parasites), liver damage (hepatitis), or muscle paralysis (polio).

## GENERAL PRECAUTIONS

**Water**: The following beverages are safe to drink: boiled water or beverages made with boiled water, canned or carbonated beverages, beer, or wine. Impure water often contaminates drinking containers, ice, and tap water.

**Food**: Food that has been cooked to 165° F (74° C) is generally safe. As a reference, food at this temperature cannot be put directly into your mouth, but must cool a bit. Foods of concern are salads, uncooked vegetables and fruit, unpasteurized milk and milk products, raw meat, and shellfish. If you peel fruit yourself, it is generally safe. A simple rule of thumb is: "Boil it, cook it, peel it, or forget it."

For additional detailed precautions, be sure to read *Appendix 4, Traveler's Diarrhea & Food and Water Precautions*.

## TYPHOID FEVER

Typhoid fever is a bacterial infection transmitted to humans through contaminated food and/or water, or directly between people. Symptoms of typhoid fever include fever, headaches, fatigue, loss of appetite, and constipation. Typhoid fever can be treated effectively with antibiotics.

### Risk to Traveler

Travelers to Temperate South America are at risk for typhoid fever, especially when traveling to smaller cities, villages, or rural areas.

### Prevention

By drinking only bottled or boiled beverages and eating only thoroughly cooked food, a traveler lowers the risk of infection. Currently available vaccines have been shown to protect 70-90% of the recipients, so even vaccinated travelers should be cautious in selecting their food and water.

Two vaccines are recommended for protection against typhoid fever. An oral vaccine, **TY21a**, consists of a total of 4 capsules taken (one per day, every other day) over a seven day period, and requires a booster every five years. Reactions to the TY21a vaccine are rare but include nausea, vomiting, abdominal cramps, and skin rash.

A new single-dose injectable vaccine, **Typhim Vi** or **ViCPS**, is equally effective, and requires a booster dose every two years. Reactions to Typhim Vi are also rare, but include discomfort at the site of injection and headaches. An earlier typhoid vaccine developed years ago, which uses killed typhoid organisms and is administered in a two dose series, had more reported side effect and is currently not preferred. Instead, use one of the newer vaccines. Based on the vaccine chosen, booster doses are required every two to five years.

### Recommendations

CDC recommends a typhoid vaccination for those travelers who are going off the usual tourist itineraries, traveling to smaller cities and rural areas, or staying long term, that is, for six weeks or more. Vaccination should be completed at least two weeks before travel. Typhoid vaccination is not required for international travel.

### CHOLERA

Cholera is an acute diarrheal illness caused by an infection of the intestine with the bacterium *Vibrio cholerae*. Infection is acquired by ingesting contaminated water or food. The infection is often mild without symptoms, but sometimes can be severe. Approximately one in 20 infected persons has severe disease characterized by an abrupt onset of profuse watery diarrhea, vomiting, dehydration, and leg cramps.

### Risk to Traveler

A recent epidemic of cholera has swept through the entire South

American Area. The risk of infection to the US traveler is very low, especially those that are following the usual tourist itineraries, staying in standard accommodations, and following food and water safety instructions. A list of cholera infected countries is given in *Appendix 10, CDC's Blue Sheet.*

## Prevention

Travelers to cholera infected areas should:
- avoid eating high risk foods, especially fish and shellfish, and
- follow the standard food and water precautions of eating only thoroughly cooked food that is served hot, peeling their own fruit, and drinking beverages and ice made from boiled or chlorinated water, bottled carbonated water, or bottled carbonated soft drinks.

Persons with severe cases of cholera respond well to simple fluid and electrolyte-replacement therapy, but medical attention must be sought quickly when cholera is suspected.

The cholera vaccine licensed for use in the United States confers only brief and incomplete immunity (50% effective in reducing the illness). The risk of cholera to US travelers is so low that it is questionable whether the vaccine is of benefit, and therefore it is not recommended routinely for travelers. The primary series for this cholera vaccine is normally two injections with booster doses given every 6 months for persons who remain at high risk. **Cholera vaccine is not recommended for infants under 6 months old or for pregnant women.**

For additional information, read *Appendix 4, Traveler's Diarrhea & Food and Water Precautions*, and *Appendix 8, Cholera Information.*

## HEPATITIS A

Hepatitis A is a viral infection of the liver transmitted to humans by the fecal-oral route; through direct person-to-person contact; from contaminated water, ice, or shellfish; or from fruits or uncooked vegetables contaminated through handling. Symptoms include fatigue, fever, loss of appetite, nausea, dark urine, jaundice, vomiting, aches and pains, and light stools. No specific therapy, only supportive care, is available.

## Risk to Traveler

Travelers are at high risk for hepatitis A, especially if travel plans include visiting rural areas and extensive travel in the countryside, frequent close contact with local persons, or eating in settings of poor sanitation. Be aware that a study has shown that many cases of travel-related hepatitis A occur in travelers to developing countries with "standard" itineraries, accommodations, and food consumption behaviors.

## Prevention

The virus is inactivated by boiling or cooking to 185° F (85° C) for one minute. Therefore, eating thoroughly cooked foods and drinking only treated water serve as general precautions. In addition, **Immune globulin (IG)** *or* **hepatitis A vaccine** is recommended before travel. Two hepatitis A vaccines, **Havrix®** and **VAQTA®**, are currently licensed in the US.

Immune globulin and the hepatitis A vaccine marketed in the United States are safe. American travelers should note that IG manufactured in foreign countries may or may not meet these requirements. Therefore, American travelers who will need to receive additional doses of IG in other countries should use products that meet US standards and license requirements. For reference, the method of manufacturing IG in the US is called the **Cohn-Oncley procedure**.

## Recommendations

CDC recommends Immune globulin (IG) or hepatitis A vaccine before travel for protection against hepatitis A.

**Immune globulin** is recommended for persons of all ages who:
- desire only short term protection (one dose is effective for three months)
- need immediate protection, and
- are too young for the vaccine (less than 2 years of age).

**Hepatitis A vaccine** is preferred for persons two years of age and older who plan to travel repeatedly or reside for long periods of time in intermediate or high risk areas. Bear in mind:
- The complete hepatitis A vaccine series requires a minimum of six months to complete.
- For these travelers over 18 years of age, hepatitis A vaccine should be given in a two-dose series with the second dose administered 6-12 months after the first.
- For children and adolescents between ages 2 through 18, a two or three dose series of hepatitis A vaccine is recommended depending on the vaccine chosen.

Travelers can be considered to be protected four weeks after receiving the initial vaccine dose. If the vaccine is administered less than four weeks

before travel, then IG should also be given. The vaccine series must be completed for long-term protection. Hepatitis A vaccination is not required for travel to any country.

In addition to receiving IG or the vaccine, all travelers should follow the food and water precautions as described in *Appendix 4, Traveler's Diarrhea & Food and Water Precautions.*

Additional IG and hepatitis A information covering the vaccine and its safety are found in *Appendix 9, Hepatitis A Vaccine & Immune Globulin (IG) - Disease and Vaccine Information.*

## PARASITES
Parasitic infections are acquired by eating or drinking contaminated food or water, through direct contact with soil or water containing parasites or their larva, or by contact with biting insects. Symptoms and evidence of infection may include, but are not limited to: fever, swollen lymph nodes, rashes or itchy skin, digestive problems such as abdominal pain or diarrhea, eye problems, and anemia.

### Risk to Traveler
Travelers to Temperate South America are at risk of parasitic infections. There are many types of parasites and infection may occur in several ways: by eating undercooked meats infected with parasites or their larva; by eating food or drinking water contaminated with parasites or their eggs; by contact with soil or water infected with parasites; or through insect bites. Several types of parasites, for example schistosomiasis, can penetrate intact human skin and travelers are advised to wear shoes and avoid swimming, wading, or washing in fresh water.

### Prevention
Travelers should eat only thoroughly cooked food, drink safe water, wear shoes, refrain from swimming in fresh water, and avoid contact with insects, particularly mosquitoes, biting flies, gnats, and midges.

## DISEASES TRANSMITTED THROUGH INTIMATE CONTACT WITH PEOPLE
### HIV/AIDS
Human immunodeficiency virus, or HIV, which causes acquired immunodeficiency syndrome or AIDS, is found primarily in blood, semen, and vaginal secretions of an infected person. HIV is spread by sexual contact with an infected person, by needle-sharing among injecting drug users,

and through transfusions of infected blood and blood clotting factors. Babies born to HIV-infected women may become infected before, during, or shortly after birth.

In the United States, blood is screened for HIV antibodies, but this screening may not take place in all countries. Scientific studies have revealed no evidence that HIV is transmitted by air, food, water, insects, inanimate objects or casual contact. Even though HIV antibodies are normally detected on a test within 6 months after infection, the period between infection and development of disease symptoms (incubation period) may be 10 years or longer. Treatment has prolonged the survival of some HIV infected persons but there is no known cure or vaccine available. For additional information, see *Appendix 7, HIV/AIDS Information.*

### Risk to Traveler
AIDS is found throughout the region. In Temperate South America, sexual transmission accounts for the majority of the cases. Heterosexual transmission is increasing. The risk to a traveler depends on whether the traveler will be involved in sexual or needle-sharing contact with a person who is infected with HIV. Receipt of unscreened blood for transfusion poses a risk for HIV infection.

### Prevention
No effective vaccine has been developed for HIV. Travelers should avoid sexual or needle-sharing contact with a person who is infected with HIV. If a blood transfusion is necessary, screened blood should come from an HIV-negative blood donor.

### Recommendations
Travelers should avoid activities known to carry risks for infection with HIV.

## OTHER DISEASES
## RABIES
Rabies is a viral infection that affects the central nervous system. It is transmitted to humans by warm-blooded animal (mammal) bites that introduce the virus into the wound. Although dogs are the main reservoir of the disease, all warm-blooded animal bites should be suspect.

### Risk to Traveler
For countries in Temperate South America, there is a risk of rabies

infection, particularly in rural areas or in areas where large numbers of dogs are found.

## Prevention

Do not handle animals! Any animal bite should receive prompt medical attention. When wounds are thoroughly cleaned with large amounts of soap and water, the risk of rabies infection is reduced. Exposed individuals should receive prompt medical attention and advice on post-exposure preventive treatment.

## Recommendations

There are no requirements for vaccination, but pre-exposure vaccination is recommended for:

- travelers visiting foreign areas where dog rabies is known to exist and whose activities may place them at high risk of exposure;
- veterinarians and animal handlers;
- spelunkers; and
- certain rabies laboratory workers.

Pre-exposure vaccination does not nullify the need for post-exposure vaccine, but reduces the number of injections and may provide protection under circumstances in which rabies exposure is unrecognized. For additional rabies information, refer to *Appendix 11, Rabies Information.*

---

### SUMMARY OF RECOMMENDATIONS FOR TEMPERATE SOUTH AMERICA

*Travelers should:*

- *take the appropriate country specific malaria prevention measures (chloroquine, northern Argentina only)*
- *follow precautions to prevent insect bites*
- *pay attention to the quality of their drinking water and food*
- *have a dose of Immune Globulin (IG) or the hepatitis A vaccine, and consider booster doses of tetanus (Td) and polio (eIPV) vaccines.*
- *Depending on the locations to be visited, planned activities, and health of the traveler, the following vaccines should be considered: Hepatitis B, Yellow Fever, Typhoid, Rabies (pre-exposure), and Cholera.*
- *Finally, the normal "childhood" vaccines should be up-to-date: Measles, Mumps, Rubella (MMR Vaccine); Diphtheria, Tetanus, Pertussis (DTP Vaccine if traveler is less than 7 years of age, or Td if older than 7 years of age), and Polio vaccine. For additional information on these "childhood" vaccines, refer to Appendix 5, Vaccine Recommendations.*

# 12. EAST ASIA

## COUNTRIES IN THIS REGION
China
Hong Kong
Japan
Democratic People's Republic of Korea (North Korea)
Republic of Korea (South Korea)
Macau
Mongolia
Taiwan

**EAST ASIA TRAVELER'S OVERVIEW**

*Travelers to East Asia may be exposed to potential diseases from a number of sources. The most frequently reported illness is traveler's diarrhea, but East Asia contains a variety of diseases transmitted by:*
- *insects,*
- *contaminated food and water, or*
- *close contact with infected people.*

*In this chapter, specific diseases, their causes, symptoms, geographic areas of risk, and prevention recommendations or requirement information are discussed under their topical headings. As a general guideline, in order to reduce the risk of infection, travelers must:*
- *protect themselves from insects*
- *ensure the quality of their food and drinking water*
- *be knowledgeable about potential diseases in the region to be visited*
- *receive all recommended vaccines and preventive medications.*

*In addition, travelers should note that diseases are not restricted to cleanly defined geographical areas. For example, mosquitoes can fly over city or country borders, so all travelers should protect themselves by taking the basic preventive precautions as described under each section and disease. Where appropriate, more detailed information is referenced in the Appendices.*

## DISEASES TRANSMITTED BY INSECTS

Many diseases are transmitted through the bite of infected insects such as mosquitoes, flies, fleas, ticks and lice. In general, **travelers must protect themselves from insect bites**. Travelers are at a higher risk for insect bites if they participate in outdoor activities during night time hours from dusk to dawn when mosquitoes bite, or if their living accommodations are unscreened. If a mosquito net is unlikely to be available, consider buying a portable mosquito net.

## PREVENTING INSECT BITES

To reduce the risk of mosquito bites, travelers should remain in well-screened areas, use mosquito nets, and wear clothes that cover most of the body. Travelers should also take insect repellent with them to use on any exposed areas of the skin. The most effective compound in a repellent is **DEET**, which may be listed as an ingredient on repellant labels as "**N,N-diethyl meta-toluamide.**" Check the repellent label to ensure DEET is an ingredient.

Travelers should note, however, that insect repellents containing DEET should always be used according to label directions and sparingly on children. **Avoid applying high-concentration (greater than 35%) products to the skin, particularly on children, and refrain from applying repellent to portions of the hands that are likely to come in contact with the eyes and mouth.** Pediatric insect repellents with 6-10% DEET are available without prescription in many drug stores. In rare instances, toxic reactions or other problems have developed after contact with DEET.

Travelers should also purchase a flying insect-killing spray to use in living and sleeping areas during the evening and night. For greater protection, clothing and bednets can be soaked in or sprayed with **permethrin**, which is an insect repellent licensed for use on clothing. If applied according to the directions, permethrin will repel insects from clothing for several weeks. Portable mosquito bednets, repellents containing DEET, and permethrin can be purchased in hardware, backpacking, and military surplus stores.

## MALARIA

Malaria is a serious parasitic infection transmitted to humans by an Anopheles mosquito. These mosquitoes bite at night, from dusk to dawn. Symptoms of malaria range from flu-like symptoms with fever, general achiness, headache, and fatigue, to a cycle of shaking chills, high fever, and sweating. If left untreated, malaria can cause anemia, kidney failure, coma, and death. Drugs are available to help prevent a malaria infection.

However, in spite of all protective measures, travelers occasionally develop malaria. Therefore, while traveling and up to one year after returning home, travelers should seek medical evaluation for any flu-like illness.

### Risk to Traveler

*Areas of Risk*

- **China** – Travelers visiting cities and popular rural sites on usual tourist routes are generally not at risk, and taking drugs to prevent malaria is therefore not recommended. Malaria risk is found in rural areas only, except no risk in provinces bordering Mongolia and in the western provinces of Heilungkiang, Kirin, Ningsia Hui, Tibet and Tsinghai. For rural Chinese areas other than those listed above: North of 33°N latitude, transmission occurs between July and November; in the region between 33°N and 25°N latitude, transmission occurs from May to December; in the region south of 25°N latitude, transmission occurs year-round. (For China, see specific instructions in the Prevention section below.)

*No Risk*
Hong Kong, Japan, North Korea, South Korea, Macao, Mongolia and Taiwan.

## Prevention & Recommendations

Since malaria transmission in China is largely confined to the rural areas not visited by most travelers, taking drugs to prevent malaria is only recommended for travelers who will have outdoor exposure during evening and nighttime hours in rural areas.

Travelers to China at risk of malaria should take one of two drugs to prevent malaria transmission:
  • If traveling to rural areas other than those listed above, travelers should take a weekly **chloroquine** tablet. The weekly dosage for an adult is 500 mg (salt) once a week. This drug should be taken one week before entering a malarious area, weekly while there, and weekly for 4 weeks after leaving the malarious area.
  • Travelers to southern China, Hainan Island, and provinces bordering Laos, Myanmar (Burma), and Vietnam should take **mefloquine** to prevent malaria.

Mefloquine should not be used by travelers with a:
  • history of epilepsy or psychiatric disorder,
  • known hypersensitivity to mefloquine.

In consultation with a physician, mefloquine may be used by pregnant women and children weighing less than 30 pounds, when travel to an area with chloroquine-resistant malaria is unavoidable. Travelers who cannot take mefloquine should read the section "Prescription Drugs for Malaria" found in *Appendix 1, Malaria Information.*

In addition to using drugs to prevent malaria and treat a possible malaria attack, travelers should use measures to reduce exposure to malaria-carrying mosquitoes and protect themselves from mosquito bites. Remember, these mosquitoes bite mainly during the evening and night, from dusk to dawn.

Additional general malaria information, as well as specific information for women who are pregnant or children, is found in *Appendix 1, Malaria Information.*

## YELLOW FEVER

Yellow fever is a viral disease found in parts of Africa and South America. It is transmitted to humans by a mosquito bite. Even though there is no risk of becoming infected while traveling in East Asian countries, some countries require a yellow fever vaccination when travelers arrive from certain South American and African countries.

If you are **only** traveling from the United States to an East Asian country, CDC does not recommend, and you are not required to have, a yellow fever vaccination. If your travel plans include traveling to or from countries in South America or Africa, you may be required to have a yellow fever vaccination. Therefore, you should review the comprehensive country-by-country yellow fever vaccine requirements in *Appendix 2, Yellow Fever Requirements*.

## DENGUE FEVER

Dengue fever is a viral infection transmitted to humans by mosquito bites. These mosquitoes are most active during the day, especially around dawn and dusk, and are frequently found in or around residential areas. The illness is flu-like and characterized by sudden onset, high fever, severe headaches, joint and muscle pain, and rash. Severe cases of dengue hemorrhagic fever produce shock, internal bleeding, and death. The rash appears 3-4 days after the onset of fever. Since there is no vaccine or specific treatment available, prevention is important.

### Risk to Traveler

Dengue fever occurs in parts of **southern China** and **Taiwan**. The risk of infection is small for most travelers except during periods of epidemic transmission.

### Prevention

There is no vaccine for dengue fever, therefore, the traveler should avoid mosquito bites. These mosquitoes may bite anytime during the day, especially in shady areas, indoors, or when the sky is overcast, but prefer feeding around dawn and dusk. For additional information on dengue fever, refer to *Appendix 12, Dengue Fever*.

## JAPANESE ENCEPHALITIS

Japanese Encephalitis is a mosquito-borne viral disease that occurs in rural areas. These mosquitoes are most often found in rice growing areas and bite in the late afternoon and early evening. Symptoms range from: no symptoms to headache, fever, and flu-like symptoms. More serious complications involve a swelling of the brain (encephalitis). There is no specific drug to treat Japanese Encephalitis.

## Risk to Traveler

Transmission is usually seasonal (associated with the rainy season). There is a risk for travelers to **rural areas of Asian countries**. In all areas, Japanese Encephalitis is primarily a rural disease. The chance that a traveler to Asia will develop Japanese Encephalitis is extremely small.

## Prevention & Recommendations

The vaccine **JE-VAX** is licensed and available in the United States. Vaccination should be considered for persons who plan long-term residence in rural areas. Travelers who visit rural farming areas for 4 weeks or more during the transmission season should consider immunization. Travelers who remain un-immunized should wear mosquito repellents, sleep under bed-nets, and bring insecticidal sprays to use in their sleeping quarters.

The vaccine is given in 3 doses on days 0, 7, and 30. Protection can be expected 10 days following the last dose. A shorter course of vaccination (Day 0, 7, and 14) can be used, but protection and duration is less than the normal schedule. Fever and local reactions such as redness, swelling, and pain are reported in fewer than 10% of those vaccinated. More severe allergic reactions have been reported in persons with a history of insect or food allergies. These reactions have been life-threatening on occasion. Once vaccinated, you should have access to medical care, if needed, for 2-3 days after vaccination.

*The Japanese Encephalitis vaccine should not be given to*:
- Those acutely ill or with active infections.
- Persons with heart, kidney, or liver disorders.
- Persons with generalized cancerous malignancies such as leukemia and lymphoma.
- Persons with a history of multiple allergies or hypersensitivity to components of the vaccine.
- Pregnant women, unless there is a high risk of Japanese Encephalitis during the woman's stay.

For additional information on Japanese Encephalitis, refer to *Appendix 13, Japanese Encephalitis*.

## OTHER INSECT DISEASES
### Risks to Traveler
Other diseases spread by mosquitoes, sand flies, black flies, or other insects are prevalent, especially in rural areas. These diseases include: *filariasis* (mosquito), *leishmaniasis* (sandfly), *Congo-Crimean hemorrhagic fever* (tick), *typhus* (lice), and *plague* (fleas).

### Prevention
For most of these diseases, a vaccine is not available and treatment is limited. Therefore, travelers must follow the guidelines under "Preventing Insect Bites." For additional detailed information of these and other insect diseases, please read *Appendix 3, Other Insect Diseases.*

## DISEASES TRANSMITTED THROUGH FOOD & WATER
Food and waterborne diseases are the number one cause of illness to travelers and are very common in East Asia. **Traveler's diarrhea is the most frequent health problem for travelers.** It can be caused by viruses, bacteria, or parasites that are found universally throughout the region. Transmission is most often through contaminated food or water. Infections may cause diarrhea and vomiting (typhoid fever, cholera, and parasites), liver damage (hepatitis), or muscle paralysis (polio).

### GENERAL PRECAUTIONS
**Water**: The following beverages are safe to drink: boiled water or beverages made with boiled water, canned or carbonated beverages, beer, or wine. Impure water often contaminates drinking containers, ice, and tap water.

**Food**: Food that has been cooked to 165° F (74° C) is generally safe. As a reference, food at this temperature cannot be put directly into your mouth, but must cool a bit. Foods of concern are salads, uncooked vegetables and fruit, unpasteurized milk and milk products, raw meat, and shellfish. If you peel fruit yourself, it is generally safe. A simple rule of thumb is: "Boil it, cook it, peel it, or forget it."

For additional detailed precautions, be sure to read *Appendix 4, Traveler's Diarrhea & Food and Water Precautions.*

### TYPHOID FEVER
Typhoid fever is a bacterial infection transmitted to humans through contaminated food and/or water, or directly between people. Symptoms

of typhoid fever include fever, headaches, fatigue, loss of appetite, and constipation. Typhoid fever can be treated effectively with antibiotics.

## Risk to Traveler

Travelers to East Asia are at risk for typhoid fever, especially when traveling to smaller cities, villages, or rural areas.

## Prevention

By drinking only bottled or boiled beverages and eating only thoroughly cooked food, a traveler lowers the risk of infection. Currently available vaccines have been shown to protect 70-90% of the recipients, so even vaccinated travelers should be cautious in selecting their food and water.

Two vaccines are recommended for protection against typhoid fever. An oral vaccine, **TY21a**, consists of a total of 4 capsules taken (one per day, every other day) over a seven day period, and requires a booster every five years. Reactions to the TY21a vaccine are rare but include nausea, vomiting, abdominal cramps, and skin rash.

A new single-dose injectable vaccine, **Typhim Vi** or **ViCPS**, is equally effective, and requires a booster dose every two years. Reactions to Typhim Vi are also rare, but include discomfort at the site of injection and headaches. An earlier typhoid vaccine developed years ago, which uses killed typhoid organisms and is administered in a two dose series, had more reported side effect and is currently not preferred. Instead, use one of the newer vaccines. Based on the vaccine chosen, booster doses are required every two to five years.

## Recommendations

CDC recommends a typhoid vaccination for those travelers who are going off the usual tourist itineraries, traveling to smaller cities and rural areas, or staying long term, that is, for six weeks or more. Vaccination should be completed at least two weeks before travel. Typhoid vaccination is not required for international travel.

## CHOLERA

Cholera is an acute diarrheal illness caused by an infection of the intestine with the bacterium *Vibrio cholerae*. Infection is acquired by ingesting contaminated water or food. The infection is often mild without symptoms, but sometimes can be severe. Approximately one in 20 infected persons has severe disease characterized by an abrupt onset of profuse watery diarrhea, vomiting, dehydration, and leg cramps.

## Risk to Traveler

Cholera cases have been reported from some countries of East Asia. The risk of infection to the US traveler is very low, especially those that are following the usual tourist itineraries, staying in standard accommodations, and following food and water safety instructions. A list of cholera infected countries is given in *Appendix 10, CDC's Blue Sheet*.

## Prevention

Travelers to cholera infected areas should:
- avoid eating high risk foods, especially fish and shellfish, and
- follow the standard food and water precautions of eating only thoroughly cooked food that is served hot, peeling their own fruit, and drinking beverages and ice made from boiled or chlorinated water, bottled carbonated water, or bottled carbonated soft drinks.

Persons with severe cases of cholera respond well to simple fluid and electrolyte-replacement therapy, but medical attention must be sought quickly when cholera is suspected.

The cholera vaccine licensed for use in the United States confers only brief and incomplete immunity (50% effective in reducing the illness). The risk of cholera to US travelers is so low that it is questionable whether the vaccine is of benefit, and therefore it is not recommended routinely for travelers. The primary series for this cholera vaccine is normally two injections with booster doses given every 6 months for persons who remain at high risk. **Cholera vaccine is not recommended for infants under 6 months old or for pregnant women.**

For additional information, read *Appendix 4, Traveler's Diarrhea & Food and Water Precautions*, and *Appendix 8, Cholera Information*.

## HEPATITIS A

Hepatitis A is a viral infection of the liver transmitted to humans by the fecal-oral route; through direct person-to-person contact; from contaminated water, ice, or shellfish; or from fruits or uncooked vegetables contaminated through handling. Symptoms include fatigue, fever, loss of appetite, nausea, dark urine, jaundice, vomiting, aches and pains, and light stools. No specific therapy, only supportive care, is available.

## Risk to Traveler

Travelers are at **high risk** for hepatitis A – **except travelers to Japan** – especially if travel plans include visiting rural areas and extensive travel in the countryside, frequent close contact with local persons, or eating in settings of poor sanitation. Be aware that a study has shown that many cases of travel-related hepatitis A occur in travelers to developing countries with "standard" itineraries, accommodations, and food consumption behaviors.

## Prevention

The virus is inactivated by boiling or cooking to 185° F (85° C) for one minute. Therefore, eating thoroughly cooked foods and drinking only treated water serve as general precautions. In addition, **Immune globulin (IG)** *or* **hepatitis A vaccine** is recommended before travel. Two hepatitis A vaccines, **Havrix®** and **VAQTA®**, are currently licensed in the US.

Immune globulin and the hepatitis A vaccine marketed in the United States are safe. American travelers should note that IG manufactured in foreign countries may or may not meet these requirements. Therefore, American travelers who will need to receive additional doses of IG in other countries should use products that meet US standards and license requirements. For reference, the method of manufacturing IG in the US is called the **Cohn-Oncley procedure.**

## Recommendations

CDC recommends Immune globulin (IG) or hepatitis A vaccine before travel for protection against hepatitis A.

**Immune globulin** is recommended for persons of all ages who:
- desire only short term protection (one dose is effective for three months)
- need immediate protection, and
- are too young for the vaccine (less than 2 years of age).

**Hepatitis A vaccine** is preferred for persons two years of age and older who plan to travel repeatedly or reside for long periods of time in intermediate or high risk areas. Bear in mind:
- The complete hepatitis A vaccine series requires a minimum of six months to complete.
- For these travelers over 18 years of age, hepatitis A vaccine should be given in a two-dose series with the second dose administered 6-12 months after the first.
- For children and adolescents between ages 2 through 18, a two or three dose series of hepatitis A vaccine is recommended depending on the vaccine chosen.

Travelers can be considered to be protected four weeks after receiving the initial vaccine dose. If the vaccine is administered less than four weeks before travel, then IG should also be given. The vaccine series must be completed for long-term protection. Hepatitis A vaccination is not required for travel to any country.

In addition to receiving IG or the vaccine, all travelers should follow the food and water precautions as described in *Appendix 4, Traveler's Diarrhea & Food and Water Precautions.*

Additional IG and hepatitis A information covering the vaccine and its safety are found in *Appendix 9, Hepatitis A Vaccine & Immune Globulin (IG) - Disease and Vaccine Information.*

## PARASITES

Parasitic infections are acquired by eating or drinking contaminated food or water, through direct contact with soil or water containing parasites or their larva, or by contact with biting insects. Symptoms and evidence of infection may include, but are not limited to: fever, swollen lymph nodes, rashes or itchy skin, digestive problems such as abdominal pain or diarrhea, eye problems, and anemia.

### Risk to Traveler

Travelers to East Asia are at risk of parasitic infections. There are many types of parasites and infection may occur in several ways: by eating undercooked meats infected with parasites or their larva; by eating food or drinking water contaminated with parasites or their eggs; by contact with soil or water infected with parasites; or through insect bites. Several types of parasites, for example schistosomiasis, can penetrate intact human skin and travelers are advised to wear shoes and avoid swimming, wading, or washing in fresh water.

### Prevention

Travelers should eat only thoroughly cooked food, drink safe water, wear shoes, refrain from swimming in fresh water, and avoid contact with insects, particularly mosquitoes, biting flies, gnats, and midges.

## DISEASES TRANSMITTED THROUGH INTIMATE CONTACT WITH PEOPLE

### HIV/AIDS

Human immunodeficiency virus, or HIV, which causes acquired immunodeficiency syndrome or AIDS, is found primarily in blood, semen, and vaginal secretions of an infected person. HIV is spread by sexual contact with an infected person, by needle-sharing among injecting drug users, and through transfusions of infected blood and blood clotting factors. Babies born to HIV-infected women may become infected before, during, or shortly after birth.

In the United States, blood is screened for HIV antibodies, but this screening may not take place in all countries. Scientific studies have revealed no evidence that HIV is transmitted by air, food, water, insects, inanimate objects or casual contact. Even though HIV antibodies are normally detected on a test within 6 months after infection, the period between infection and development of disease symptoms (incubation period) may be 10 years or longer. Treatment has prolonged the survival of some HIV infected persons but there is no known cure or vaccine available. For additional information, see *Appendix 7, HIV/AIDS Information.*

### Risk to Traveler
AIDS is found in some parts of this region. In East Asia, the predominant modes of transmission are not fully defined due to the recent spread of HIV into these areas. The risk to a traveler depends on whether the traveler will be involved in sexual or needle-sharing contact with a person who is infected with HIV. Receipt of unscreened blood for transfusion poses a risk for HIV infection.

### Prevention
No effective vaccine has been developed for HIV. Travelers should avoid sexual or needle-sharing contact with a person who is infected with HIV. If a blood transfusion is necessary, screened blood should come from an HIV-negative blood donor.

### Recommendations
Travelers should avoid activities known to carry risks for infection with HIV.

## HEPATITIS B
Hepatitis B is a viral infection of the liver. Hepatitis B is transmitted to humans primarily through behavior that result in the exchange of blood or fluids containing blood. Risky behavior includes heterosexual or homosexual contact or sharing needles or drug paraphernalia with a person infected with the hepatitis B virus. Any unscreened or improperly screened blood or blood product, as well as unsterilized needles, or

contact with potentially infected people who have open skin sores due to impetigo, scabies, and scratched insect bites, heightens the potential for infection to the traveler. An effective vaccine for prevention of hepatitis B is available.

## Risk to Traveler

Hepatitis B rates are high for most countries in this region, **especially China**. Japan reports a lower rate than the other countries. The risk to the individual international traveler is greater if the traveler:
- has direct contact with blood or fluids containing blood;
- has intimate sexual contact with an infected person;
- remains in the country for longer than six months or has close contact with the local population.

## Prevention

**Hepatitis B vaccine** should be considered for those traveling to countries with high to intermediate rates of hepatitis B infection. For those travelers expecting to reside in countries of high risk, as well as all health workers, vaccination is strongly recommended.

Vaccination should ideally begin 6 months before travel, in order to complete the full series, which is needed for optimal protection. The three intramuscular doses of vaccine should be spaced so that the second dose is given one month after the first. The final dose is given 6 months after the first. The vaccination schedule should be initiated even if it will not be completed before travel begins. There is an alternative four-dose schedule that may provide protection if the first three doses can be delivered before departure. After completing the primary series, booster doses of the vaccine are not necessary.

## Recommendations

CDC recommends vaccination for any of the following people:
- any health care worker (medical, dental, or laboratory) whose activities might result in blood exposure;
- any traveler who may have intimate sexual contact with the local population;
- any long-term (6 months or more) traveler, e.g. teachers, who will reside in rural areas or have daily physical contact with the local population; or
- any traveler who is likely to seek either medical, dental, or other treatment in local facilities during their stay.

Hepatitis B vaccination is not required for travel to any country. Additional hepatitis B information is found in *Appendix 15, Hepatitis B.*

## OTHER DISEASES
## SCHISTOSOMIASIS

Schistosomiasis is a parasitic infection that develops after the larvae of a flatworm have penetrated the human skin. These larvae live in fresh water lakes, ponds, and streams and can penetrate unbroken skin. Water treated with chlorine or iodine is virtually safe, and salt water poses no risk.

### Risk to Traveler

Schistosomiasis infection is found in some parts of China, **including many rivers and lakes of southeastern and eastern China along the valley of Chang Jiang (Yangtze) river and its tributaries.** The risk is a function of the frequency and degree of contact with contaminated fresh water for bathing, wading, or swimming.

### Prevention

The traveler cannot distinguish between infested and non-infested water. Therefore, swimming in fresh water in rural areas should be avoided. Bath water should either be heated to 50° (122° F) for five minutes or treated with chlorine or iodine as done for drinking water. If exposed, immediate and vigorous towel drying or application of rubbing alcohol to the exposed areas may reduce the risk of infection. Screening procedures are available for those who suspect infection, and schistosomiasis is treatable with drugs.

### Recommendations

Avoid contact with potentially contaminated water, such as swimming in lakes, ponds, rivers, etc.

## RABIES

Rabies is a viral infection that affects the central nervous system. It is transmitted to humans by warm-blooded animal (mammal) bites that introduce the virus into the wound. Although dogs are the main reservoir of the disease, all warm-blooded animal bites should be suspect.

### Risk to Traveler

For some countries in East Asia, there is a risk of rabies infection, particularly in rural areas or in areas where large numbers of dogs are found. There is no risk in Japan and Taiwan.

## Prevention

Do not handle animals! Any animal bite should receive prompt medical attention. When wounds are thoroughly cleaned with large amounts of soap and water, the risk of rabies infection is reduced. Exposed individuals should receive prompt medical attention and advice on post-exposure preventive treatment.

## Recommendations

There are no requirements for vaccination, but pre-exposure vaccination is recommended for:
- travelers visiting foreign areas where dog rabies is known to exist and whose activities may place them at high risk of exposure;
- veterinarians and animal handlers;
- spelunkers; and
- certain rabies laboratory workers.

Pre-exposure vaccination does not nullify the need for post-exposure vaccine, but reduces the number of injections and may provide protection under circumstances in which rabies exposure is unrecognized. For additional rabies information, refer to *Appendix 11, Rabies Information.*

---

### SUMMARY OF RECOMMENDATIONS FOR EAST ASIA

*Travelers should:*
- *take the appropriate country specific malaria prevention measures (chloroquine or mefloquine, China only)*
- *follow precautions to prevent insect bites*
- *pay attention to the quality of their drinking water and food*
- *have a dose of Immune Globulin (IG) or the hepatitis A vaccine, and consider booster doses of tetanus (Td) and polio (eIPV) vaccines.*
- *Depending on the locations to be visited, planned activities, and health of the traveler, the following vaccines should be considered: Hepatitis B, Yellow Fever, Typhoid, Rabies (pre-exposure), and Cholera.*
- *Finally, the normal "childhood" vaccines should be up-to-date: Measles, Mumps, Rubella (MMR Vaccine); Diphtheria, Tetanus, Pertussis (DTP Vaccine if traveler is less than 7 years of age, or Td if older than 7 years of age), and Polio vaccine. For additional information on these "childhood" vaccines, refer to Appendix 5, Vaccine Recommendations.*

# 13. SOUTHEAST ASIA

## COUNTRIES IN THIS REGION
Brunei Darussalam
Cambodia
Indonesia
Lao People's Democratic Republic (Laos)
Malaysia
Myanmar (Burma)
Philippines
Singapore
Thailand
Vietnam

## SOUTHEAST ASIA TRAVELER'S OVERVIEW

*Travelers to Southeast Asia may be exposed to potential diseases from a number of sources.* **The most frequently reported illness is traveler's diarrhea,** *but Southeast Asia contains a variety of diseases transmitted by:*

- *insects,*
- *contaminated food and water, or*
- *close contact with infected people.*

*In this chapter, specific diseases, their causes, symptoms, geographic areas of risk, and prevention recommendations or requirement information are discussed under their topical headings. As a general guideline, in order to reduce the risk of infection, travelers must:*

- *protect themselves from insects*
- *ensure the quality of their food and drinking water*
- *be knowledgeable about potential diseases in the region to be visited*
- *receive all recommended vaccines and preventive medications.*

*In addition, travelers should note that diseases are not restricted to cleanly defined geographical areas. For example, mosquitoes can fly over city or country borders, so all travelers should protect themselves by taking the basic preventive precautions as described under each section and disease. Where appropriate, more detailed information is referenced in the Appendices.*

## DISEASES TRANSMITTED BY INSECTS

Many diseases are transmitted through the bite of infected insects such as mosquitoes, flies, fleas, ticks and lice. In general, **travelers must protect themselves from insect bites**. Travelers are at a higher risk for insect bites if they participate in outdoor activities during night time hours from dusk to dawn when mosquitoes bite, or if their living accommodations are unscreened. If a mosquito net is unlikely to be available, consider buying a portable mosquito net.

## PREVENTING INSECT BITES

To reduce the risk of mosquito bites, travelers should remain in well-screened areas, use mosquito nets, and wear clothes that cover most of the body. Travelers should also take insect repellent with them to use on any exposed areas of the skin. The most effective compound in a repellent is **DEET**, which may be listed as an ingredient on repellant labels as **"N,N-diethyl meta-toluamide."** Check the repellent label to ensure DEET is an ingredient.

Travelers should note, however, that insect repellents containing DEET should always be used according to label directions and sparingly on children. **Avoid applying high-concentration (greater than 35%) products to the skin, particularly on children, and refrain from applying repellent to portions of the hands that are likely to come in contact with the eyes and mouth.** Pediatric insect repellents with 6-10% DEET are available without prescription in many drug stores. In rare instances, toxic reactions or other problems have developed after contact with DEET.

Travelers should also purchase a flying insect-killing spray to use in living and sleeping areas during the evening and night. For greater protection, clothing and bednets can be soaked in or sprayed with **permethrin**, which is an insect repellent licensed for use on clothing. If applied according to the directions, permethrin will repel insects from clothing for several weeks. Portable mosquito bednets, repellents containing DEET, and permethrin can be purchased in hardware, backpacking, and military surplus stores.

## MALARIA

Malaria is a serious parasitic infection transmitted to humans by an Anopheles mosquito. These mosquitoes bite at night, from dusk to dawn. Symptoms of malaria range from flu-like symptoms with fever, general achiness, headache, and fatigue, to a cycle of shaking chills, high fever, and sweating. If left untreated, malaria can cause anemia, kidney failure, coma, and death. Drugs are available to help prevent a malaria infection.

However, in spite of all protective measures, travelers occasionally develop malaria. While traveling and up to one year after returning home, travelers should seek medical evaluation for any flu-like illness.

### Risk to Traveler

A risk for malaria exists throughout the year in all parts of these countries, including some urban areas. In this region the dominant form of malaria is *P. falciparum* (the most dangerous type), which has been reported to be resistant to the drug chloroquine.

*Areas of Risk*
- **Cambodia** – malaria risk in all areas, except Phnom Penh.
- **Indonesia** – in general, malaria risk in rural areas only (largely confined to rural areas not visited by most travelers; most travel to rural areas is in the daytime hours when there is minimal risk of exposure, except high risk in all areas of Irian Jaya (western half of the island of New Guinea); no risk in the big cities and resort areas of Java and Bali.

- **Lao People's Democratic Republic** – malaria risk in all areas, except no risk in city of Vientiane.
- **Malaysia** – for peninsular Malaysia and Sarawak (northwest Borneo) malaria risk is limited to the rural hinterlands; urban and coastal areas are malaria free; Sabah (northeast Borneo) has malaria throughout.
- **Myanmar (Burma)** – malaria risk in rural areas only (largely confined to rural areas not visited by most travelers; most travel to rural areas is in the daytime hours when there is minimal risk of exposure).
- **Philippines** – malaria risk in rural areas only, except no risk in provinces of Bohol, Catanduanes, Cebu and Leyte. Malaria transmission is largely confined to rural areas not visited by most travelers; most travel to rural areas is in the daytime hours when there is minimal risk of exposure. See specific instructions in the prevention section below.)
- **Thailand** – malaria transmission is confined to the forested areas of its borders with Cambodia and Myanmar (Burma). These areas are not visited by most travelers. Therefore, most travelers to Thailand are not at risk for malaria. (In Thailand, use Doxycycline for malaria prevention; see prevention section below).
- **Vietnam** – malaria risk in rural areas only, except no risk in the Red and Mekong Deltas.

*No Risk*
Brunei Darussalam and Singapore.

## Prevention & Recommendations

Travelers to Cambodia, Indonesia, Lao Peoples' Democratic Republic, Malaysia, Myanmar and Vietnam at risk for malaria should take **mefloquine** to prevent malaria. For travelers to the Philippines and Thailand, different prevention instructions apply; see below. This drug is marketed in the United States under the name Lariam™. The adult dosage is 250 mg (one tablet) once a week.

Mefloquine should not be used by travelers with a:
- history of epilepsy or psychiatric disorder,
- known hypersensitivity to mefloquine.

In consultation with a physician, mefloquine may be used by pregnant women and children weighing less than 30 pounds, when travel to an area with chloroquine-resistant malaria is unavoidable. Travelers who cannot take mefloquine should read the section "Prescription Drugs for Malaria" found in *Appendix 1, Malaria Information.*

Travelers to **Thailand** who overnight in the few areas of risk (see risk section) should take **Doxycycline**. This drug is taken every day at a dose of 100 mg, to begin on the day before entering the malarious area, while there, and continued for 4 weeks after leaving. If Doxycycline is used, there is no need to take other preventive drugs, such as chloroquine.

Possible side effects include skin photosensitivity that may result in an exaggerated sunburn reaction. This risk can be minimized by wearing a hat and using sunscreens. Women who take Doxycycline for long periods may develop vaginal yeast infections and should discuss this with their doctor before using Doxycycline.

*Doxycycline should not be used by:*
- pregnant women,
- children under 8 years of age, or
- travelers with a known hypersensitivity to Doxycycline.

In the **Philippines**, since malaria transmission is largely confined to the rural areas not visited by most travelers, taking drugs to prevent malaria is only recommended for travelers who will have outdoor exposure during evening and nighttime hours in rural areas. Travelers to the rural areas of the Philippines at risk of malaria should take one of two drugs to prevent malaria transmission:
- If traveling to rural areas of the Philippines other than those listed below, travelers should take a weekly **chloroquine** tablet. The weekly dosage for an adult is 500 mg (salt) once a week. This drug should be taken one week before entering a malarious area, weekly while there, and weekly for 4 weeks after leaving the malarious area.
- Travelers to the rural areas on the Philippine Islands of Luzon, Basilian, Mindoro, Palawan, Mindanao, and to Sulu Archipelago should take **mefloquine** for prevention of malaria. For mefloquine details, see above.

In addition to using drugs to prevent malaria and treat a possible malaria attack, travelers should use measures to reduce exposure to malaria-carrying mosquitoes and protect themselves from mosquito bites. Remember, these mosquitoes bite mainly during the evening and night, from dusk to dawn.

Additional general malaria information, as well as specific information for women who are pregnant or children, is found in *Appendix 1, Malaria Information.*

## YELLOW FEVER

Yellow fever is a viral disease found in parts of Africa and South America. It is transmitted to humans by a mosquito bite. Even though there is no risk of becoming infected while traveling in East Asian countries, some countries require a yellow fever vaccination when travelers arrive from certain South American and African countries.

If you are **only** traveling from the United States to a Southeast Asian country, CDC does not recommend, and you are not required to have, a yellow fever vaccination. If your travel plans include traveling to or from countries in South America or Africa, you may be required to have a yellow fever vaccination. Therefore, you should review the comprehensive country-by-country yellow fever vaccine requirements in *Appendix 2, Yellow Fever Requirements.*

## DENGUE FEVER

Dengue fever is a viral infection transmitted to humans by mosquito bites. These mosquitoes are most active during the day, especially around dawn and dusk, and are frequently found in or around residential areas. The illness is flu-like and characterized by sudden onset, high fever, severe headaches, joint and muscle pain, and rash. Severe cases of dengue hemorrhagic fever produce shock, internal bleeding, and death. The rash appears 3-4 days after the onset of fever. Since there is no vaccine or specific treatment available, prevention is important.

### Risk to Traveler

Dengue fever occurs throughout Southeast Asia, with epidemics most recently in **Cambodia**, **Indonesia**, **Laos**, **East and West Malaysia**, **Myanmar**, **Philippines**, **Singapore**, **Thailand**, and **Vietnam**. The risk of infection is small for most travelers, except during periods of epidemic transmission.

### Prevention

There is no vaccine for dengue fever, therefore, the traveler should avoid mosquito bites. These mosquitoes may bite anytime during the day, especially in shady areas, indoors, or when the sky is overcast, but prefer feeding around dawn and dusk. For additional information on dengue fever, refer to *Appendix 12, Dengue Fever.*

## JAPANESE ENCEPHALITIS

Japanese Encephalitis is a mosquito-borne viral disease that occurs in rural areas. These mosquitoes are most often found in rice growing areas and bite in the late afternoon and early evening. Symptoms range from:

no symptoms to headache, fever, and flu-like symptoms. More serious complications involve a swelling of the brain (encephalitis). There is no specific drug to treat Japanese Encephalitis.

## Risk to Traveler

Transmission is usually seasonal (associated with the rainy season). There is a risk for travelers to rural areas of Southeast Asian countries, especially **Burma**, **Thailand**, **Cambodia**, **Indonesia**, **Laos**, **Malaysia**, **Philippines**, **Thailand**, and **Vietnam**. The chance that a traveler to Southeast Asia will develop Japanese Encephalitis is extremely small.

## Prevention & Recommendations

The vaccine **JE-VAX** is licensed and available in the United States. Vaccination should be considered for persons who plan long-term residence in rural areas. Travelers who visit rural farming areas for 4 weeks or more during the transmission season should consider immunization. Travelers who remain un-immunized should wear mosquito repellents, sleep under bed-nets, and bring insecticidal sprays to use in their sleeping quarters.

The vaccine is given in 3 doses on days 0, 7, and 30. Protection can be expected 10 days following the last dose. A shorter course of vaccination (Day 0, 7, and 14) can be used, but protection and duration is less than the normal schedule. Fever and local reactions such as redness, swelling, and pain are reported in fewer than 10% of those vaccinated. More severe allergic reactions have been reported in persons with a history of insect or food allergies. These reactions have been life-threatening on occasion. Once vaccinated, you should have access to medical care, if needed, for 2-3 days after vaccination.

*The Japanese Encephalitis vaccine should not be given to*:
- Those acutely ill or with active infections.
- Persons with heart, kidney, or liver disorders.
- Persons with generalized cancerous malignancies such as leukemia and lymphoma.
- Persons with a history of multiple allergies or hypersensitivity to components of the vaccine.
- Pregnant women, unless there is a high risk of Japanese Encephalitis during the woman's stay.

For additional information on Japanese Encephalitis, refer to *Appendix 13, Japanese Encephalitis.*

## OTHER INSECT DISEASES
### Risks to Traveler
Other diseases spread by mosquitoes, sand flies, black flies, or other insects are prevalent, especially in rural areas.. These diseases include: *filariasis* (mosquito), *leishmaniasis* (sandfly), *Congo-Crimean hemorrhagic fever* (tick), *typhus* (lice), and *plague* (fleas).

### Prevention
For most of these diseases, a vaccine is not available and treatment is limited. Therefore, travelers must follow the guidelines under "Preventing Insect Bites." For additional detailed information of these and other insect diseases, please read *Appendix 3, Other Insect Diseases.*

## DISEASES TRANSMITTED THROUGH FOOD & WATER
Food and waterborne diseases are the number one cause of illness to travelers and are very common in Southeast Asia. **Traveler's diarrhea is the most frequent health problem for travelers.** It can be caused by viruses, bacteria, or parasites that are found universally throughout the region. Transmission is most often through contaminated food or water. Infections may cause diarrhea and vomiting (typhoid fever, cholera, and parasites), liver damage (hepatitis), or muscle paralysis (polio).

## GENERAL PRECAUTIONS
**Water**: The following beverages are safe to drink: boiled water or beverages made with boiled water, canned or carbonated beverages, beer, or wine. Impure water often contaminates drinking containers, ice, and tap water.

**Food**: Food that has been cooked to 165° F (74° C) is generally safe. As a reference, food at this temperature cannot be put directly into your mouth, but must cool a bit. Foods of concern are salads, uncooked vegetables and fruit, unpasteurized milk and milk products, raw meat, and shellfish. If you peel fruit yourself, it is generally safe. A simple rule of thumb is: "Boil it, cook it, peel it, or forget it."

For additional detailed precautions, be sure to read *Appendix 4, Traveler's Diarrhea & Food and Water Precautions.*

## TYPHOID FEVER
Typhoid fever is a bacterial infection transmitted to humans through contaminated food and/or water, or directly between people. Symptoms

of typhoid fever include fever, headaches, fatigue, loss of appetite, and constipation. Typhoid fever can be treated effectively with antibiotics.

## Risk to Traveler
Travelers to Southeast Asia are at risk for typhoid fever, especially when traveling to smaller cities, villages, or rural areas.

## Prevention
By drinking only bottled or boiled beverages and eating only thoroughly cooked food, a traveler lowers the risk of infection. Currently available vaccines have been shown to protect 70-90% of the recipients, so even vaccinated travelers should be cautious in selecting their food and water.

Two vaccines are recommended for protection against typhoid fever. An oral vaccine, **TY21a**, consists of a total of 4 capsules taken (one per day, every other day) over a seven day period, and requires a booster every five years. Reactions to the TY21a vaccine are rare but include nausea, vomiting, abdominal cramps, and skin rash.

A new single-dose injectable vaccine, **Typhim Vi** or **ViCPS**, is equally effective, and requires a booster dose every two years. Reactions to Typhim Vi are also rare, but include discomfort at the site of injection and headaches. An earlier typhoid vaccine developed years ago, which uses killed typhoid organisms and is administered in a two dose series, had more reported side effect and is currently not preferred. Instead, use one of the newer vaccines. Based on the vaccine chosen, booster doses are required every two to five years.

## Recommendations
CDC recommends a typhoid vaccination for those travelers who are going off the usual tourist itineraries, traveling to smaller cities and rural areas, or staying long term, that is, for six weeks or more. Vaccination should be completed at least two weeks before travel. Typhoid vaccination is not required for international travel.

## CHOLERA
Cholera is an acute diarrheal illness caused by an infection of the intestine with the bacterium *Vibrio cholerae*. Infection is acquired by ingesting contaminated water or food. The infection is often mild without symptoms, but sometimes can be severe. Approximately one in 20 infected persons has severe disease characterized by an abrupt onset of profuse watery diarrhea, vomiting, dehydration, and leg cramps.

## Risk to Traveler

Cholera cases have been reported from some countries of Southeast Asia. The risk of infection to the US traveler is very low, especially those that are following the usual tourist itineraries, staying in standard accommodations, and following food and water safety instructions. A list of cholera infected countries is given in *Appendix 10, CDC's Blue Sheet*.

## Prevention

Travelers to cholera infected areas should:
- avoid eating high risk foods, especially fish and shellfish, and
- follow the standard food and water precautions of eating only thoroughly cooked food that is served hot, peeling their own fruit, and drinking beverages and ice made from boiled or chlorinated water, bottled carbonated water, or bottled carbonated soft drinks.

Persons with severe cases of cholera respond well to simple fluid and electrolyte-replacement therapy, but medical attention must be sought quickly when cholera is suspected.

The cholera vaccine licensed for use in the United States confers only brief and incomplete immunity (50% effective in reducing the illness). The risk of cholera to US travelers is so low that it is questionable whether the vaccine is of benefit, and therefore it is not recommended routinely for travelers. The primary series for this cholera vaccine is normally two injections with booster doses given every 6 months for persons who remain at high risk. **Cholera vaccine is not recommended for infants under 6 months old or for pregnant women**.

For additional information, read *Appendix 4, Traveler's Diarrhea & Food and Water Precautions*, and *Appendix 8, Cholera Information*.

## HEPATITIS A

Hepatitis A is a viral infection of the liver transmitted to humans by the fecal-oral route; through direct person-to-person contact; from contaminated water, ice, or shellfish; or from fruits or uncooked vegetables contaminated through handling. Symptoms include fatigue, fever, loss of appetite, nausea, dark urine, jaundice, vomiting, aches and pains, and light stools. No specific therapy, only supportive care, is available.

## Risk to Traveler

Travelers are at **high risk** for hepatitis A especially if travel plans include visiting rural areas and extensive travel in the countryside, frequent close contact with local persons, or eating in settings of poor sanitation. Be aware that a study has shown that many cases of travel-related hepatitis A occur in travelers to developing countries with "standard" itineraries, accommodations, and food consumption behaviors.

## Prevention

The virus is inactivated by boiling or cooking to 185° F (85° C) for one minute. Therefore, eating thoroughly cooked foods and drinking only treated water serve as general precautions. In addition, **Immune globulin (IG)** *or* **hepatitis A vaccine** is recommended before travel. Two hepatitis A vaccines, **Havrix®** and **VAQTA®**, are currently licensed in the United States.

Immune globulin and the hepatitis A vaccine marketed in the United States are safe. American travelers should note that IG manufactured in foreign countries may or may not meet these requirements. Therefore, American travelers who will need to receive additional doses of IG in other countries should use products that meet US standards and license requirements. For reference, the method of manufacturing IG in the US is called the **Cohn-Oncley procedure**.

## Recommendations

CDC recommends Immune globulin (IG) or hepatitis A vaccine before travel for protection against hepatitis A.

**Immune globulin** is recommended for persons of all ages who:
- desire only short term protection (one dose is effective for three months)
- need immediate protection, and
- are too young for the vaccine (less than 2 years of age).

**Hepatitis A vaccine** is preferred for persons two years of age and older who plan to travel repeatedly or reside for long periods of time in intermediate or high risk areas. Bear in mind:
- The complete hepatitis A vaccine series requires a minimum of six months to complete.
- For these travelers over 18 years of age, hepatitis A vaccine should be given in a two-dose series with the second dose administered 6-12 months after the first.
- For children and adolescents between ages 2 through 18, a two or three dose series of hepatitis A vaccine is recommended depending on the vaccine chosen.

Travelers can be considered to be protected four weeks after receiving the initial vaccine dose. If the vaccine is administered less than four weeks before travel, then IG should also be given. The vaccine series must be completed for long-term protection. Hepatitis A vaccination is not required for travel to any country.

In addition to receiving IG or the vaccine, all travelers should follow the food and water precautions as described in *Appendix 4, Traveler's Diarrhea & Food and Water Precautions.*

Additional IG and hepatitis A information covering the vaccine and its safety are found in *Appendix 9, Hepatitis A Vaccine & Immune Globulin (IG) - Disease and Vaccine Information.*

## PARASITES

Parasitic infections are acquired by eating or drinking contaminated food or water, through direct contact with soil or water containing parasites or their larva, or by contact with biting insects. Symptoms and evidence of infection may include, but are not limited to: fever, swollen lymph nodes, rashes or itchy skin, digestive problems such as abdominal pain or diarrhea, eye problems, and anemia.

### Risk to Traveler

Travelers to Southeast Asia are at risk of parasitic infections. There are many types of parasites and infection may occur in several ways: by eating undercooked meats infected with parasites or their larva; by eating food or drinking water contaminated with parasites or their eggs; by contact with soil or water infected with parasites; or through insect bites. Several types of parasites, for example schistosomiasis, can penetrate intact human skin and travelers are advised to wear shoes and avoid swimming, wading, or washing in fresh water.

### Prevention

Travelers should eat only thoroughly cooked food, drink safe water, wear shoes, refrain from swimming in fresh water, and avoid contact with insects, particularly mosquitoes, biting flies, gnats, and midges.

## DISEASES TRANSMITTED THROUGH INTIMATE CONTACT WITH PEOPLE

### HIV/AIDS

Human immunodeficiency virus, or HIV, which causes acquired immunodeficiency syndrome or AIDS, is found primarily in blood, semen, and vaginal secretions of an infected person. HIV is spread by sexual contact with an infected person, by needle-sharing among injecting drug users, and through transfusions of infected blood and blood clotting factors. Babies born to HIV-infected women may become infected before, during, or shortly after birth.

In the United States, blood is screened for HIV antibodies, but this screening may not take place in all countries. Scientific studies have revealed no evidence that HIV is transmitted by air, food, water, insects, inanimate objects or casual contact. Even though HIV antibodies are normally detected on a test within 6 months after infection, the period between infection and development of disease symptoms (incubation period) may be 10 years or longer. Treatment has prolonged the survival of some HIV infected persons but there is no known cure or vaccine available. For additional information, see *Appendix 7, HIV/AIDS Information.*

## Risk to Traveler
AIDS is found throughout the region. In Southeast Asia, heterosexual transmission is now the predominant mode of transmission, and there are high numbers of HIV-positive injecting drug users. The risk to a traveler depends on whether the traveler will be involved in sexual or needle-sharing contact with a person who is infected with HIV. Receipt of unscreened blood for transfusion poses a risk for HIV infection.

## Prevention
No effective vaccine has been developed for HIV. Travelers should avoid sexual or needle-sharing contact with a person who is infected with HIV. If a blood transfusion is necessary, screened blood should come from an HIV-negative blood donor.

## Recommendations
Travelers should avoid activities known to carry risks for infection with HIV.

## HEPATITIS B
Hepatitis B is a viral infection of the liver. Hepatitis B is transmitted to humans primarily through behavior that result in the exchange of blood or fluids containing blood. Risky behavior includes heterosexual or homosexual contact or sharing needles or drug paraphernalia with a person infected with the hepatitis B virus. Any unscreened or improperly screened blood or blood product, as well as unsterilized needles, or

contact with potentially infected people who have open skin sores due to impetigo, scabies, and scratched insect bites, heightens the potential for infection to the traveler. An effective vaccine for prevention of hepatitis B is available.

## Risk to Traveler

The risk of hepatitis B virus infection is **high** for Southeast Asia. The risk to the individual international traveler is greater if the traveler:
- has direct contact with blood or fluids containing blood;
- has intimate sexual contact with an infected person;
- remains in the country for longer than six months or has close contact with the local population.

## Prevention

**Hepatitis B vaccine** should be considered for those traveling to countries with high to intermediate rates of hepatitis B infection. For those travelers expecting to reside in countries of high risk, as well as all health workers, vaccination is strongly recommended.

Vaccination should ideally begin 6 months before travel, in order to complete the full series, which is needed for optimal protection. The three intramuscular doses of vaccine should be spaced so that the second dose is given one month after the first. The final dose is given 6 months after the first. The vaccination schedule should be initiated even if it will not be completed before travel begins. There is an alternative four-dose schedule that may provide protection if the first three doses can be delivered before departure. After completing the primary series, booster doses of the vaccine are not necessary.

## Recommendations

CDC recommends vaccination for any of the following people:
- any health care worker (medical, dental, or laboratory) whose activities might result in blood exposure;
- any traveler who may have intimate sexual contact with the local population;
- any long-term (6 months or more) traveler, e.g. teachers, who will reside in rural areas or have daily physical contact with the local population; or
- any traveler who is likely to seek either medical, dental, or other treatment in local facilities during their stay.

Hepatitis B vaccination is not required for travel to any country. Additional hepatitis B information is found in *Appendix 15, Hepatitis B*.

## OTHER DISEASES
## SCHISTOSOMIASIS

Schistosomiasis is a parasitic infection that develops after the larvae of a flatworm have penetrated the human skin. These larvae live in fresh water lakes, ponds, and streams and can penetrate unbroken skin. Water treated with chlorine or iodine is virtually safe, and salt water poses no risk.

### Risk to Traveler

Schistosomiasis infection is found in some parts of a few Southeast Asian countries. **Cambodia**, **Indonesia**, **Laos**, **Philippines**, and **Thailand** all have specific areas of potential infection. The risk is a function of the frequency and degree of contact with contaminated fresh water for bathing, wading, or swimming.

### Prevention

The traveler cannot distinguish between infested and non-infested water. Therefore, swimming in fresh water in rural areas should be avoided. Bath water should either be heated to 50° (122° F) for five minutes or treated with chlorine or iodine as done for drinking water. If exposed, immediate and vigorous towel drying or application of rubbing alcohol to the exposed areas may reduce the risk of infection. Screening procedures are available for those who suspect infection, and schistosomiasis is treatable with drugs.

### Recommendations

Avoid contact with potentially contaminated water, such as swimming in lakes, ponds, rivers, etc.

## RABIES

Rabies is a viral infection that affects the central nervous system. It is transmitted to humans by warm-blooded animal (mammal) bites that introduce the virus into the wound. Although dogs are the main reservoir of the disease, all warm-blooded animal bites should be suspect.

### Risk to Traveler

For most countries in Southeast Asia, there is a risk of rabies infection, particularly in rural areas or in areas where large numbers of dogs are found. **Singapore, the Malaysian Islands, and parts of Indonesia** (excluding Java, Sumatra, Sulawesi, and Kalimantan) have not reported rabies cases for at least the past two years.

## Prevention

Do not handle animals! Any animal bite should receive prompt medical attention. When wounds are thoroughly cleaned with large amounts of soap and water, the risk of rabies infection is reduced. Exposed individuals should receive prompt medical attention and advice on post-exposure preventive treatment.

## Recommendations

There are no requirements for vaccination, but pre-exposure vaccination is recommended for:

- travelers visiting foreign areas where dog rabies is known to exist and whose activities may place them at high risk of exposure;
- veterinarians and animal handlers;
- spelunkers; and
- certain rabies laboratory workers.

Pre-exposure vaccination does not nullify the need for post-exposure vaccine, but reduces the number of injections and may provide protection under circumstances in which rabies exposure is unrecognized. For additional rabies information, refer to *Appendix 11, Rabies Information.*

### SUMMARY OF RECOMMENDATIONS FOR SOUTHEAST ASIA

*Travelers should:*
- *take the appropriate country specific malaria prevention measures (mefloquine, doxycycline, or chloroquine),*
- *follow precautions to prevent insect bites*
- *pay attention to the quality of their drinking water and food*
- *have a dose of Immune Globulin (IG) or the hepatitis A vaccine, and consider booster doses of tetanus (Td) and polio (eIPV) vaccines.*
- *Depending on the locations to be visited, planned activities, and health of the traveler, the following vaccines should be considered: Hepatitis B, Typhoid, Rabies (pre-exposure), and Cholera.*
- *Finally, the normal "childhood" vaccines should be up-to-date: Measles, Mumps, Rubella (MMR Vaccine); Diphtheria, Tetanus, Pertussis (DTP Vaccine if traveler is less than 7 years of age, or Td if older than 7 years of age), and Polio vaccine. For additional information on these "childhood" vaccines, refer to Appendix 5, Vaccine Recommendations.*

# 14. AUSTRALIA & THE SOUTH PACIFIC

## COUNTRIES IN THIS REGION

Australia
Christmas Island
Cook Island
Fiji
Guam
Kiribati
Marshall Islands
Nauru
New Caledonia
New Zealand
Niue
Northern Mariana Islands
Palau
Papua New Guinea
Pitcairn
Samoa
American Samoa
Solomon Islands
Tahiti
Tokelau
Tonga
Tuvalu
US Trust Territory of the Pacific Islands
Vanuatu
Wake Island
Wallis and Futuna

## AUSTRALIA & SOUTH PACIFIC
## TRAVELER'S OVERVIEW

*Travelers to Australia & the South Pacific may be exposed to potential diseases from a number of sources.* **The most frequently reported illness is traveler's diarrhea,** *but Australia & the South Pacific contains a variety of diseases transmitted by:*

- *insects,*
- *contaminated food and water, or*
- *close contact with infected people.*

*In this chapter, specific diseases, their causes, symptoms, geographic areas of risk, and prevention recommendations or requirement information are discussed under their topical headings. As a general guideline, in order to reduce the risk of infection, travelers must:*

- *protect themselves from insects*
- *ensure the quality of their food and drinking water*
- *be knowledgeable about potential diseases in the region to be visited*
- *receive all recommended vaccines and preventive medications.*

*In addition, travelers should note that diseases are not restricted to cleanly defined geographical areas. For example, mosquitoes can fly over city or country borders, so all travelers should protect themselves by taking the basic preventive precautions as described under each section and disease. Where appropriate, more detailed information is referenced in the Appendices.*

## DISEASES TRANSMITTED BY INSECTS

Many diseases are transmitted through the bite of infected insects such as mosquitoes, flies, fleas, ticks and lice. In general, **travelers must protect themselves from insect bites**. Travelers are at a higher risk for insect bites if they participate in outdoor activities during night time hours from dusk to dawn when mosquitoes bite, or if their living accommodations are unscreened. If a mosquito net is unlikely to be available, consider buying a portable mosquito net.

## PREVENTING INSECT BITES

To reduce the risk of mosquito bites, travelers should remain in well-screened areas, use mosquito nets, and wear clothes that cover most of the body. Travelers should also take insect repellent with them to use on any exposed areas of the skin. The most effective compound in a repellent is **DEET**, which may be listed as an ingredient on repellant labels as **"N,N-diethyl meta-toluamide."** Check the repellent label to ensure DEET is an ingredient.

Travelers should note, however, that insect repellents containing DEET should always be used according to label directions and sparingly on children. **Avoid applying high-concentration (greater than 35%) products to the skin, particularly on children, and refrain from applying repellent to portions of the hands that are likely to come in contact with the eyes and mouth.** Pediatric insect repellents with 6-10% DEET are available without prescription in many drug stores. In rare instances, toxic reactions or other problems have developed after contact with DEET.

Travelers should also purchase a flying insect-killing spray to use in living and sleeping areas during the evening and night. For greater protection, clothing and bednets can be soaked in or sprayed with **permethrin**, which is an insect repellent licensed for use on clothing. If applied according to the directions, permethrin will repel insects from clothing for several weeks. Portable mosquito bednets, repellents containing DEET, and permethrin can be purchased in hardware, backpacking, and military surplus stores.

## MALARIA
Malaria is a serious parasitic infection transmitted to humans by an Anopheles mosquito. These mosquitoes bite at night, from dusk to dawn. Symptoms of malaria range from flu-like symptoms with fever, general achiness, headache, and fatigue, to a cycle of shaking chills, high fever, and sweating. If left untreated, malaria can cause anemia, kidney failure, coma, and death. Drugs are available to help prevent a malaria infection.

However, in spite of all protective measures, travelers occasionally develop malaria. Therefore, while traveling and up to one year after returning home, travelers should seek medical evaluation for any flu-like illness.

### Risk to Traveler
*High Risk*
In **Papua New Guinea, the Solomon Islands, and Vanuatu (except Fortuna Island)**, there is a high risk for malaria in all parts of these countries including urban areas. The dominant form is *P. falciparum* (the most dangerous type), which has been reported to be resistant to the drug chloroquine.

*No Risk*
Australia, Christmas Island, Cook Island, Fiji, Guam, Kiribati, Marshall Islands, Nauru, New Caledonia, New Zealand, Niue, Northern Mariana

Islands, Palau, Pitcairn, Samoa, American Samoa, Tahiti, Tokelau, Tonga, Tuvalu, US Trust Territory of the Pacific Islands, Wake Island, and Wallis & Futuna.

## Prevention & Recommendations

Travelers at risk for malaria should take **mefloquine** to prevent malaria. Mefloquine is marketed in the United States under the name **Lariam™**. The adult dosage is 250 mg (one tablet) once a week. Mefloquine should be taken one week before leaving, weekly while in the malarious area, and weekly for 4 weeks after leaving the malarious area.

Minor side effects one may experience while taking mefloquine include gastrointestinal disturbances and dizziness. More serious side effects at the recommended dosage have rarely occurred. Consult a physician for other precautions.

Mefloquine should not be used by travelers with a:
- history of epilepsy or psychiatric disorder,
- known hypersensitivity to mefloquine.

In consultation with a physician, mefloquine may be used by pregnant women and children weighing less than 30 pounds, when travel to an area with chloroquine-resistant malaria is unavoidable. Travelers who cannot take mefloquine should read the section "Prescription Drugs for Malaria" found in *Appendix 1, Malaria Information*.

In addition to using drugs to prevent malaria and treat a possible malaria attack, travelers should use measures to reduce exposure to malaria-carrying mosquitoes and protect themselves from mosquito bites. Remember, these mosquitoes bite mainly during the evening and night, from dusk to dawn.

Additional general malaria information, as well as specific information for women who are pregnant or children, is found in *Appendix 1, Malaria Information*.

## YELLOW FEVER

Yellow fever is a viral disease found in parts of Africa and South America. It is transmitted to humans by a mosquito bite. Even though there is no risk of becoming infected while traveling in Australia and the South Pacific, some countries require a yellow fever vaccination when travelers arrive from certain South American and African countries.

If you are **only** traveling from the United States to Australia and the South Pacific, CDC does not recommend, and you are not required to have, a yellow fever vaccination. If your travel plans include traveling to or from countries in South America or Africa, you may be required to have a yellow fever vaccination. Therefore, you should review the comprehensive country-by-country yellow fever vaccine requirements in *Appendix 2, Yellow Fever Requirements*.

## DENGUE FEVER

Dengue fever is a viral infection transmitted to humans by mosquito bites. These mosquitoes are most active during the day, especially around dawn and dusk, and are frequently found in or around residential areas. The illness is flu-like and characterized by sudden onset, high fever, severe headaches, joint and muscle pain, and rash. Severe cases of dengue hemorrhagic fever produce shock, internal bleeding, and death. The rash appears 3-4 days after the onset of fever. Si ice there is no vaccine or specific treatment available, prevention is important.

### Risk to Traveler

Dengue fever occurs sporadically throughout the region: **Australia (in parts of northern Queensland and the Torres Strait Islands of Australia), Cook Islands, Fiji, Kiribati, Kosrae, New Caledonia, Niue, Palau, Papua New Guinea, Samoa, Tahiti, Tokelau, US Trust Territory of the Pacific Islands, Vanuatu, Wallis and Futuna.** The risk of infection is small for most travelers except during periods of epidemic transmission.

New Zealand and the rest of the island groups are free of Dengue.

### Prevention

There is no vaccine for dengue fever, therefore, the traveler should avoid mosquito bites. These mosquitoes may bite anytime during the day, especially in shady areas, indoors, or when the sky is overcast, but prefer feeding around dawn and dusk. For additional information on dengue fever, refer to *Appendix 12, Dengue Fever*.

## OTHER INSECT DISEASES
### Risks to Traveler

Other diseases spread by mosquitoes, sand flies, black flies, or other insects are prevalent, especially in rural areas. Other diseases spread by mosquitoes, sand flies, black flies, or other insects are prevalent, especially in rural areas. These diseases include: *filariasis* and *Ross River Virus* (mosquito), and *typhus* (lice).

## Prevention

For most of these diseases, a vaccine is not available and treatment is limited. Therefore, travelers must follow the guidelines under "Preventing Insect Bites." For additional detailed information of these and other insect diseases please read *Appendix 3, Other Insect Diseases.*

## DISEASES TRANSMITTED THROUGH FOOD & WATER

Food and waterborne diseases are the number one cause of illness to travelers and are very common in Australia and the South Pacific. **Traveler's diarrhea is the most frequent health problem for travelers.** It can be caused by viruses, bacteria, or parasites that are found universally throughout the region. Transmission is most often through contaminated food or water. Infections may cause diarrhea and vomiting (typhoid fever, cholera, and parasites), liver damage (hepatitis), or muscle paralysis (polio).

## GENERAL PRECAUTIONS

**Water**: The following beverages are safe to drink: boiled water or beverages made with boiled water, canned or carbonated beverages, beer, or wine. Impure water often contaminates drinking containers, ice, and tap water.

**Food**: Food that has been cooked to 165° F (74° C) is generally safe. As a reference, food at this temperature cannot be put directly into your mouth, but must cool a bit. Foods of concern are salads, uncooked vegetables and fruit, unpasteurized milk and milk products, raw meat, and shellfish. If you peel fruit yourself, it is generally safe. A simple rule of thumb is: "Boil it, cook it, peel it, or forget it."

For additional detailed precautions, be sure to read *Appendix 4, Traveler's Diarrhea & Food and Water Precautions.*

## TYPHOID FEVER

Typhoid fever is a bacterial infection transmitted to humans through contaminated food and/or water, or directly between people. Symptoms of typhoid fever include fever, headaches, fatigue, loss of appetite, and constipation. Typhoid fever can be treated effectively with antibiotics.

### Risk to Traveler

Travelers to many of the **South Pacific islands** are at risk for typhoid fever, especially when traveling to smaller cities, villages, or rural areas. Typhoid fever is rare in Australia and New Zealand.

## Prevention

By drinking only bottled or boiled beverages and eating only thoroughly cooked food, a traveler lowers the risk of infection. Currently available vaccines have been shown to protect 70-90% of the recipients, so even vaccinated travelers should be cautious in selecting their food and water.

Two vaccines are recommended for protection against typhoid fever. An oral vaccine, **TY21a**, consists of a total of 4 capsules taken (one per day, every other day) over a seven day period, and requires a booster every five years. Reactions to the TY21a vaccine are rare but include nausea, vomiting, abdominal cramps, and skin rash.

A new single-dose injectable vaccine, **Typhim Vi** or **ViCPS**, is equally effective, and requires a booster dose every two years. Reactions to Typhim Vi are also rare, but include discomfort at the site of injection and headaches. An earlier typhoid vaccine developed years ago, which uses killed typhoid organisms and is administered in a two dose series, had more reported side effect and is currently not preferred. Instead, use one of the newer vaccines. Based on the vaccine chosen, booster doses are required every two to five years.

## Recommendations

CDC recommends a typhoid vaccination for those travelers who are going off the usual tourist itineraries, traveling to smaller cities and rural areas, or staying long term, that is, for six weeks or more. Vaccination should be completed at least two weeks before travel. Typhoid vaccination is not required for international travel.

## CHOLERA

Cholera is an acute diarrheal illness caused by an infection of the intestine with the bacterium *Vibrio cholerae*. Infection is acquired by ingesting contaminated water or food. The infection is often mild without symptoms, but sometimes can be severe. Approximately one in 20 infected persons has severe disease characterized by an abrupt onset of profuse watery diarrhea, vomiting, dehydration, and leg cramps.

## Risk to Traveler

Cholera cases have been reported from several islands in the South Pacific. The risk of infection to the US traveler is very low, especially those that are following the usual tourist itineraries, staying in standard accommodations, and following food and water safety instructions. A list of cholera infected countries is given in *Appendix 10, CDC's Blue Sheet.*

### Prevention

Travelers to cholera infected areas should:
- avoid eating high risk foods, especially fish and shellfish, and
- follow the standard food and water precautions of eating only thoroughly cooked food that is served hot, peeling their own fruit, and drinking beverages and ice made from boiled or chlorinated water, bottled carbonated water, or bottled carbonated soft drinks.

Persons with severe cases of cholera respond well to simple fluid and electrolyte-replacement therapy, but medical attention must be sought quickly when cholera is suspected.

The cholera vaccine licensed for use in the United States confers only brief and incomplete immunity (50% effective in reducing the illness). The risk of cholera to US travelers is so low that it is questionable whether the vaccine is of benefit, and therefore it is not recommended routinely for travelers. The primary series for this cholera vaccine is normally two injections with booster doses given every 6 months for persons who remain at high risk. **Cholera vaccine is not recommended for infants under 6 months old or for pregnant women.**

For additional information about cholera, read *Appendix 4, Traveler's Diarrhea & Food and Water Precautions*, and *Appendix 8, Cholera Information*.

## HEPATITIS A

Hepatitis A is a viral infection of the liver transmitted to humans by the fecal-oral route; through direct person-to-person contact; from contaminated water, ice, or shellfish; or from fruits or uncooked vegetables contaminated through handling. Symptoms include fatigue, fever, loss of appetite, nausea, dark urine, jaundice, vomiting, aches and pains, and light stools. No specific therapy, only supportive care, is available.

### Risk to Traveler

Travelers are at **high risk** for hepatitis A, **except for travel to Australia and New Zealand**, especially if travel plans include visiting rural areas and extensive travel in the countryside, frequent close contact with local persons, or eating in settings of poor sanitation. Be aware that a study has shown that many cases of travel-related hepatitis A occur in travelers to developing countries with "standard" itineraries, accommodations, and food consumption behaviors.

## Prevention

The virus is inactivated by boiling or cooking to 185° F (85° C) for one minute. Therefore, eating thoroughly cooked foods and drinking only treated water serve as general precautions. In addition, **Immune globulin (IG)** *or* **hepatitis A vaccine** is recommended before travel. Two hepatitis A vaccines, **Havrix®** and **VAQTA®**, are currently licensed in the United States.

Immune globulin and the hepatitis A vaccine marketed in the United States are safe. American travelers should note that IG manufactured in foreign countries may or may not meet these requirements. Therefore, American travelers who will need to receive additional doses of IG in other countries should use products that meet US standards and license requirements. For reference, the method of manufacturing IG in the US is called the **Cohn-Oncley procedure**.

## Recommendations

CDC recommends Immune globulin (IG) or hepatitis A vaccine before travel for protection against hepatitis A.

**Immune globulin** is recommended for persons of all ages who:
- desire only short term protection (one dose is effective for three months)
- need immediate protection, and
- are too young for the vaccine (less than 2 years of age).

**Hepatitis A vaccine** is preferred for persons two years of age and older who plan to travel repeatedly or reside for long periods of time in intermediate or high risk areas. Bear in mind:
- The complete hepatitis A vaccine series requires a minimum of six months to complete.
- For these travelers over 18 years of age, hepatitis A vaccine should be given in a two-dose series with the second dose administered 6-12 months after the first.
- For children and adolescents between ages 2 through 18, a two or three dose series of hepatitis A vaccine is recommended depending on the vaccine chosen.

Travelers can be considered to be protected four weeks after receiving the initial vaccine dose. If the vaccine is administered less than four weeks before travel, then IG should also be given. The vaccine series must be completed for long-term protection. Hepatitis A vaccination is not required for travel to any country.

In addition to receiving IG or the vaccine, all travelers should follow the food and water precautions as described in *Appendix 4, Traveler's Diarrhea & Food and Water Precautions.*

Additional IG and hepatitis A information covering the vaccine and its safety are found in *Appendix 9, Hepatitis A Vaccine & Immune Globulin (IG) - Disease and Vaccine Information.*

## PARASITES

Parasitic infections are acquired by eating or drinking contaminated food or water, through direct contact with soil or water containing parasites or their larva, or by contact with biting insects. Symptoms and evidence of infection may include, but are not limited to: fever, swollen lymph nodes, rashes or itchy skin, digestive problems such as abdominal pain or diarrhea, eye problems, and anemia.

### Risk to Traveler

Travelers to many of the **South Pacific islands** are at risk of parasitic infection. Travelers to Australia and New Zealand have little or no risk. There are many types of parasites and infection may occur in several ways: by eating undercooked meats infected with parasites or their larva; by eating food or drinking water contaminated with parasites or their eggs; by contact with soil or water infected with parasites; or through insect bites. Several types of parasites can penetrate intact human skin and travelers are advised to wear shoes.

### Prevention

Travelers should eat only thoroughly cooked food, drink safe water, wear shoes, refrain from swimming in fresh water, and avoid contact with insects, particularly mosquitoes, biting flies, gnats, and midges.

## DISEASES TRANSMITTED THROUGH INTIMATE CONTACT WITH PEOPLE

### HIV/AIDS

Human immunodeficiency virus, or HIV, which causes acquired immunodeficiency syndrome or AIDS, is found primarily in blood, semen, and vaginal secretions of an infected person. HIV is spread by sexual contact with an infected person, by needle-sharing among injecting drug users, and through transfusions of infected blood and blood clotting factors. Babies born to HIV-infected women may become infected before, during, or shortly after birth.

In the United States, blood is screened for HIV antibodies, but this screening may not take place in all countries. Scientific studies have revealed no evidence that HIV is transmitted by air, food, water, insects, inanimate objects or casual contact. Even though HIV antibodies are normally detected on a test within 6 months after infection, the period between infection and development of disease symptoms (incubation period) may be 10 years or longer. Treatment has prolonged the survival of some HIV infected persons but there is no known cure or vaccine available. For additional information, see *Appendix 7, HIV/AIDS Information.*

### Risk to Traveler
AIDS is found throughout the region. In Australia and New Zealand, sexual transmission accounts for the majority of the cases. For the remaining countries, little information is available regarding the rates of infection or the extent of high risk behaviors. The risk to a traveler depends on whether the traveler will be involved in sexual or needle-sharing contact with a person who is infected with HIV. Receipt of unscreened blood for transfusion poses a risk for HIV infection.

### Prevention
No effective vaccine has been developed for HIV. Travelers should avoid sexual or needle-sharing contact with a person who is infected with HIV. If a blood transfusion is necessary, screened blood should come from an HIV-negative blood donor.

### Recommendations
Travelers should avoid activities known to carry risks for infection with HIV.

### HEPATITIS B
Hepatitis B is a viral infection of the liver. Hepatitis B is transmitted to humans primarily through behavior that result in the exchange of blood or fluids containing blood. Risky behavior includes heterosexual or homosexual contact or sharing needles or drug paraphernalia with a person infected with the hepatitis B virus. Any unscreened or improperly screened blood or blood product, as well as unsterilized needles, or contact with potentially infected people who have open skin sores due to impetigo, scabies, and scratched insect bites, heightens the potential for infection to the traveler. An effective vaccine for prevention of hepatitis B is available.

## Risk to Traveler

Hepatitis B rates are **high for the South Pacific islands**, but rates are low in Australia and New Zealand. The risk to the individual international traveler is greater if the traveler:
- has direct contact with blood or fluids containing blood;
- has intimate sexual contact with an infected person;
- remains in the country for longer than six months or has close contact with the local population.

## Prevention

**Hepatitis B vaccine** should be considered for those traveling to countries with high to intermediate rates of hepatitis B infection. For those travelers expecting to reside in countries of high risk, as well as all health workers, vaccination is strongly recommended.

Vaccination should ideally begin 6 months before travel, in order to complete the full series, which is needed for optimal protection. The three intramuscular doses of vaccine should be spaced so that the second dose is given one month after the first. The final dose is given 6 months after the first. The vaccination schedule should be initiated even if it will not be completed before travel begins. There is an alternative four-dose schedule that may provide protection if the first three doses can be delivered before departure. After completing the primary series, booster doses of the vaccine are not necessary.

## Recommendations

CDC recommends vaccination for any of the following people:
- any health care worker (medical, dental, or laboratory) whose activities might result in blood exposure;
- any traveler who may have intimate sexual contact with the local population;
- any long-term (6 months or more) traveler, e.g. teachers, who will reside in rural areas or have daily physical contact with the local population; or
- any traveler who is likely to seek either medical, dental, or other treatment in local facilities during their stay.

Hepatitis B vaccination is not required for travel to any country. Additional hepatitis B information is found in *Appendix 15, Hepatitis B.*

## SUMMARY OF RECOMMENDATIONS
## FOR AUSTRALIA & THE SOUTH PACIFIC

*Travelers should:*

- *take the appropriate country specific malaria prevention measures (mefloquine or equivalent)*
- *follow precautions to prevent insect bites*
- *pay attention to the quality of their drinking water and food*
- *have a dose of Immune Globulin (IG) or the hepatitis A vaccine (except Australia and New Zealand), and consider booster doses of tetanus (Td) and polio (eIPV) vaccines.*
- *Depending on the locations to be visited, planned activities, and health of the traveler, the following vaccines should be considered: Hepatitis B, Typhoid, and Cholera.*
- *Finally, the normal "childhood" vaccines should be up-to-date: Measles, Mumps, Rubella (MMR Vaccine); Diphtheria, Tetanus, Pertussis (DTP Vaccine if traveler is less than 7 years of age, or Td if older than 7 years of age), and Polio vaccine. For additional information on these "childhood" vaccines, refer to Appendix 5, Vaccine Recommendations.*

# 15. THE INDIAN SUBCONTINENT (SOUTH ASIA)

## COUNTRIES IN THIS REGION
Afghanistan
Bangladesh
Bhutan
India
Maldives
Nepal
Pakistan
Sri Lanka

**INDIAN SUBCONTINENT TRAVELER'S OVERVIEW**

*Travelers to the Indian Subcontinent may be exposed to potential diseases from a number of sources. **The most frequently reported illness is traveler's diarrhea,** but the Indian Subcontinent contains a variety of diseases transmitted by:*

- *insects,*
- *contaminated food and water, or*
- *close contact with infected people.*

*In this chapter, specific diseases, their causes, symptoms, geographic areas of risk, and prevention recommendations or requirement information are discussed under their topical headings. As a general guideline, in order to reduce the risk of infection, travelers must:*

- *protect themselves from insects*
- *ensure the quality of their food and drinking water*
- *be knowledgeable about potential diseases in the region to be visited*
- *receive all recommended vaccines and preventive medications.*

*In addition, travelers should note that diseases are not restricted to cleanly defined geographical areas. For example, mosquitoes can fly over city or country borders, so all travelers should protect themselves by taking the basic preventive precautions as described under each section and disease. Where appropriate, more detailed information is referenced in the Appendices.*

## DISEASES TRANSMITTED BY INSECTS

Many diseases are transmitted through the bite of infected insects such as mosquitoes, flies, fleas, ticks and lice. In general, **travelers must protect themselves from insect bites**. Travelers are at a higher risk for insect bites if they participate in outdoor activities during night time hours from dusk to dawn when mosquitoes bite, or if their living accommodations are unscreened. If a mosquito net is unlikely to be available, consider buying a portable mosquito net.

### PREVENTING INSECT BITES

To reduce the risk of mosquito bites, travelers should remain in well-screened areas, use mosquito nets, and wear clothes that cover most of the body. Travelers should also take insect repellent with them to use on any exposed areas of the skin. The most effective compound in a repellent is **DEET**, which may be listed as an ingredient on repellant labels as **"N,N-diethyl meta-toluamide."** Check the repellent label to ensure DEET is an ingredient.

Travelers should note, however, that insect repellents containing DEET should always be used according to label directions and sparingly on children. **Avoid applying high-concentration (greater than 35%) products to the skin, particularly on children, and refrain from applying repellent to portions of the hands that are likely to come in contact with the eyes and mouth.** Pediatric insect repellents with 6-10% DEET are available without prescription in many drug stores. In rare instances, toxic reactions or other problems have developed after contact with DEET.

Travelers should also purchase a flying insect-killing spray to use in living and sleeping areas during the evening and night. For greater protection, clothing and bednets can be soaked in or sprayed with **permethrin**, which is an insect repellent licensed for use on clothing. If applied according to the directions, permethrin will repel insects from clothing for several weeks. Portable mosquito bednets, repellents containing DEET, and permethrin can be purchased in hardware, backpacking, and military surplus stores.

## MALARIA

Malaria is a serious parasitic infection transmitted to humans by an Anopheles mosquito. These mosquitoes bite at night, from dusk to dawn. Symptoms of malaria range from flu-like symptoms with fever, general achiness, headache, and fatigue, to a cycle of shaking chills, high fever, and sweating. If left untreated, malaria can cause anemia, kidney failure, coma, and death. Drugs are available to help prevent a malaria infection.

However, in spite of all protective measures, travelers occasionally develop malaria. Therefore, while traveling and up to one year after returning home, travelers should seek medical evaluation for any flu-like illness.

### Risk to Traveler

The risk of a malaria infection is relatively low for most travelers to the Indian subcontinent. *P. falciparum* (the most dangerous type), is present in all countries (except Maldives) and has been reported to be resistant to the drug chloroquine.

*Areas of Risk*
- **Afghanistan** – all areas.
- **Bangladesh** – all areas, except no risk in the city of Dhaka.
- **Bhutan** – rural areas in districts bordering India.
- **India** – all areas, except no risk in parts of the States of Himechel, Pradesh, Jammu, Kashmir, and Sikkim.

- **Nepal** – in Terai and Hill Districts below 1200 meters (3900 feet), no risk in Katmandu.
- **Pakistan** – all areas.
- **Sri Lanka** – malaria risk in all areas except Colombo, Kalutara, and Nuwara Eliya.

*No Risk*
Maldives.

## Prevention & Recommendations
Travelers at risk for malaria should take mefloquine to prevent malaria. This drug is marketed in the United States under the name Lariam™. The adult dosage is 250 mg (one tablet) once a week.

Mefloquine should not be used by travelers with a:
- history of epilepsy or psychiatric disorder,
- known hypersensitivity to mefloquine.

In consultation with a physician, mefloquine may be used by pregnant women and children weighing less than 30 pounds, when travel to an area with chloroquine-resistant malaria is unavoidable. Travelers who cannot take mefloquine should read the section "Prescription Drugs for Malaria" found in *Appendix 1, Malaria Information*.

Minor side effects one may experience while taking mefloquine include gastrointestinal disturbances and dizziness. More serious side effects at the recommended dosage have rarely occurred. Consult a physician for other precautions.

In addition to using drugs to prevent malaria and treat a possible malaria attack, travelers should use measures to reduce exposure to malaria-carrying mosquitoes and protect themselves from mosquito bites. Remember, these mosquitoes bite mainly during the evening and night, from dusk to dawn.

Additional general malaria information, as well as specific information for women who are pregnant or children, is found in *Appendix 1, Malaria Information*.

## YELLOW FEVER
Yellow fever is a viral disease found in parts of Africa and South America. It is transmitted to humans by a mosquito bite. Even though there is no risk of becoming infected while traveling in the Indian Subcontinent,

some countries require a yellow fever vaccination when travelers arrive from certain South American and African countries.

If you are **only** traveling from the United States to a country in the Indian Subcontinent, CDC does not recommend, and you are not required to have, a yellow fever vaccination. If your travel plans include traveling to or from countries in South America or Africa, you may be required to have a yellow fever vaccination. Therefore, you should review the comprehensive country-by-country yellow fever vaccine requirements in *Appendix 2, Yellow Fever Requirements*.

## DENGUE FEVER

Dengue fever is a viral infection transmitted to humans by mosquito bites. These mosquitoes are most active during the day, especially around dawn and dusk, and are frequently found in or around residential areas. The illness is flu-like and characterized by sudden onset, high fever, severe headaches, joint and muscle pain, and rash. Severe cases of dengue hemorrhagic fever produce shock, internal bleeding, and death. The rash appears 3-4 days after the onset of fever. Since there is no vaccine or specific treatment available, prevention is important.

### Risk to Traveler

Dengue fever occurs sporadically in parts of **Bangladesh**, **India**, **Maldives**, and **Sri Lanka**. Recently Sri Lanka has reported increased activity. The risk of infection is small for most travelers except during periods of epidemic transmission.

### Prevention

There is no vaccine for dengue fever, therefore, the traveler should avoid mosquito bites. These mosquitoes may bite anytime during the day, especially in shady areas, indoors, or when the sky is overcast, but prefer feeding around dawn and dusk. For additional information on dengue fever, refer to *Appendix 12, Dengue Fever*.

## JAPANESE ENCEPHALITIS

Japanese Encephalitis is a mosquito-borne viral disease that occurs in rural areas. These mosquitoes are most often found in rice growing areas and bite in the late afternoon and early evening. Symptoms range from: no symptoms to headache, fever, and flu-like symptoms. More serious complications involve a swelling of the brain (encephalitis). There is no specific drug to treat Japanese Encephalitis.

## Risk to Traveler

Transmission is usually seasonal (associated with the rainy season). There is a risk for travelers to rural areas including **Bangladesh, India, southern Nepal**, and **Sri Lanka**. In all areas, Japanese Encephalitis is primarily a rural disease. The chance that a traveler to the Indian Subcontinent will develop Japanese Encephalitis is probably very small.

## Prevention & Recommendations

The vaccine **JE-VAX** is licensed and available in the United States. Vaccination should be considered for persons who plan long-term residence in rural areas. Travelers who visit rural farming areas for 4 weeks or more during the transmission season should consider immunization. Travelers who remain un-immunized should wear mosquito repellents, sleep under bed-nets, and bring insecticidal sprays to use in their sleeping quarters.

The vaccine is given in 3 doses on days 0, 7, and 30. Protection can be expected 10 days following the last dose. A shorter course of vaccination (Day 0, 7, and 14) can be used, but protection and duration is less than the normal schedule. Fever and local reactions such as redness, swelling, and pain are reported in fewer than 10% of those vaccinated. More severe allergic reactions have been reported in persons with a history of insect or food allergies. These reactions have been life-threatening on occasion. Once vaccinated, you should have access to medical care, if needed, for 2-3 days after vaccination.

*The Japanese Encephalitis vaccine should not be given to*:
- Those acutely ill or with active infections.
- Persons with heart, kidney, or liver disorders.
- Persons with generalized cancerous malignancies such as leukemia and lymphoma.
- Persons with a history of multiple allergies or hypersensitivity to components of the vaccine.
- Pregnant women, unless there is a high risk of Japanese Encephalitis during the woman's stay.

For additional information on Japanese Encephalitis, refer to *Appendix 13, Japanese Encephalitis*.

## OTHER INSECT DISEASES

### Risks to Traveler

Other diseases spread by mosquitoes, sand flies, black flies, or other insects are prevalent, especially in rural areas. These diseases include: *filariasis* and *Chikungunya* (mosquito), *leishmaniasis* (sand fly), *Congo-Crimean hemorrhagic fever* (tick), *typhus* (lice), and *plague* (fleas).

## Prevention

For most of these diseases, a vaccine is not available and treatment is limited. Therefore, travelers must follow the guidelines under "Preventing Insect Bites." For additional detailed information of these and other insect diseases please read *Appendix 3, Other Insect Diseases.*

## DISEASES TRANSMITTED THROUGH FOOD & WATER

Food and waterborne diseases are the number one cause of illness to travelers and are very common in the Indian Subcontinent. **Traveler's diarrhea is the most frequent health problem for travelers.** It can be caused by viruses, bacteria, or parasites that are found universally throughout the region. Transmission is most often through contaminated food or water. Infections may cause diarrhea and vomiting (typhoid fever, cholera, and parasites), liver damage (hepatitis), or muscle paralysis (polio).

## GENERAL PRECAUTIONS

**Water**: The following beverages are safe to drink: boiled water or beverages made with boiled water, canned or carbonated beverages, beer, or wine. Impure water often contaminates drinking containers, ice, and tap water.

**Food**: Food that has been cooked to 165° F (74° C) is generally safe. As a reference, food at this temperature cannot be put directly into your mouth, but must cool a bit. Foods of concern are salads, uncooked vegetables and fruit, unpasteurized milk and milk products, raw meat, and shellfish. If you peel fruit yourself, it is generally safe. A simple rule of thumb is: "Boil it, cook it, peel it, or forget it."

For additional detailed precautions, be sure to read *Appendix 4, Traveler's Diarrhea & Food and Water Precautions.*

## TYPHOID FEVER

Typhoid fever is a bacterial infection transmitted to humans through contaminated food and/or water, or directly between people. Symptoms of typhoid fever include fever, headaches, fatigue, loss of appetite, and constipation. Typhoid fever can be treated effectively with antibiotics.

## Risk to Traveler

Travelers to the Indian Subcontinent are at increased risk for typhoid fever, especially when traveling to smaller cities, villages, or rural areas.

## Prevention

By drinking only bottled or boiled beverages and eating only thoroughly cooked food, a traveler lowers the risk of infection. Currently available vaccines have been shown to protect 70-90% of the recipients. Therefore, even vaccinated travelers should be cautious in selecting their food and water.

Two vaccines are recommended for protection against typhoid fever. An oral vaccine, **TY21a**, consists of a total of 4 capsules taken (one per day, every other day) over a seven day period, and requires a booster every five years. Reactions to the TY21a vaccine are rare but include nausea, vomiting, abdominal cramps, and skin rash.

A new single-dose injectable vaccine, **Typhim Vi** or **ViCPS**, is equally effective, and requires a booster dose every two years. Reactions to Typhim Vi are also rare, but include discomfort at the site of injection and headaches. An earlier typhoid vaccine developed years ago, which uses killed typhoid organisms and is administered in a two dose series, had more reported side effect and is currently not preferred. Instead, use one of the newer vaccines. Based on the vaccine chosen, booster doses are required every two to five years.

## Recommendations

CDC recommends a typhoid vaccination for those travelers who are going off the usual tourist itineraries, traveling to smaller cities and rural areas, or staying long term, that is, for six weeks or more. Vaccination should be completed at least two weeks before travel. Typhoid vaccination is not required for international travel.

## CHOLERA

Cholera is an acute diarrheal illness caused by an infection of the intestine with the bacterium *Vibrio cholerae*. Infection is acquired by ingesting contaminated water or food. The infection is often mild without symptoms, but sometimes can be severe. Approximately one in 20 infected persons has severe disease characterized by an abrupt onset of profuse watery diarrhea, vomiting, dehydration, and leg cramps.

## Risk to Traveler

Cholera cases have been reported from most of the countries of the Indian Subcontinent. The risk of infection to the US traveler is very low, especially those that are following the usual tourist itineraries, staying in standard accommodations, and following food and water safety instructions. A list of cholera infected countries is given in *Appendix 10, CDC's Blue Sheet*.

## Prevention

Travelers to cholera infected areas should:
- avoid eating high risk foods, especially fish and shellfish, and
- follow the standard food and water precautions of eating only thoroughly cooked food that is served hot, peeling their own fruit, and drinking beverages and ice made from boiled or chlorinated water, bottled carbonated water, or bottled carbonated soft drinks.

Persons with severe cases of cholera respond well to simple fluid and electrolyte-replacement therapy, but medical attention must be sought quickly when cholera is suspected.

The cholera vaccine licensed for use in the United States confers only brief and incomplete immunity (50% effective in reducing the illness). The risk of cholera to US travelers is so low that it is questionable whether the vaccine is of benefit, and therefore it is not recommended routinely for travelers. The primary series for this cholera vaccine is normally two injections with booster doses given every 6 months for persons who remain at high risk. **Cholera vaccine is not recommended for infants under 6 months old or for pregnant women.**

For additional information about cholera, read *Appendix 4, Traveler's Diarrhea & Food and Water Precautions*, and *Appendix 8, Cholera Information*.

## HEPATITIS A

Hepatitis A is a viral infection of the liver transmitted to humans by the fecal-oral route; through direct person-to-person contact; from contaminated water, ice, or shellfish; or from fruits or uncooked vegetables contaminated through handling. Symptoms include fatigue, fever, loss of appetite, nausea, dark urine, jaundice, vomiting, aches and pains, and light stools. No specific therapy, only supportive care, is available.

## Risk to Traveler

Travelers are at **high risk** for hepatitis A especially if travel plans include visiting rural areas and extensive travel in the countryside, frequent close contact with local persons, or eating in settings of poor sanitation. Be aware that a study has shown that many cases of travel-related hepatitis A occur in travelers to developing countries with "standard" itineraries, accommodations, and food consumption behaviors.

## Prevention

The virus is inactivated by boiling or cooking to 185° F (85° C) for one minute. Therefore, eating thoroughly cooked foods and drinking only treated water serve as general precautions. In addition, **Immune globulin (IG)** *or* **hepatitis A vaccine** is recommended before travel. Two hepatitis A vaccines, **Havrix®** and **VAQTA®**, are currently licensed in the United States.

Immune globulin and the hepatitis A vaccine marketed in the United States are safe. American travelers should note that IG manufactured in foreign countries may or may not meet these requirements. Therefore, American travelers who will need to receive additional doses of IG in other countries should use products that meet US standards and license requirements. For reference, the method of manufacturing IG in the US is called the **Cohn-Oncley procedure.**

## Recommendations

CDC recommends Immune globulin (IG) or hepatitis A vaccine before travel for protection against hepatitis A.

**Immune globulin** is recommended for persons of all ages who:
- desire only short term protection (one dose is effective for three months)
- need immediate protection, and
- are too young for the vaccine (less than 2 years of age).

**Hepatitis A vaccine** is preferred for persons two years of age and older who plan to travel repeatedly or reside for long periods of time in intermediate or high risk areas. Bear in mind:
- The complete hepatitis A vaccine series requires a minimum of six months to complete.
- For these travelers over 18 years of age, hepatitis A vaccine should be given in a two-dose series with the second dose administered 6-12 months after the first.

•   For children and adolescents between ages 2 through 18, a two or three dose series of hepatitis A vaccine is recommended depending on the vaccine chosen.

Travelers can be considered to be protected four weeks after receiving the initial vaccine dose. If the vaccine is administered less than four weeks before travel, then IG should also be given. The vaccine series must be completed for long-term protection. Hepatitis A vaccination is not required for travel to any country.

In addition to receiving IG or the vaccine, all travelers should follow the food and water precautions as described in *Appendix 4, Traveler's Diarrhea & Food and Water Precautions.*

Additional IG and hepatitis A information covering the vaccine and its safety are found in *Appendix 9, Hepatitis A Vaccine & Immune Globulin (IG) - Disease and Vaccine Information.*

## PARASITES
Parasitic infections are acquired by eating or drinking contaminated food or water, through direct contact with soil or water containing parasites or their larva, or by contact with biting insects. Symptoms and evidence of infection may include, but are not limited to: fever, swollen lymph nodes, rashes or itchy skin, digestive problems such as abdominal pain or diarrhea, eye problems, and anemia.

### Risk to Traveler
Travelers to the Indian Subcontinent are at risk of parasitic infections. There are many types of parasites and infection may occur in several ways: by eating undercooked meats infected with parasites or their larva; by eating food or drinking water contaminated with parasites or their eggs; by contact with soil or water infected with parasites; or through insect bites. Several types of parasites can penetrate intact human skin and travelers are advised to wear shoes.

### Prevention
Travelers should eat only thoroughly cooked food, drink safe water, wear shoes, refrain from swimming in fresh water, and avoid contact with insects, particularly mosquitoes, biting flies, gnats, and midges.

## DISEASES TRANSMITTED THROUGH INTIMATE CONTACT WITH PEOPLE

### HIV/AIDS

Human immunodeficiency virus, or HIV, which causes acquired immunodeficiency syndrome or AIDS, is found primarily in blood, semen, and vaginal secretions of an infected person. HIV is spread by sexual contact with an infected person, by needle-sharing among injecting drug users, and through transfusions of infected blood and blood clotting factors. Babies born to HIV-infected women may become infected before, during, or shortly after birth.

In the US, blood is screened for HIV antibodies, but this screening may not take place in all countries. Scientific studies have revealed no evidence that HIV is transmitted by air, food, water, insects, inanimate objects or casual contact. Even though HIV antibodies are normally detected on a test within 6 months after infection, the period between infection and development of disease symptoms (incubation period) may be 10 years or longer. Treatment has prolonged the survival of some HIV infected persons but there is no known cure or vaccine available. For additional information, see *Appendix 7, HIV/AIDS Information.*

### Risk to Traveler

AIDS is found throughout the region. In the Indian Subcontinent, heterosexual transmission is prevalent, with some transmission in injecting drug users. The risk to a traveler depends on whether the traveler will be involved in sexual or needle-sharing contact with a person who is infected with HIV. Receipt of unscreened blood for transfusion poses a risk for HIV infection.

### Prevention

No effective vaccine has been developed for HIV. Travelers should avoid sexual or needle-sharing contact with a person who is infected with HIV. If a blood transfusion is necessary, screened blood should come from an HIV-negative blood donor.

### Recommendations

Travelers should avoid activities known to carry risks for infection with HIV.

### HEPATITIS B

Hepatitis B is a viral infection of the liver. Hepatitis B is transmitted to humans primarily through behavior that result in the exchange of blood or fluids containing blood. Risky behavior includes heterosexual or homosexual contact or sharing needles or drug paraphernalia with a person infected with the hepatitis B virus. Any unscreened or improperly screened blood or blood product, as well as unsterilized needles, or contact with potentially infected people who have open skin sores due to impetigo, scabies, and scratched insect bites, heightens the potential for infection to the traveler. An effective vaccine for prevention of hepatitis B is available.

## Risk to Traveler
The risk of hepatitis B virus infection is **high** for the Indian Subcontinent. The risk to the individual international traveler is greater if the traveler:
- has direct contact with blood or fluids containing blood;
- has intimate sexual contact with an infected person;
- remains in the country for longer than six months or has close contact with the local population.

## Prevention
**Hepatitis B vaccine** should be considered for those traveling to countries with high to intermediate rates of hepatitis B infection. For those travelers expecting to reside in countries of high risk, as well as all health workers, vaccination is strongly recommended.

Vaccination should ideally begin 6 months before travel, in order to complete the full series, which is needed for optimal protection. The three intramuscular doses of vaccine should be spaced so that the second dose is given one month after the first. The final dose is given 6 months after the first. The vaccination schedule should be initiated even if it will not be completed before travel begins. There is an alternative four-dose schedule that may provide protection if the first three doses can be delivered before departure. After completing the primary series, booster doses of the vaccine are not necessary.

## Recommendations
CDC recommends vaccination for any of the following people:
- any health care worker (medical, dental, or laboratory) whose activities might result in blood exposure;
- any traveler who may have intimate sexual contact with the local population;
- any long-term (6 months or more) traveler, e.g. teachers, who will reside in rural areas or have daily physical contact with the local population; or

- any traveler who is likely to seek either medical, dental, or other treatment in local facilities during their stay.

Hepatitis B vaccination is not required for travel to any country. Additional hepatitis B information is found in *Appendix 15, Hepatitis B*.

## MENINGOCOCCAL DISEASE

Meningococcal disease (bacterial meningitis) is a bacterial infection in the lining of the brain or spinal cord. Early symptoms are headache, stiff neck, a rash, and fever. The bacteria is transmitted to humans through respiratory droplets when an infected person sneezes or coughs on you.

### Risk to Traveler

There is a **year-round risk** of meningococcal disease in parts of the Indian Subcontinent, **primarily in India and Nepal**. When a traveler lives and works around the local population, the risk increases.

### Prevention

A one dose meningococcal vaccine called **Menomune** is available.

### Recommendations

Vaccination is not required for entry into any country in this region. CDC recommends vaccination with meningococcal vaccine for travelers going to Nepal and the Delhi region of India.

## OTHER DISEASES

## RABIES

Rabies is a viral infection that affects the central nervous system. It is transmitted to humans by warm-blooded animal (mammal) bites that introduce the virus into the wound. Although dogs are the main reservoir of the disease, all warm-blooded animal bites should be suspect.

### Risk to Traveler

For countries in the Indian Subcontinent, there is a risk of rabies infection, particularly in rural areas or in areas where large numbers of dogs are found. Rabies is not reported in the Maldives.

### Prevention

Do not handle animals! Any animal bite should receive prompt medical attention. When wounds are thoroughly cleaned with large amounts of soap and water, the risk of rabies infection is reduced. Exposed individuals should receive prompt medical attention and advice on post-exposure preventive treatment.

## Recommendations

There are no requirements for vaccination, but pre-exposure vaccination is recommended for:

- travelers visiting foreign areas where dog rabies is known to exist and whose activities may place them at high risk of exposure;
- veterinarians and animal handlers;
- spelunkers; and
- certain rabies laboratory workers.

Pre-exposure vaccination does not nullify the need for post-exposure vaccine, but reduces the number of injections and may provide protection under circumstances in which rabies exposure is unrecognized. For additional rabies information, refer to *Appendix 11, Rabies Information.*

---

### SUMMARY OF RECOMMENDATIONS FOR THE INDIAN SUBCONTINENT

*Travelers should:*

- *take mefloquine (or equivalent) for malaria prevention,*
- *follow precautions to prevent insect bites*
- *pay attention to the quality of their drinking water and food*
- *have a dose of Immune Globulin (IG) or the hepatitis A vaccine, and consider booster doses of tetanus (Td) and polio (eIPV) vaccines.*
- *Depending on the locations to be visited, planned activities, and health of the traveler, the following vaccines should be considered: Hepatitis B, Japanese Encephalitis, Typhoid, Meningococcal, Rabies (pre-exposure), and Cholera.*
- *Finally, the normal "childhood" vaccines should be up-to-date: Measles, Mumps, Rubella (MMR Vaccine); Diphtheria, Tetanus, Pertussis (DTP Vaccine if traveler is less than 7 years of age, or Td if older than 7 years of age), and Polio vaccine. For additional information on these "childhood" vaccines, refer to Appendix 5, Vaccine Recommendations.*

---

# 16. THE MIDDLE EAST

## COUNTRIES IN THIS REGION

Bahrain
Cyprus
Iran
Iraq
Israel
Jordan
Kuwait
Lebanon
Oman
Qatar
Saudi Arabia
Syrian Arab Republic
Turkey
United Arab Emirates
Yemen

## MIDDLE EAST TRAVELER'S OVERVIEW

*Travelers to the Middle East may be exposed to potential diseases from a number of sources. **The most frequently reported illness is traveler's diarrhea**, but the Middle East contains a variety of diseases transmitted by:*

- *insects,*
- *contaminated food and water, or*
- *close contact with infected people.*

*In this chapter, specific diseases, their causes, symptoms, geographic areas of risk, and prevention recommendations or requirement information are discussed under their topical headings. As a general guideline, in order to reduce the risk of infection, travelers must:*

- *protect themselves from insects*
- *ensure the quality of their food and drinking water*
- *be knowledgeable about potential diseases in the region to be visited*
- *receive all recommended vaccines and preventive medications.*

*In addition, travelers should note that diseases are not restricted to cleanly defined geographical areas. For example, mosquitoes can fly over city or country borders, so all travelers should protect themselves by taking the basic preventive precautions as described under each section and disease. Where appropriate, more detailed information is referenced in the Appendices.*

## DISEASES TRANSMITTED BY INSECTS

Many diseases are transmitted through the bite of infected insects such as mosquitoes, flies, fleas, ticks and lice. In general, **travelers must protect themselves from insect bites**. Travelers are at a higher risk for insect bites if they participate in outdoor activities during night time hours from dusk to dawn when mosquitoes bite, or if their living accommodations are unscreened. If a mosquito net is unlikely to be available, consider buying a portable mosquito net.

### PREVENTING INSECT BITES

To reduce the risk of mosquito bites, travelers should remain in well-screened areas, use mosquito nets, and wear clothes that cover most of the body. Travelers should also take insect repellent with them to use on any exposed areas of the skin. The most effective compound in a repellent is **DEET**, which may be listed as an ingredient on repellant labels as "**N,N-diethyl meta-toluamide**." Check the repellent label to ensure DEET is an ingredient.

Travelers should note, however, that insect repellents containing DEET should always be used according to label directions and sparingly on children. **Avoid applying high-concentration (greater than 35%) products to the skin, particularly on children, and refrain from applying repellent to portions of the hands that are likely to come in contact with the eyes and mouth.** Pediatric insect repellents with 6-10% DEET are available without prescription in many drug stores. In rare instances, toxic reactions or other problems have developed after contact with DEET.

Travelers should also purchase a flying insect-killing spray to use in living and sleeping areas during the evening and night. For greater protection, clothing and bednets can be soaked in or sprayed with **permethrin**, which is an insect repellent licensed for use on clothing. If applied according to the directions, permethrin will repel insects from clothing for several weeks. Portable mosquito bednets, repellents containing DEET, and permethrin can be purchased in hardware, backpacking, and military surplus stores.

## MALARIA
Malaria is a serious parasitic infection transmitted to humans by an Anopheles mosquito. These mosquitoes bite at night, from dusk to dawn. Symptoms of malaria range from flu-like symptoms with fever, general achiness, headache, and fatigue, to a cycle of shaking chills, high fever, and sweating. If left untreated, malaria can cause anemia, kidney failure, coma, and death. Drugs are available to help prevent a malaria infection.

However, in spite of all protective measures, travelers occasionally develop malaria. Therefore, while traveling and up to one year after returning home, travelers should seek medical evaluation for any flu-like illness.

### Risk to Traveler
A low risk for malaria exists in parts of these countries. The dominant form is *P. falciparum* (the most dangerous type), which has been reported to be resistant to the drug **chloroquine**.

*Areas of Risk*
- **Iran** – in rural areas only in the provinces of Sistan-Baluchestan and Hormozgan, the southern parts of Fars, Kohgiluyeh-Boyar, Lorestan, and Chahar Mahal-Bakhtiara, and the north of Khuzestan.
- **Iraq** – in all areas in the northern region, i.e., Dahuk, Erbil, At-ta'min (Kirkuk), Ninawa, Sulaimaniya Provinces.

- **Oman** – all areas.
- **Saudi Arabia** – all areas in the western provinces, except no risk in the high altitude areas of Asir Province (Yemen border), and the urban areas of Jeddah, Mecca, Medina, and Taif.
- **Syrian Arab Republic** – rural areas only, except no risk in the southern and western Districts of Deir-es-zor and Sweida;
- **Turkey** – a risk in southeast Anatolia from the coastal city of Mersin to the Iraqi border (Cukurova/Amikova Areas);
- **United Arab Emirates** – risk in the Northern Emirates, except no risk in the cities of Dubai, Sharjah, Ajman, Umm al Qaiwan and the Emirate of Abu Dhabi;
- **Yemen** – all areas, except Aden and the airport perimeter.

*No Risk*
Bahrain, Cyprus, Israel, Jordan, Kuwait, Lebanon and Qatar.

## Prevention & Recommendations
Prevention information is specific to countries; please read this information carefully.

Travelers to **Iran, Oman,** and **Yemen** at risk for malaria should take **mefloquine** to prevent malaria. This drug is marketed in the United States under the name Lariam™. The adult dosage is 250 mg (one tablet) once a week.

Mefloquine should not be used by travelers with a:
- history of epilepsy or psychiatric disorder,
- known hypersensitivity to mefloquine.

In consultation with a physician, mefloquine may be used by pregnant women and children weighing less than 30 pounds, when travel to an area with chloroquine-resistant malaria is unavoidable. Travelers who cannot take mefloquine should read the section "Prescription Drugs for Malaria" found in *Appendix 1, Malaria Information.*

Travelers to **Iraq, Saudi Arabia, Syria, Turkey,** and **United Arab Emirates** at risk for malaria should take **chloroquine** to prevent malaria. The weekly dosage for an adult is 500 mg (salt) once a week. This drug should be taken one week before entering a malarious area, weekly while there, and weekly for 4 weeks after leaving the malarious area. No other anti-malarial drugs are needed.

In addition to using drugs to prevent malaria and treat a possible malaria attack, travelers should use measures to reduce exposure to malaria-carrying mosquitoes and protect themselves from mosquito bites. Remember, these mosquitoes bite mainly during the evening and night, from dusk to dawn.

Additional general malaria information, as well as specific information for women who are pregnant or children, is found in Appendix 1, *Malaria Information*.

## YELLOW FEVER

Yellow fever is a viral disease found in parts of Africa and South America. It is transmitted to humans by a mosquito bite. Even though there is no risk of becoming infected while traveling in East Asian countries, some countries require a yellow fever vaccination when travelers arrive from certain South American and African countries.

If you are **only** traveling from the United States to an East Asian country, CDC does not recommend, and you are not required to have, a yellow fever vaccination. If your travel plans include traveling to or from countries in South America or Africa, you may be required to have a yellow fever vaccination. Therefore, you should review the comprehensive country-by-country yellow fever vaccine requirements in *Appendix 2, Yellow Fever Requirements*.

## DENGUE FEVER

Dengue fever is a viral infection transmitted to humans by mosquito bites. These mosquitoes are most active during the day, especially around dawn and dusk, and are frequently found in or around residential areas. The illness is flu-like and characterized by sudden onset, high fever, severe headaches, joint and muscle pain, and rash. Severe cases of dengue hemorrhagic fever produce shock, internal bleeding, and death. The rash appears 3-4 days after the onset of fever. Since there is no vaccine or specific treatment available, prevention is important.

### Risk to Traveler

Dengue fever occurs sporadically only in **Yemen**. The risk of infection is small for most travelers except during periods of epidemic transmission.

### Prevention

There is no vaccine for dengue fever, therefore, the traveler should avoid mosquito bites. These mosquitoes may bite anytime during the day, especially in shady areas, indoors, or when the sky is overcast, but prefer feeding around dawn and dusk. For additional information on dengue fever, refer to *Appendix 12, Dengue Fever*.

## OTHER INSECT DISEASES
### Risks to Traveler
Other diseases spread by mosquitoes, sand flies, black flies, or other insects are prevalent, especially in rural areas. These diseases include: *filariasis* (mosquito), *leishmaniasis* (sand fly), *onchocerciasis* (black flies), *Congo-Crimean hemorrhagic fever* (tick), *typhus* (lice), and *plague* (fleas).

### Prevention
For most of these diseases, a vaccine is not available and treatment is limited. Therefore, travelers must follow the guidelines under "Preventing Insect Bites." For additional detailed information of these and other insect diseases please read *Appendix 3, Other Insect Diseases*.

## DISEASES TRANSMITTED THROUGH FOOD & WATER
Food and waterborne diseases are the number one cause of illness to travelers and are very common in the Middle East. **Traveler's diarrhea is the most frequent health problem for travelers**. It can be caused by viruses, bacteria, or parasites that are found universally throughout the region. Transmission is most often through contaminated food or water. Infections may cause diarrhea and vomiting (typhoid fever, cholera, and parasites), liver damage (hepatitis), or muscle paralysis (polio).

## GENERAL PRECAUTIONS
**Water**: The following beverages are safe to drink: boiled water or beverages made with boiled water, canned or carbonated beverages, beer, or wine. Impure water often contaminates drinking containers, ice, and tap water.

**Food**: Food that has been cooked to 165° F (74° C) is generally safe. As a reference, food at this temperature cannot be put directly into your mouth, but must cool a bit. Foods of concern are salads, uncooked vegetables and fruit, unpasteurized milk and milk products, raw meat, and shellfish. If you peel fruit yourself, it is generally safe. A simple rule of thumb is: "Boil it, cook it, peel it, or forget it."

For additional detailed precautions, be sure to read *Appendix 4, Traveler's Diarrhea & Food and Water Precautions*.

## TYPHOID FEVER

Typhoid fever is a bacterial infection transmitted to humans through contaminated food and/or water, or directly between people. Symptoms of typhoid fever include fever, headaches, fatigue, loss of appetite, and constipation. Typhoid fever can be treated effectively with antibiotics.

### Risk to Traveler

Travelers to the Middle East are at increased risk for typhoid fever, especially when traveling to smaller cities, villages, or rural areas.

### Prevention

By drinking only bottled or boiled beverages and eating only thoroughly cooked food, a traveler lowers the risk of infection. Currently available vaccines have been shown to protect 70-90% of the recipients. Therefore, even vaccinated travelers should be cautious in selecting their food and water.

Two vaccines are recommended for protection against typhoid fever. An oral vaccine, **TY21a**, consists of a total of 4 capsules taken (one per day, every other day) over a seven day period, and requires a booster every five years. Reactions to the TY21a vaccine are rare but include nausea, vomiting, abdominal cramps, and skin rash.

A new single-dose injectable vaccine, **Typhim Vi** or **ViCPS**, is equally effective, and requires a booster dose every two years. Reactions to Typhim Vi are also rare, but include discomfort at the site of injection and headaches. An earlier typhoid vaccine developed years ago, which uses killed typhoid organisms and is administered in a two dose series, had more reported side effect and is currently not preferred. Instead, use one of the newer vaccines. Based on the vaccine chosen, booster doses are required every two to five years.

### Recommendations

CDC recommends a typhoid vaccination for those travelers who are going off the usual tourist itineraries, traveling to smaller cities and rural areas, or staying long term, that is, for six weeks or more. Vaccination should be completed at least two weeks before travel. Typhoid vaccination is not required for international travel.

## CHOLERA

Cholera is an acute diarrheal illness caused by an infection of the intestine with the bacterium *Vibrio cholerae*. Infection is acquired by ingesting contaminated water or food. The infection is often mild without symptoms, but sometimes can be severe. Approximately one in 20 infected persons has severe disease characterized by an abrupt onset of profuse watery diarrhea, vomiting, dehydration, and leg cramps.

## Risk to Traveler

Cholera cases have been reported from some of the countries of the Middle East. The risk of infection to the US traveler is very low, especially those that are following the usual tourist itineraries, staying in standard accommodations, and following food and water safety instructions. A list of cholera infected countries is given in *Appendix 10, CDC's Blue Sheet.*

## Prevention

Travelers to cholera infected areas should:
- avoid eating high risk foods, especially fish and shellfish, and
- follow the standard food and water precautions of eating only thoroughly cooked food that is served hot, peeling their own fruit, and drinking beverages and ice made from boiled or chlorinated water, bottled carbonated water, or bottled carbonated soft drinks.

Persons with severe cases of cholera respond well to simple fluid and electrolyte-replacement therapy, but medical attention must be sought quickly when cholera is suspected.

The cholera vaccine licensed for use in the United States confers only brief and incomplete immunity (50% effective in reducing the illness). The risk of cholera to US travelers is so low that it is questionable whether the vaccine is of benefit, and therefore it is not recommended routinely for travelers. The primary series for this cholera vaccine is normally two injections with booster doses given every 6 months for persons who remain at high risk. **Cholera vaccine is not recommended for infants under 6 months old or for pregnant women.**

For additional information about cholera, read *Appendix 4, Traveler's Diarrhea & Food and Water Precautions*, and *Appendix 8, Cholera Information*.

## HEPATITIS A

Hepatitis A is a viral infection of the liver transmitted to humans by the fecal-oral route; through direct person-to-person contact; from contaminated water, ice, or shellfish; or from fruits or uncooked vegetables contaminated through handling. Symptoms include fatigue, fever, loss of appetite, nausea, dark urine, jaundice, vomiting, aches and pains, and light stools. No specific therapy, only supportive care, is available.

## Risk to Traveler

Travelers are at intermediate to high risk for hepatitis A, especially if travel plans include visiting rural areas and extensive travel in the countryside, frequent close contact with local persons, or eating in settings of poor sanitation. Be aware that a study has shown that many cases of travel-related hepatitis A occur in travelers to developing countries with "standard" itineraries, accommodations, and food consumption behaviors.

## Prevention

The virus is inactivated by boiling or cooking to 185° F (85° C) for one minute. Therefore, eating thoroughly cooked foods and drinking only treated water serve as general precautions. In addition, **Immune globulin (IG)** *or* **hepatitis A vaccine** is recommended before travel. Two hepatitis A vaccines, **Havrix®** and **VAQTA®**, are currently licensed in the US.

Immune globulin and the hepatitis A vaccine marketed in the United States are safe. American travelers should note that IG manufactured in foreign countries may or may not meet these requirements. Therefore, American travelers who will need to receive additional doses of IG in other countries should use products that meet US standards and license requirements. For reference, the method of manufacturing IG in the US is called the **Cohn-Oncley procedure**.

## Recommendations

CDC recommends Immune globulin (IG) or hepatitis A vaccine before travel for protection against hepatitis A.

**Immune globulin** is recommended for persons of all ages who:
- desire only short term protection (one dose is effective for three months)
- need immediate protection, and
- are too young for the vaccine (less than 2 years of age).

**Hepatitis A vaccine** is preferred for persons two years of age and older who plan to travel repeatedly or reside for long periods of time in intermediate or high risk areas. Bear in mind:
- The complete hepatitis A vaccine series requires a minimum of six months to complete.

- For these travelers over 18 years of age, hepatitis A vaccine should be given in a two-dose series with the second dose administered 6-12 months after the first.
- For children and adolescents between ages 2 through 18, a two or three dose series of hepatitis A vaccine is recommended depending on the vaccine chosen.

Travelers can be considered to be protected four weeks after receiving the initial vaccine dose. If the vaccine is administered less than four weeks before travel, then IG should also be given. The vaccine series must be completed for long-term protection. Hepatitis A vaccination is not required for travel to any country.

In addition to receiving IG or the vaccine, all travelers should follow the food and water precautions as described in *Appendix 4, Traveler's Diarrhea & Food and Water Precautions.*

Additional IG and hepatitis A information covering the vaccine and its safety are found in *Appendix 9, Hepatitis A Vaccine & Immune Globulin (IG) - Disease and Vaccine Information.*

## PARASITES

Parasitic infections are acquired by eating or drinking contaminated food or water, through direct contact with soil or water containing parasites or their larva, or by contact with biting insects. Symptoms and evidence of infection may include, but are not limited to: fever, swollen lymph nodes, rashes or itchy skin, digestive problems such as abdominal pain or diarrhea, eye problems, and anemia.

### Risk to Traveler

Travelers to the Middle East are at risk of parasitic infections. There are many types of parasites and infection may occur in several ways: by eating undercooked meats infected with parasites or their larva; by eating food or drinking water contaminated with parasites or their eggs; by contact with soil or water infected with parasites; or through insect bites. Several types of parasites can penetrate intact human skin and travelers are advised to wear shoes.

### Prevention

Travelers should eat only thoroughly cooked food, drink safe water, wear shoes, refrain from swimming in fresh water, and avoid contact with insects, particularly mosquitoes, biting flies, gnats, and midges.

## DISEASES TRANSMITTED THROUGH INTIMATE CONTACT WITH PEOPLE
### HIV/AIDS

Human immunodeficiency virus, or HIV, which causes acquired immunodeficiency syndrome or AIDS, is found primarily in blood, semen, and vaginal secretions of an infected person. HIV is spread by sexual contact with an infected person, by needle-sharing among injecting drug users, and through transfusions of infected blood and blood clotting factors. Babies born to HIV-infected women may become infected before, during, or shortly after birth.

In the US, blood is screened for HIV antibodies, but this screening may not take place in all countries. Scientific studies have revealed no evidence that HIV is transmitted by air, food, water, insects, inanimate objects or casual contact. Even though HIV antibodies are normally detected on a test within 6 months after infection, the period between infection and development of disease symptoms (incubation period) may be 10 years or longer. Treatment has prolonged the survival of some HIV infected persons but there is no known cure or vaccine available. For additional information, see *Appendix 7, HIV/AIDS Information.*

### Risk to Traveler

AIDS is found throughout the Middle East. However, little information is available regarding the rates of infection or the extent of high risk behaviors. The risk to a traveler depends on whether the traveler will be involved in sexual or needle-sharing contact with a person who is infected with HIV. Receipt of unscreened blood for transfusion poses a risk for HIV infection.

### Prevention

No effective vaccine has been developed for HIV. Travelers should avoid sexual or needle-sharing contact with a person who is infected with HIV. If a blood transfusion is necessary, screened blood should come from an HIV-negative blood donor.

### Recommendations

Travelers should avoid activities known to carry risks for infection with HIV.

### HEPATITIS B

Hepatitis B is a viral infection of the liver. Hepatitis B is transmitted to humans primarily through behavior that result in the exchange of blood or fluids containing blood. Risky behavior includes heterosexual or homosexual contact or sharing needles or drug paraphernalia with a person infected with the hepatitis B virus. Any unscreened or improperly screened blood or blood product, as well as unsterilized needles, or contact with potentially infected people who have open skin sores due to impetigo, scabies, and scratched insect bites, heightens the potential for infection to the traveler. An effective vaccine for prevention of hepatitis B is available.

### Risk to Traveler
Hepatitis B rates **moderate to high** for countries in the Middle East. The risk to the individual international traveler is greater if the traveler:
- has direct contact with blood or fluids containing blood;
- has intimate sexual contact with an infected person;
- remains in the country for longer than six months or has close contact with the local population.

### Prevention
**Hepatitis B vaccine** should be considered for those traveling to countries with high to intermediate rates of hepatitis B infection. For those travelers expecting to reside in countries of high risk, as well as all health workers, vaccination is strongly recommended.

Vaccination should ideally begin 6 months before travel, in order to complete the full series, which is needed for optimal protection. The three intramuscular doses of vaccine should be spaced so that the second dose is given one month after the first. The final dose is given 6 months after the first. The vaccination schedule should be initiated even if it will not be completed before travel begins. There is an alternative four-dose schedule that may provide protection if the first three doses can be delivered before departure. After completing the primary series, booster doses of the vaccine are not necessary.

### Recommendations
CDC recommends vaccination for any of the following people:
- any health care worker (medical, dental, or laboratory) whose activities might result in blood exposure;
- any traveler who may have intimate sexual contact with the local population;
- any long-term (6 months or more) traveler, e.g. teachers, who will reside in rural areas or have daily physical contact with the local population; or

- any traveler who is likely to seek either medical, dental, or other treatment in local facilities during their stay.

Hepatitis B vaccination is not required for travel to any country. Additional hepatitis B information is found in *Appendix 15, Hepatitis B*.

## MENINGOCOCCAL DISEASE

Meningococcal disease (bacterial meningitis) is a bacterial infection in the lining of the brain or spinal cord. Early symptoms are headache, stiff neck, a rash, and fever. The bacteria is transmitted to humans through respiratory droplets when an infected person sneezes or coughs on you.

### Risk to Traveler

There is **very low risk** of meningococcal disease in most of the Middle East, however, vaccination is required for pilgrims to the city of Mecca in Saudi Arabia for the annual Hajj (pilgrimage). When a traveler lives and works around the local population, the risk increases.

### Prevention

A one dose vaccine called **Menomune** is available.

### Requirements

Except for Saudi Arabia, vaccination is not required for entry into any country. Except as required, CDC normally does not recommend vaccination with meningococcal vaccine for travelers to most of the Middle Eastern countries. Travelers to the city of Mecca in Saudi Arabia should have a Meningococcal Vaccine Certificate showing vaccination within the last three years. The vaccine must be administered at least 10 days before arriving.

## OTHER DISEASES

## SCHISTOSOMIASIS

Schistosomiasis is a parasitic infection that develops after the larvae of a flatworm have penetrated the human skin. These larvae live in fresh water lakes, ponds, and streams, and can penetrate unbroken skin. Water treated with chlorine or iodine is virtually safe, and salt water poses no risk.

### Risk to Traveler

Schistosomiasis infection is localized to certain areas of the Middle East. It can be found in parts of **Iran, Iraq, Lebanon, Oman, Saudi Arabia,**

**Syria, Turkey, and Yemen.** The risk is a function of the frequency and degree of contact with contaminated fresh water for bathing, wading, or swimming.

## Prevention
The traveler cannot distinguish between infested and non-infested water. Therefore, swimming in fresh water in rural areas should be avoided. Bath water should either be heated to 50° (122° F) for five minutes or treated with chlorine or iodine as done for drinking water. If exposed, immediate and vigorous towel drying or application of rubbing alcohol to the exposed areas may reduce the risk of infection. Screening procedures are available for those who suspect infection, and schistosomiasis is treatable with drugs.

## Recommendations
Avoid contact with potentially contaminated water, such as swimming in lakes, ponds, rivers, etc.

## RABIES
Rabies is a viral infection that affects the central nervous system. It is transmitted to humans by warm-blooded animal (mammal) bites that introduce the virus into the wound. Although dogs are the main reservoir of the disease, all warm-blooded animal bites should be suspect.

### Risk to Traveler
For all countries in the Middle East, there is a risk of rabies infection, particularly in rural areas or in areas where large numbers of dogs are found. Bahrain and Cyprus have reported no rabies cases for at least the past two years.

### Prevention
Do not handle animals! Any animal bite should receive prompt medical attention. When wounds are thoroughly cleaned with large amounts of soap and water, the risk of rabies infection is reduced. Exposed individuals should receive prompt medical attention and advice on post-exposure preventive treatment.

### Recommendations
There are no requirements for vaccination, but pre-exposure vaccination is recommended for:
  • travelers visiting foreign areas where dog rabies is known to exist and whose activities may place them at high risk of exposure;

- veterinarians and animal handlers;
- spelunkers; and
- certain rabies laboratory workers.

Pre-exposure vaccination does not nullify the need for post-exposure vaccine, but reduces the number of injections and may provide protection under circumstances in which rabies exposure is unrecognized. For additional rabies information, refer to *Appendix 11, Rabies Information.*

---

## SUMMARY OF RECOMMENDATIONS FOR THE MIDDLE EAST

*Travelers should:*

- *take appropriate country specific malaria prevention measures mefloquine (or equivalent) or chloroquine,*
- *follow precautions to prevent insect bites*
- *pay attention to the quality of their drinking water and food*
- *have a dose of Immune Globulin (IG) or the hepatitis A vaccine, and consider booster doses of tetanus (Td) and polio (eIPV) vaccines.*
- *Depending on the locations to be visited, planned activities, and health of the traveler, the following vaccines should be considered: Hepatitis B, Typhoid, Meningococcal, Rabies (pre-exposure), and Cholera. Travelers to Saudi Arabia during the Hajj season should read Appendix 6: "Saudi Arabia Hajj Requirements."*
- *Finally, the normal "childhood" vaccines should be up-to-date: Measles, Mumps, Rubella (MMR Vaccine); Diphtheria, Tetanus, Pertussis (DTP Vaccine if traveler is less than 7 years of age, or Td if older than 7 years of age), and Polio vaccine. For additional information on these "childhood" vaccines, refer to Appendix 5, Vaccine Recommendations.*

# 17. EASTERN EUROPE & THE NEW INDEPENDENT STATES OF THE FORMER SOVIET UNION (NIS)

## COUNTRIES IN THIS REGION

Albania
Armenia
Azerbaijan
Belarus
Bosnia/Herzegovina
Bulgaria
Croatia
Czech Republic
Estonia
Georgia
Hungary
Kazakhstan
Kyrgyzstan

Latvia
Lithuania
Moldova
Poland
Romania
Russia
Serbia/Montenegro
Slovak Republic
Slovenia
Tajikistan
Turkmenistan
Ukraine
Uzbekistan

## EASTERN EUROPE & NIS TRAVELER'S OVERVIEW

*Travelers to Eastern Europe and the NIS may be exposed to potential diseases from a number of sources. The most frequently reported illness is traveler's diarrhea, but Eastern Europe and the NIS contain a variety of diseases transmitted by:*

- *insects,*
- *contaminated food and water, or*
- *close contact with infected people.*

*In this chapter, specific diseases, their causes, symptoms, geographic areas of risk, and prevention recommendations or requirement information are discussed under their topical headings. As a general guideline, in order to reduce the risk of infection, travelers must:*

- *protect themselves from insects*
- *ensure the quality of their food and drinking water*
- *be knowledgeable about potential diseases in the region to be visited*
- *receive all recommended vaccines and preventive medications.*

*In addition, travelers should note that diseases are not restricted to cleanly defined geographical areas. For example, mosquitoes can fly over city or country borders, so all travelers should protect themselves by taking the basic preventive precautions as described under each section and disease. Where appropriate, more detailed information is referenced in the Appendices.*

*Please Note: An **outbreak of diphtheria** began in 1990 and is occurring in all the New Independent States of the former Soviet Union. Travelers should have their diphtheria immunization up-to-date.*

## DISEASES TRANSMITTED BY INSECTS

Many diseases are transmitted through the bite of infected insects such as mosquitoes, flies, fleas, ticks and lice. In general, **travelers must protect themselves from insect bites**. Travelers are at a higher risk for insect bites if they participate in outdoor activities during night time hours from dusk to dawn when mosquitoes bite, or if their living accommodations are unscreened. If a mosquito net is unlikely to be available, consider buying a portable mosquito net.

### PREVENTING INSECT BITES

To reduce the risk of mosquito bites, travelers should remain in well-screened areas, use mosquito nets, and wear clothes that cover most of the body. Travelers should also take insect repellent with them to use on any exposed areas of the skin. The most effective compound in a repellent is **DEET**, which may be listed as an ingredient on repellant labels as "**N,N-diethyl meta-toluamide.**" Check the repellent label to ensure DEET is an ingredient.

Travelers should note, however, that insect repellents containing DEET should always be used according to label directions and sparingly on children. **Avoid applying high-concentration (greater than 35%) products to the skin, particularly on children, and refrain from applying repellent to portions of the hands that are likely to come in contact with the eyes and mouth.** Pediatric insect repellents with 6-10% DEET are available without prescription in many drug stores. In rare instances, toxic reactions or other problems have developed after contact with DEET.

Travelers should also purchase a flying insect-killing spray to use in living and sleeping areas during the evening and night. For greater protection, clothing and bednets can be soaked in or sprayed with **permethrin**, which is an insect repellent licensed for use on clothing. If applied according to the directions, permethrin will repel insects from clothing for several weeks. Portable mosquito bednets, repellents containing DEET, and permethrin can be purchased in hardware, backpacking, and military surplus stores.

## MALARIA

Malaria is a serious parasitic infection transmitted to humans by an Anopheles mosquito. These mosquitoes bite at night, from dusk to dawn. Symptoms of malaria range from flu-like symptoms with fever, general achiness, headache, and fatigue, to a cycle of shaking chills, high fever, and sweating. If left untreated, malaria can cause anemia, kidney failure, coma, and death. Drugs are available to help prevent a malaria infection.

However, in spite of all protective measures, travelers occasionally develop malaria. Therefore, while traveling and up to one year after returning home, travelers should seek medical evaluation for any flu-like illness.

### Risk to Traveler

*Areas of Risk*
In **Azerbaijan** and **Tajikistan**, the risk of malaria infection exists in some very small southern border areas.

*No Risk*
There is no risk of malaria in the other countries of this region.

## Prevention & Recommendations

Travelers at risk for malaria should take the prescription drug **chloroquine** to prevent malaria. The weekly dosage for an adult is 500 mg (salt) once a week. This drug should be taken one week before entering a malarious area, weekly while there, and weekly for 4 weeks after leaving the malarious area. No other anti-malarial drugs are needed.

In addition to using drugs to prevent malaria and treat a possible malaria attack, travelers should use measures to reduce exposure to malaria-carrying mosquitoes and protect themselves from mosquito bites. Remember, these mosquitoes bite mainly during the evening and night, from dusk to dawn.

Additional general malaria information, as well as specific information for women who are pregnant or children, is found in *Appendix 1, Malaria Information.*

## TICKBORNE ENCEPHALITIS

Tickborne encephalitis is a viral infection of the central nervous system. Infections are transmitted to humans by tick bites or by consumption of unpasteurized dairy products from cows, sheep, or goats. Symptoms range from: no symptoms to abrupt onset of headache, fever, and flu-like symptoms to more serious complications involving a swelling of the brain (encephalitis). There is no specific drug to treat tickborne encephalitis, but a vaccine is available in Europe.

### Risk to Traveler

The risk to travelers who do not visit or work in forested areas and who avoid unpasteurized dairy products is apparently low. Tickborne encephalitis occurs chiefly in Central and Eastern Europe, including the countries of the former Soviet Union. Travelers are at risk in **Hungary, Poland, Czech Republic, Slovak Republic, the former Soviet Union** and **Yugoslavia**. Tickborne encephalitis is found less frequently in Bulgaria and Romania. Transmission occurs in the summer months. Travelers are at risk if their plans include hiking, camping, or working in or around forested regions. The chance that a traveler to eastern Europe and the NIS will develop tickborne encephalitis is probably very small.

### Prevention

Preventing tick bites is sufficient protection for nearly all travelers to tickborne encephalitis infested areas. Vaccines are produced in Austria and Germany, but are not available in the United States. They can be obtained in Europe. Persons at risk should arrange to receive the vaccine at the country of destination; however, for most tourists, the immunization schedule is impractical and the vaccine unnecessary. Travelers who remain unimmunized should protect themselves from ticks and check for ticks daily.

The vaccine is given in three doses spaced over many months and is generally impractical for most travelers. No serious permanent side effects are known to be associated with the vaccine. Fever and local reactions such as redness, swelling, and pain are reported in fewer than 10% of those vaccinated. CDC does not have any direct information on the safety or effectiveness of the vaccine.

## LYME DISEASE
Lyme disease is a bacterial infection caused by the bite of certain, very small infected ticks. The illness is characterized by a circular rash of 2 inches or more with a bullseye appearance. The rash is often accompanied by "flu-like" symptoms of fever, headache, fatigue, and sometimes generalized aches and pains. If untreated, Lyme disease can cause further problems involving the heart, joints, and nervous system. Lyme disease can be treated effectively with antibiotics.

### Risk
Travelers visiting Eastern Europe and the NIS countries who will be **hiking, camping, or visiting rural areas** are at risk of Lyme disease.

### Prevention
Travelers should take precautions to prevent tick bites (see "Preventing Insect Bites" above).

## YELLOW FEVER
Yellow fever is a viral disease found in parts of Africa and South America. It is transmitted to humans by a mosquito bite. Even though there is no risk of becoming infected while traveling in Eastern Europe and the NIS, some countries require a yellow fever vaccination when travelers arrive from certain South American and African countries.

If you are **only** traveling from the United States to a country in Eastern Europe and the NIS, CDC does not recommend, and you are not required to have, a yellow fever vaccination. If your travel plans include traveling to or from countries in South America or Africa, you may be required to have a yellow fever vaccination. Therefore, you should review the comprehensive country-by-country yellow fever vaccine requirements in *Appendix 2, Yellow Fever Requirements.*

## DISEASES TRANSMITTED THROUGH FOOD & WATER

Food and waterborne diseases are the number one cause of illness to travelers and are very common in Eastern Europe and the NIS. **Traveler's diarrhea is the most frequent health problem for travelers.** It can be caused by viruses, bacteria, or parasites that are found universally throughout the region. Transmission is most often through contaminated food or water. Infections may cause diarrhea and vomiting (typhoid fever, cholera, and parasites), liver damage (hepatitis), or muscle paralysis (polio).

## GENERAL PRECAUTIONS

**Water**: The following beverages are safe to drink: boiled water or beverages made with boiled water, canned or carbonated beverages, beer, or wine. Impure water often contaminates drinking containers, ice, and tap water.

**Food**: Food that has been cooked to 165° F (74° C) is generally safe. As a reference, food at this temperature cannot be put directly into your mouth, but must cool a bit. Foods of concern are salads, uncooked vegetables and fruit, unpasteurized milk and milk products, raw meat, and shellfish. If you peel fruit yourself, it is generally safe. A simple rule of thumb is: "Boil it, cook it, peel it, or forget it."

For additional detailed precautions, be sure to read *Appendix 4, Traveler's Diarrhea & Food and Water Precautions.*

## TYPHOID FEVER

Typhoid fever is a bacterial infection transmitted to humans through contaminated food and/or water, or directly between people. Symptoms of typhoid fever include fever, headaches, fatigue, loss of appetite, and constipation. Typhoid fever can be treated effectively with antibiotics.

### Risk to Traveler

Travelers to Eastern Europe and the NIS countries are at risk for typhoid fever, especially when traveling to smaller cities, villages, or rural areas.

### Prevention

By drinking only bottled or boiled beverages and eating only thoroughly cooked food, a traveler lowers the risk of infection. Currently available vaccines have been shown to protect 70-90% of the recipients. Therefore, even vaccinated travelers should be cautious in selecting their food and water.

Two vaccines are recommended for protection against typhoid fever. An oral vaccine, **TY21a**, consists of a total of 4 capsules taken (one per day, every other day) over a seven day period, and requires a booster every five years. Reactions to the TY21a vaccine are rare but include nausea, vomiting, abdominal cramps, and skin rash.

A new single-dose injectable vaccine, **Typhim Vi** or **ViCPS**, is equally effective, and requires a booster dose every two years. Reactions to Typhim Vi are also rare, but include discomfort at the site of injection and headaches. An earlier typhoid vaccine developed years ago, which uses killed typhoid organisms and is administered in a two dose series, had more reported side effect and is currently not preferred. Instead, use one of the newer vaccines. Based on the vaccine chosen, booster doses are required every two to five years.

### Recommendations

CDC recommends a typhoid vaccination for those travelers who are going off the usual tourist itineraries, traveling to smaller cities and rural areas, or staying long term, that is, for six weeks or more. Vaccination should be completed at least two weeks before travel. Typhoid vaccination is not required for international travel.

### CHOLERA

Cholera is an acute diarrheal illness caused by an infection of the intestine with the bacterium *Vibrio cholerae*. Infection is acquired by ingesting contaminated water or food. The infection is often mild without symptoms, but sometimes can be severe. Approximately one in 20 infected persons has severe disease characterized by an abrupt onset of profuse watery diarrhea, vomiting, dehydration, and leg cramps.

### Risk to Traveler

Cholera cases have been reported from some of the countries of Eastern Europe and the NIS. The risk of infection to the US traveler is very low, especially those that are following the usual tourist itineraries, staying in standard accommodations, and following food and water safety instructions. A list of cholera infected countries is given in *Appendix 10, CDC's Blue Sheet*.

## Prevention

Travelers to cholera infected areas should:
- avoid eating high risk foods, especially fish and shellfish, and
- follow the standard food and water precautions of eating only thoroughly cooked food that is served hot, peeling their own fruit, and drinking beverages and ice made from boiled or chlorinated water, bottled carbonated water, or bottled carbonated soft drinks.

Persons with severe cases of cholera respond well to simple fluid and electrolyte-replacement therapy, but medical attention must be sought quickly when cholera is suspected.

The cholera vaccine licensed for use in the United States confers only brief and incomplete immunity (50% effective in reducing the illness). The risk of cholera to US travelers is so low that it is questionable whether the vaccine is of benefit, and therefore it is not recommended routinely for travelers. The primary series for this cholera vaccine is normally two injections with booster doses given every 6 months for persons who remain at high risk. **Cholera vaccine is not recommended for infants under 6 months old or for pregnant women.**

For additional information about cholera, read *Appendix 4, Traveler's Diarrhea & Food and Water Precautions*, and *Appendix 8, Cholera Information.*

## HEPATITIS A

Hepatitis A is a viral infection of the liver transmitted to humans by the fecal-oral route; through direct person-to-person contact; from contaminated water, ice, or shellfish; or from fruits or uncooked vegetables contaminated through handling. Symptoms include fatigue, fever, loss of appetite, nausea, dark urine, jaundice, vomiting, aches and pains, and light stools. No specific therapy, only supportive care, is available.

### Risk to Traveler

Compared to Northern and Western Europe, there is an increased risk in Eastern Europe and the NIS countries, where there are **intermediate rates** of hepatitis A infection. Risk is even greater if travel plans include visiting rural areas and extensive travel in the countryside, frequent close contact with local persons, or eating in settings of poor sanitation. Be aware that a study has shown that many cases of travel-related hepatitis A occur in travelers to developing countries with "standard" itineraries, accommodations, and food consumption behaviors.

## Prevention

The virus is inactivated by boiling or cooking to 185° F (85° C) for one minute. Therefore, eating thoroughly cooked foods and drinking only treated water serve as general precautions. In addition, **Immune globulin (IG)** *or* **hepatitis A vaccine** is recommended before travel. Two hepatitis A vaccines, **Havrix®** and **VAQTA®**, are currently licensed in the United States.

Immune globulin and the hepatitis A vaccine marketed in the United States are safe. American travelers should note that IG manufactured in foreign countries may or may not meet these requirements. Therefore, American travelers who will need to receive additional doses of IG in other countries should use products that meet US standards and license requirements. For reference, the method of manufacturing IG in the US is called the **Cohn-Oncley procedure**.

## Recommendations

CDC recommends Immune globulin (IG) or hepatitis A vaccine before travel for protection against hepatitis A.

**Immune globulin** is recommended for persons of all ages who:
- desire only short term protection (one dose is effective for three months)
- need immediate protection, and
- are too young for the vaccine (less than 2 years of age).

**Hepatitis A vaccine** is preferred for persons two years of age and older who plan to travel repeatedly or reside for long periods of time in intermediate or high risk areas. Bear in mind:
- The complete hepatitis A vaccine series requires a minimum of six months to complete.
- For these travelers over 18 years of age, hepatitis A vaccine should be given in a two-dose series with the second dose administered 6-12 months after the first.
- For children and adolescents between ages 2 through 18, a two or three dose series of hepatitis A vaccine is recommended depending on the vaccine chosen.

Travelers can be considered to be protected four weeks after receiving the initial vaccine dose. If the vaccine is administered less than four weeks before travel, then IG should also be given. The vaccine series must be completed for long-term protection. Hepatitis A vaccination is not required for travel to any country.

In addition to receiving IG or the vaccine, all travelers should follow the food and water precautions as described in *Appendix 4, Traveler's Diarrhea & Food and Water Precautions.*

Additional IG and hepatitis A information covering the vaccine and its safety are found in *Appendix 9, Hepatitis A Vaccine & Immune Globulin (IG) - Disease and Vaccine Information.*

## PARASITES

Parasitic infections are acquired by eating or drinking contaminated food or water, through direct contact with soil or water containing parasites or their larva, or by contact with biting insects. Symptoms and evidence of infection may include, but are not limited to: fever, swollen lymph nodes, rashes or itchy skin, digestive problems such as abdominal pain or diarrhea, eye problems, and anemia.

### Risk to Traveler

Travelers to Eastern Europe and the NIS countries are at risk of parasitic infections. There are many types of parasites and infection may occur in several ways: by eating undercooked meats infected with parasites or their larva; by eating food or drinking water contaminated with parasites or their eggs; or through insect bites.

### Prevention

Travelers should eat only thoroughly cooked food, drink safe water, wear shoes, refrain from swimming in fresh water, and avoid contact with insects, particularly mosquitoes, biting flies, gnats, and midges.

## DISEASES TRANSMITTED THROUGH INTIMATE CONTACT WITH PEOPLE

### HIV/AIDS

Human immunodeficiency virus, or HIV, which causes acquired immunodeficiency syndrome or AIDS, is found primarily in blood, semen, and vaginal secretions of an infected person. HIV is spread by sexual contact with an infected person, by needle-sharing among injecting drug users, and through transfusions of infected blood and blood clotting factors. Babies born to HIV-infected women may become infected before, during, or shortly after birth.

In the US, blood is screened for HIV antibodies, but this screening may not take place in all countries. Scientific studies have revealed no evidence that HIV is transmitted by air, food, water, insects, inanimate objects or casual contact. Even though HIV antibodies are normally detected on a test within 6 months after infection, the period between infection and development of disease symptoms (incubation period) may be 10 years or longer. Treatment has prolonged the survival of some HIV infected persons but there is no known cure or vaccine available. For additional information, see *Appendix 7, HIV/AIDS Information.*

### Risk to Traveler
AIDS is found in Eastern Europe and the NIS countries, but the magnitude and transmission modes are not well defined. The risk to a traveler depends on whether the traveler will be involved in sexual or needle-sharing contact with a person who is infected with HIV. Receipt of unscreened blood for transfusion poses a risk for HIV infection.

### Prevention
No effective vaccine has been developed for HIV. Travelers should avoid sexual or needle-sharing contact with a person who is infected with HIV. If a blood transfusion is necessary, screened blood should come from an HIV-negative blood donor.

### Recommendations
Travelers should avoid activities known to carry risks for infection with HIV.

## HEPATITIS B
Hepatitis B is a viral infection of the liver. Hepatitis B is transmitted to humans primarily through behavior that result in the exchange of blood or fluids containing blood. Risky behavior includes heterosexual or homosexual contact or sharing needles or drug paraphernalia with a person infected with the hepatitis B virus. Any unscreened or improperly screened blood or blood product, as well as unsterilized needles, or contact with potentially infected people who have open skin sores due to impetigo, scabies, and scratched insect bites, heightens the potential for infection to the traveler. An effective vaccine for prevention of hepatitis B is available.

### Risk to Traveler
Hepatitis B rates are **moderate** for Eastern Europe and the NIS. The risk to the individual international traveler is greater if the traveler:
- has direct contact with blood or fluids containing blood;
- has intimate sexual contact with an infected person;

- remains in the country for longer than six months or has close contact with the local population.

## Prevention

**Hepatitis B vaccine** should be considered for those traveling to countries with high to intermediate rates of hepatitis B infection. For those travelers expecting to reside in countries of high risk, as well as all health workers, vaccination is strongly recommended.

Vaccination should ideally begin 6 months before travel, in order to complete the full series, which is needed for optimal protection. The three intramuscular doses of vaccine should be spaced so that the second dose is given one month after the first. The final dose is given 6 months after the first. The vaccination schedule should be initiated even if it will not be completed before travel begins. There is an alternative four-dose schedule that may provide protection if the first three doses can be delivered before departure. After completing the primary series, booster doses of the vaccine are not necessary.

## Recommendations

CDC recommends vaccination for any of the following people:
- any health care worker (medical, dental, or laboratory) whose activities might result in blood exposure;
- any traveler who may have intimate sexual contact with the local population;
- any long-term (6 months or more) traveler, e.g. teachers, who will reside in rural areas or have daily physical contact with the local population; or
- any traveler who is likely to seek either medical, dental, or other treatment in local facilities during their stay.

Hepatitis B vaccination is not required for travel to any country. Additional hepatitis B information is found in *Appendix 15, Hepatitis B.*

## OTHER DISEASES
## RABIES

Rabies is a viral infection that affects the central nervous system. It is transmitted to humans by warm-blooded animal (mammal) bites that introduce the virus into the wound. Although dogs are the main reservoir of the disease, all warm-blooded animal bites should be suspect.

## Risk to Traveler

For most countries of Eastern Europe and the NIS there is a risk of rabies infection, particularly in rural areas or in areas where large numbers of dogs are found.

## Prevention

Do not handle animals! Any animal bite should receive prompt medical attention. When wounds are thoroughly cleaned with large amounts of soap and water, the risk of rabies infection is reduced. Exposed individuals should receive prompt medical attention and advice on post-exposure preventive treatment.

## Recommendations

There are no requirements for vaccination, but pre-exposure vaccination is recommended for:
- travelers visiting foreign areas where dog rabies is known to exist and whose activities may place them at high risk of exposure;
- veterinarians and animal handlers;
- spelunkers; and
- certain rabies laboratory workers.

Pre-exposure vaccination does not nullify the need for post-exposure vaccine, but reduces the number of injections and may provide protection under circumstances in which rabies exposure is unrecognized. For additional rabies information, refer to *Appendix 11, Rabies Information.*

---

### SUMMARY OF RECOMMENDATIONS FOR EASTERN EUROPE & THE NIS

*Travelers should:*
- *follow precautions to prevent insect bites*
- *pay attention to the quality of their drinking water and food*
- *have a dose of Immune Globulin (IG) or the hepatitis A vaccine, and consider booster doses of tetanus (Td) and polio (eIPV) vaccines.*
- *Depending on the locations to be visited, planned activities, and health of the traveler, the following vaccines should be considered: Hepatitis B, Rabies (pre-exposure), and Typhoid.*
- *Finally, the normal "childhood" vaccines should be up-to-date: Measles, Mumps, Rubella (MMR Vaccine); Diphtheria, Tetanus, Pertussis (DTP Vaccine if traveler is less than 7 years of age, or Td if older than 7 years of age), and Polio vaccine. For additional information on these "childhood" vaccines, refer to Appendix 5, Vaccine Recommendations.*

# 18. WESTERN EUROPE

## COUNTRIES IN THIS REGION

Andorra
Austria
Azores
Belgium
Denmark
Faroe Island
Finland
France
Germany
Gibraltar
Greece
Greenland
Iceland
Ireland

Italy
Liechtenstein
Luxembourg
Madeira
Malta
Monaco
Netherlands
Norway
Portugal
San Marino
Spain
Sweden
Switzerland
United Kingdom

## WESTERN EUROPE TRAVELER'S OVERVIEW

*Travelers to Western Europe may be exposed to potential diseases from a number of sources. **The most frequently reported illness is traveler's diarrhea**, but Western Europe contains a variety of diseases transmitted by:*
- *insects,*
- *contaminated food and water, or*
- *close contact with infected people.*

*In this chapter, specific diseases, their causes, symptoms, geographic areas of risk, and prevention recommendations or requirement information are discussed under their topical headings. As a general guideline, in order to reduce the risk of infection, travelers must:*
- *protect themselves from insects*
- *ensure the quality of their food and drinking water*
- *be knowledgeable about potential diseases in the region to be visited*
- *receive all recommended vaccines and preventive medications.*

*In addition, travelers should note that diseases are not restricted to cleanly defined geographical areas. For example, mosquitoes can fly over city or country borders, so all travelers should protect themselves by taking the basic preventive precautions as described under each section and disease. Where appropriate, more detailed information is referenced in the Appendices.*

## DISEASES TRANSMITTED BY INSECTS

Many diseases are transmitted through the bite of infected insects such as mosquitoes, flies, fleas, ticks and lice. In general, **travelers must protect themselves from insect bites**. Travelers are at a higher risk for insect bites if they participate in outdoor activities during night time hours from dusk to dawn when mosquitoes bite, or if their living accommodations are unscreened. If a mosquito net is unlikely to be available, consider buying a portable mosquito net.

## PREVENTING INSECT BITES

To reduce the risk of mosquito bites, travelers should remain in well-screened areas, use mosquito nets, and wear clothes that cover most of the body. Travelers should also take insect repellent with them to use on any exposed areas of the skin. The most effective compound in a repellent is **DEET**, which may be listed as an ingredient on repellant labels as "**N,N-diethyl meta-toluamide**." Check the repellent label to ensure DEET is an ingredient.

Travelers should note, however, that insect repellents containing DEET should always be used according to label directions and sparingly on children. **Avoid applying high-concentration (greater than 35%) products to the skin, particularly on children, and refrain from applying repellent to portions of the hands that are likely to come in contact with the eyes and mouth.** Pediatric insect repellents with 6-10% DEET are available without prescription in many drug stores. In rare instances, toxic reactions or other problems have developed after contact with DEET.

Travelers should also purchase a flying insect-killing spray to use in living and sleeping areas during the evening and night. For greater protection, clothing and bednets can be soaked in or sprayed with **permethrin**, which is an insect repellent licensed for use on clothing. If applied according to the directions, permethrin will repel insects from clothing for several weeks. Portable mosquito bednets, repellents containing DEET, and permethrin can be purchased in hardware, backpacking, and military surplus stores.

## TICKBORNE ENCEPHALITIS

Tickborne encephalitis is a viral infection of the central nervous system. Infections are transmitted to humans by tick bites or by consumption of unpasteurized dairy products from cows, sheep, or goats. Symptoms range from: no symptoms to abrupt onset of headache, fever, and flu-like symptoms to more serious complications involving a swelling of the brain (encephalitis). There is no specific drug to treat tickborne encephalitis, but a vaccine is available in Europe.

### Risk to Traveler

The risk to travelers who do not visit or work in forested areas and who avoid unpasteurized dairy products is apparently low. Tickborne encephalitis occurs chiefly in Central and Western Europe, including the countries from the Mediterranean to Scandinavia. It occurs more frequently in **Austria**, **Germany**, and **Switzerland**. Tickborne encephalitis is found less frequently in Finland and Sweden and is rare in Denmark and France. Transmission occurs in the summer months. Travelers are at risk if their plans include hiking, camping, or working in or around forested regions. The chance that a traveler to Western Europe will develop tickborne encephalitis is very small.

### Prevention

Preventing tick bites is sufficient protection for nearly all travelers to tickborne encephalitis infested areas. Vaccines are produced in Austria and Germany, but are not available in the United States. They can be obtained in Europe. Persons at risk should arrange to receive the vaccine at the country of destination; however, for most tourists, the immunization schedule is impractical and the vaccine unnecessary. Travelers who remain unimmunized should protect themselves from ticks and check for ticks daily.

The vaccine is given in three doses spaced over many months and is generally impractical for most travelers. No serious permanent side effects are known to be associated with the vaccine. Fever and local reactions such as redness, swelling, and pain are reported in fewer than 10% of those vaccinated. CDC does not have any direct information on the safety or effectiveness of the vaccine.

## LYME DISEASE

Lyme disease is a bacterial infection caused by the bite of certain, very small infected ticks. The illness is characterized by a circular rash of 2 inches or more with a bullseye appearance. The rash is often accompanied by "flu-like" symptoms of fever, headache, fatigue, and sometimes generalized aches and pains. If untreated, Lyme disease can cause further problems involving the heart, joints, and nervous system. Lyme disease can be treated effectively with antibiotics.

### Risk

Travelers visiting western European countries who will be hiking, camping, or visiting wooded parks and rural areas are at risk of Lyme disease.

### Prevention

Travelers should take precautions to prevent tick bites.

## YELLOW FEVER

Yellow fever is a viral disease found in parts of Africa and South America. It is transmitted to humans by a mosquito bite. Even though there is no risk of becoming infected while traveling in Western Europe, some countries require a yellow fever vaccination when travelers arrive from certain South American and African countries.

If you are **only** traveling from the United States to Western Europe, CDC does not recommend, and you are not required to have, a yellow fever vaccination. If your travel plans include traveling to or from countries in South America or Africa, you may be required to have a yellow fever vaccination. Therefore, you should review the comprehensive country-by-country yellow fever vaccine requirements in *Appendix 2, Yellow Fever Requirements*.

## DISEASES TRANSMITTED THROUGH FOOD & WATER

Food and waterborne diseases are the number one cause of illness to travelers and are very common in Western Europe. **Traveler's diarrhea is the most frequent health problem for travelers**. It can be caused by viruses, bacteria, or parasites that are found universally throughout the region. Transmission is most often through contaminated food or water. Infections may cause diarrhea and vomiting (typhoid fever, cholera, and parasites), liver damage (hepatitis), or muscle paralysis (polio).

### GENERAL PRECAUTIONS

**Water**: The following beverages are safe to drink: boiled water or beverages made with boiled water, canned or carbonated beverages, beer, or wine. Impure water often contaminates drinking containers, ice, and tap water.

**Food**: Food that has been cooked to 165° F (74° C) is generally safe. As a reference, food at this temperature cannot be put directly into your mouth, but must cool a bit. Foods of concern are salads, uncooked vegetables and fruit, unpasteurized milk and milk products, raw meat, and shellfish. If you peel fruit yourself, it is generally safe. A simple rule of thumb is: "Boil it, cook it, peel it, or forget it."

For additional detailed precautions, be sure to read *Appendix 4, Traveler's Diarrhea & Food and Water Precautions*.

### TYPHOID FEVER

Typhoid fever is a bacterial infection transmitted to humans through contaminated food and/or water, or directly between people. Symptoms of typhoid fever include fever, headaches, fatigue, loss of appetite, and constipation. Typhoid fever can be treated effectively with antibiotics.

#### Risk to Traveler

Typhoid fever is **rare** in Western Europe.

#### Prevention

By drinking only bottled or boiled beverages and eating only thoroughly cooked food, a traveler lowers the risk of infection. Currently available vaccines have been shown to protect 70-90% of the recipients, so even vaccinated travelers should be cautious in selecting their food and water.

Two vaccines are recommended for protection against typhoid fever. An oral vaccine, **TY21a**, consists of a total of 4 capsules taken (one per day, every other day) over a seven day period, and requires a booster every five years. Reactions to the TY21a vaccine are rare but include nausea, vomiting, abdominal cramps, and skin rash.

A new single-dose injectable vaccine, **Typhim Vi** or **ViCPS**, is equally effective, and requires a booster dose every two years. Reactions to Typhim Vi are also rare, but include discomfort at the site of injection and headaches. An earlier typhoid vaccine developed years ago, which uses killed typhoid organisms and is administered in a two dose series, had more reported side effect and is currently not preferred. Instead, use one of the newer vaccines. Based on the vaccine chosen, booster doses are required every two to five years.

## Recommendations

CDC recommends a typhoid vaccination for those travelers who are going off the usual tourist itineraries, traveling to smaller cities and rural areas, or staying long term, that is, for six weeks or more. Vaccination should be completed at least two weeks before travel. Typhoid vaccination is not required for international travel.

## HEPATITIS A

Hepatitis A is a viral infection of the liver transmitted to humans by the fecal-oral route; through direct person-to-person contact; from contaminated water, ice, or shellfish; or from fruits or uncooked vegetables contaminated through handling. Symptoms include fatigue, fever, loss of appetite, nausea, dark urine, jaundice, vomiting, aches and pains, and light stools. No specific therapy, only supportive care, is available.

### Risk to Traveler

In general, travelers to Northern and Western Europe are not at increased risk for hepatitis A. However, **increased risk does exist in Southern Europe** where there are intermediate rates of hepatitis A. Risk is even greater if travel plans include visits to rural areas, extensive travel in the countryside, frequent, close contact with local persons, or eating in settings of poor sanitation. A study has shown that many cases of travel-related hepatitis A occur in travelers to developing countries with "standard" itineraries, accommodations, and food consumption behaviors.

## Prevention

The virus is inactivated by boiling or cooking to 185° F (85° C) for one minute. Therefore, eating thoroughly cooked foods and drinking only treated water serve as general precautions. In addition, **Immune globulin (IG)** *or* **hepatitis A vaccine** is recommended before travel. Two hepatitis A vaccines, **Havrix®** and **VAQTA®**, are currently licensed in the United States.

Immune globulin and the hepatitis A vaccine marketed in the United States are safe. American travelers should note that IG manufactured in foreign countries may or may not meet these requirements. Therefore, American travelers who will need to receive additional doses of IG in other countries should use products that meet US standards and license requirements. For reference, the method of manufacturing IG in the US is called the **Cohn-Oncley procedure.**

## Recommendations

CDC recommends Immune globulin (IG) or hepatitis A vaccine before travel for protection against hepatitis A.

**Immune globulin** is recommended for persons of all ages who:
  • desire only short term protection (one dose is effective for three months)
  • need immediate protection, and
  • are too young for the vaccine (less than 2 years of age).

**Hepatitis A vaccine** is preferred for persons two years of age and older who plan to travel repeatedly or reside for long periods of time in intermediate or high risk areas. Bear in mind:
  • The complete hepatitis A vaccine series requires a minimum of six months to complete.
  • For these travelers over 18 years of age, hepatitis A vaccine should be given in a two-dose series with the second dose administered 6-12 months after the first.
  • For children and adolescents between ages 2 through 18, a two or three dose series of hepatitis A vaccine is recommended depending on the vaccine chosen.

Travelers can be considered to be protected four weeks after receiving the initial vaccine dose. If the vaccine is administered less than four weeks before travel, then IG should also be given. The vaccine series must be completed for long-term protection. Hepatitis A vaccination is not required for travel to any country.

In addition to receiving IG or the vaccine, all travelers should follow the food and water precautions as described in *Appendix 4, Traveler's Diarrhea & Food and Water Precautions.*

Additional IG and hepatitis A information covering the vaccine and its safety are found in *Appendix 9, Hepatitis A Vaccine & Immune Globulin (IG) - Disease and Vaccine Information.*

## DISEASES TRANSMITTED THROUGH INTIMATE CONTACT WITH PEOPLE
### HIV/AIDS

Human immunodeficiency virus, or HIV, which causes acquired immunodeficiency syndrome or AIDS, is found primarily in blood, semen, and vaginal secretions of an infected person. HIV is spread by sexual contact with an infected person, by needle-sharing among injecting drug users, and through transfusions of infected blood and blood clotting factors. Babies born to HIV-infected women may become infected before, during, or shortly after birth.

In the United States, blood is screened for HIV antibodies, but this screening may not take place in all countries. Scientific studies have revealed no evidence that HIV is transmitted by air, food, water, insects, inanimate objects or casual contact. Even though HIV antibodies are normally detected on a test within 6 months after infection, the period between infection and development of disease symptoms (incubation period) may be 10 years or longer. Treatment has prolonged the survival of some HIV infected persons but there is no known cure or vaccine available. For additional information, see *Appendix 7, HIV/AIDS Information.*

### Risk to Traveler

AIDS is found throughout Western Europe. The population groups predominantly affected have remained men who have sex with men and injecting drug users, although heterosexual transmission is on the rise. The risk to a traveler depends on whether the traveler will be involved in sexual or needle-sharing contact with a person who is infected with HIV. Receipt of unscreened blood for transfusion poses a risk for HIV infection.

### Prevention

No effective vaccine has been developed for HIV. Travelers should avoid sexual or needle-sharing contact with a person who is infected with HIV.

If a blood transfusion is necessary, screened blood should come from an HIV-negative blood donor.

## Recommendations
Travelers should avoid activities known to carry risks for infection with HIV.

## HEPATITIS B
Hepatitis B is a viral infection of the liver. Hepatitis B is transmitted to humans primarily through behavior that result in the exchange of blood or fluids containing blood. Risky behavior includes heterosexual or homosexual contact or sharing needles or drug paraphernalia with a person infected with the hepatitis B virus. Any unscreened or improperly screened blood or blood product, as well as unsterilized needles, or contact with potentially infected people who have open skin sores due to impetigo, scabies, and scratched insect bites, heightens the potential for infection to the traveler. An effective vaccine for prevention of hepatitis B is available.

### Risk to Traveler
Hepatitis B rates are **low** for Western Europe. The risk to the individual international traveler is greater if the traveler:
- has direct contact with blood or fluids containing blood;
- has intimate sexual contact with an infected person;
- remains in the country for longer than six months or has close contact with the local population.

### Prevention
**Hepatitis B vaccine** should be considered for those traveling to countries with high to intermediate rates of hepatitis B infection. For those travelers expecting to reside in countries of high risk, as well as all health workers, vaccination is strongly recommended.

Vaccination should ideally begin 6 months before travel, in order to complete the full series, which is needed for optimal protection. The three intramuscular doses of vaccine should be spaced so that the second dose is given one month after the first. The final dose is given 6 months after the first. The vaccination schedule should be initiated even if it will not be completed before travel begins. There is an alternative four-dose schedule that may provide protection if the first three doses can be delivered before departure. After completing the primary series, booster doses of the vaccine are not necessary.

## Recommendations

CDC recommends vaccination for any of the following people:
- any health care worker (medical, dental, or laboratory) whose activities might result in blood exposure;
- any traveler who may have intimate sexual contact with the local population;
- any long-term (6 months or more) traveler, e.g. teachers, who will reside in rural areas or have daily physical contact with the local population; or
- any traveler who is likely to seek either medical, dental, or other treatment in local facilities during their stay.

Hepatitis B vaccination is not required for travel to any country. Additional hepatitis B information is found in *Appendix 15, Hepatitis B.*

## OTHER DISEASES
## RABIES

Rabies is a viral infection that affects the central nervous system. It is transmitted to humans by warm-blooded animal (mammal) bites that introduce the virus into the wound. Although dogs are the main reservoir of the disease, all warm-blooded animal bites should be suspect.

### Risk to Traveler

There is a risk of rabies infection, particularly in rural areas or in areas where large numbers of foxes are found. There is little risk in Spain and Portugal, and some West European countries have reported no rabies cases for at least the past two years including: Cyprus, Faroe Islands, Finland, Gibraltar, Greece, Iceland, Ireland, Malta, Norway (mainland), Sweden, and the United Kingdom.

### Prevention

For most countries of Western Europe there is a risk of rabies infection, particularly in rural areas or in areas where large numbers of dogs are found.

### Prevention

Do not handle animals! Any animal bite should receive prompt medical attention. When wounds are thoroughly cleaned with large amounts of soap and water, the risk of rabies infection is reduced. Exposed individuals should receive prompt medical attention and advice on post-exposure preventive treatment.

## Recommendations

There are no requirements for vaccination, but pre-exposure vaccination is recommended for:

- travelers visiting foreign areas where dog rabies is known to exist and whose activities may place them at high risk of exposure;
  - veterinarians and animal handlers;
  - spelunkers; and
  - certain rabies laboratory workers.

Pre-exposure vaccination does not nullify the need for post-exposure vaccine, but reduces the number of injections and may provide protection under circumstances in which rabies exposure is unrecognized. For additional rabies information, refer to *Appendix 11, Rabies Information.*

---

### SUMMARY OF RECOMMENDATIONS
### FOR WESTERN EUROPE

*Travelers should:*

- *follow precautions to prevent insect bites*
- *pay attention to the quality of their drinking water and food*
- *travelers to Southern Europe should have a dose of Immune Globulin (IG) or Hepatitis A vaccine, and consider booster doses of tetanus (Td).*
- *Depending on the locations to be visited, planned activities, and health of the traveler, the following vaccines should be considered: Hepatitis B vaccine (Malta) and Rabies (pre-exposure) vaccine.*
- *Finally, the normal "childhood" vaccines should be up-to-date: Measles, Mumps, Rubella (MMR Vaccine); Diphtheria, Tetanus, Pertussis (DTP Vaccine if traveler is less than 7 years of age, or Td if older than 7 years of age), and Polio vaccine. For additional information on these "childhood" vaccines, refer to Appendix 5, Vaccine Recommendations.*

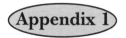

# MALARIA: GENERAL INFORMATION

**Malaria** is caused by a parasite that is transmitted from person to person by the bite of an infected **Anopheles mosquito**. These mosquitoes are present in almost all countries in the tropics and subtropics. Anopheles mosquitoes bite during nighttime hours, from dusk to dawn. Therefore, antimalarial drugs are only recommended for travelers who will have exposure during evening and nighttime hours in malaria risk areas.

Symptoms of malaria include fever, chills, headache, muscle ache, and malaise. Early stages of malaria may resemble the onset of the flu. Travelers who become ill with a fever during or after travel in a malaria risk area should seek prompt medical attention and should inform their physician of their recent travel history. Neither the traveler nor the physician should assume that the traveler has the flu or some other disease without doing a laboratory test to determine if the symptoms are caused by malaria.

Malaria can often be prevented by the use of antimalarial drugs and use of personal protection measures against mosquito bites. The risk of malaria depends on the traveler's itinerary, the duration of travel, and the place where the traveler will spend the evenings and nights.

Travelers can still get malaria despite prevention measures. Symptoms can develop as early as 6-8 days after being bitten by an infected mosquito or as late as several months after departure from a malarious area, after antimalarial drugs are discontinued. Malaria can be treated effectively in its early stages, but delaying treatment can have serious consequences.

*For additional information on the drugs used to prevent and treat malaria, see Appendix 16: Malaria Drug Information.*

## MALARIA INFORMATION: PREGNANCY & CHILDREN

### PREGNANCY

Malaria infection may pose a serious threat to a pregnant woman and her fetus. Malaria infection in pregnant women may be more severe than in nonpregnant women. Malaria may increase the risk of adverse pregnancy outcomes, including prematurity, abortion, and stillbirth. Therefore, pregnant women who are traveling to a malaria risk area should consult a physician and take prescription drugs to prevent malaria.

In areas with chloroquine-resistant *P. falciparum*, **mefloquine** or **doxycycline** are recommended as antimalarial drugs for most travelers. Mefloquine can be used during pregnancy for women traveling to areas with chloroquine-resistant *P. falciparum*. Doxycycline should not be used during the entire pregnancy. In chloroquine-sensitive areas, pregnant women should take chloroquine for malaria prevention. Neither mefloquine nor chloroquine has been demonstrated to have a harmful effect on the fetus when it is used to prevent malaria.

### BREAST-FEEDING

Very small amounts of antimalarial drugs are secreted in the breast milk of lactating women. The very small amount of drug that is transferred in breast milk is neither harmful to the infant nor does it protect the infant against malaria. Therefore, infants need to be given drugs to prevent malaria in the dosages outlined in the message on recommendations for children. Each attack of malaria must be treated promptly.

### CHILDREN

All children traveling to malaria risk areas, including young infants, should take antimalarial drugs. Therefore, the recommendations for most preventive drugs are the same as for adults, but it is essential to use the correct dosage. The dosage depends on the age and/or the weight of the child.

*Warning*: Overdoasge of antimalarial drugs can be fatal. The medication should be stored in childproof containers out of the reach of children.

**Mefloquine**: For all children, the mefloquine dosages are once-a-week. The dosage of mefloquine depends on the weight of the child: under

30lbs – 4.6 mg base (5 mg salt) per kilogram of body weight; 30-40 lbs, use 1/4 tablet; 40-60 lbs, use 1/2 tablet; 60-90 lbs, use 3/4 tablet; 90 lbs and over, use 1 tablet.

**Chloroquine:** For all children, the chloroquine dosages are once-a-week. The dosage of chloroquine depends on the weight of the child. The dosage is 8.3 mg (salt) per kilogram of body weight. In the United States, chloroquine is made only in 500 mg tablets. Pharmacists can pulverize the tablets and prepare gelatin capsules with the calculated pediatric dosages. The weekly dose should be mixed in juice, jelly, or chocolate syrup to hide the extremely bitter taste. Overseas, chloroquine is widely available as suspensions that generally contain 10 mg of chloroquine in each ml. The dosage is usually indicated on the bottle or the package.

**Doxycycline:** For all children, the doxycycline dosages are once-a-day. The dosage of doxycycline depends on the weight of the child. **Do not give Doxycycline to children under 8 years of age.** Over 8 years of age, the dosage is 2mg/kilogram of body weight, up to the adult dose of 100 mg daily.

## SELF-TREATMENT

Travelers on chloroquine or chloroquine/proguanil should be given a treatment dose of **Fansidar™**, if at any time during their travel they will be more than 24 hours from professional medical care. (Travelers with a history of sulfonamide intolerance should not be given Fansidar™.) If travelers develop a febrile illness and *if professional medical care is not readily available within 24 hours*, they should promptly take the Fansidar™. This self-treatment is **only** a temporary measure and prompt medical evaluation is *imperative*.

### FANSIDAR™ SELF-TREATMENT TABLE

| Adult Dose | Pediatric Dose | |
| --- | --- | --- |
| | *weight(kg)* | *# of tablet(s)* |
| 3 tablets (75 mg pyrimethamine | 5-10 (11-23 lbs) | 1/2 |
| and 1,500 mg sulfadoxine), | 11-20 (24-45 lbs) | 1 |
| orally as a single-dose. | 21-30 (46-67 lbs) | 1 1/2 |
| | 31-45(68-100 lbs) | 2 |
| | 45 and over | |
| | (100 lbs and over) | 3 |

## MOSQUITO PROTECTION

Travelers must also be protected from malaria-carrying mosquitoes. These mosquitoes bite during the nighttime hours, from dusk to dawn. To reduce mosquito bites, travelers should remain in well-screened areas, use mosquito nets, wear covering clothing, and use insect repellents. The most effective insect repellents contain **DEET**, the active ingredient in most insect repellents. Adults should use 30–35% DEET on exposed areas of the skin. Pediatric insect repellents with 6–10% DEET are available.

Apply repellents sparingly. Do not inhale or ingest repellents or get them in the eyes; avoid applying repellents to portions of children's hands that are likely to have contact with eyes or mouth; never use repellents on wounds or irritated skin. Wash repellent-treated skin after coming indoors.

*Additional information on the drugs used to prevent or treat malaria is found in Appendix 16, Malaria: Drug Information.*

# COMPREHENSIVE YELLOW FEVER VACCINATION REQUIREMENTS

Yellow fever vaccine is the **only** vaccine that may be officially required for entry into certain countries. Please check the following information carefully.

**Yellow fever** is a viral disease found in parts of Africa and South America. It is transmitted to humans by a mosquito bite.

In general, if you are only traveling directly from the US to countries in Europe, North Africa, the Middle East, the Indian subcontinent, East or Southeast Asia, Australia and the South Pacific, the Caribbean, most of Central America, or temperate South America, and you are not planning additional side trips to or from other countries, CDC does not recommend and you are not required to have a yellow fever vaccination.

## REQUIREMENTS
Even though there is no risk of becoming infected while traveling in countries outside of tropical South America or sub-Saharan Africa, **certain countries require** a yellow fever vaccination. Generally a country's yellow fever vaccination policy falls into one of the following groups:
- Required for all travelers;
- Required if a traveler is coming **from** the "endemic" areas of South America or Africa – the "endemic" areas where yellow fever transmission has historically occurred;

- Required if a traveler is coming **from** areas infected with yellow fever;
- Required for special situations.

## Age Requirements

Be aware that age requirements refer to the age at which vaccination is required and can vary from country to country. For example, some countries require vaccination for persons older than six months (over 6m), while other countries may require a vaccination for travelers older than one year (over 1y). In some cases the age requirement is at the country's discretion, and vaccination could be required as young as birth (over 0). If you are traveling with infants and young children, check with embassies and consulates for their specific requirements, then consult with your doctor.

## RECOMMENDATIONS

If your travel plans include traveling to or from a South American or African country that is located in areas where yellow fever transmission has occurred ("endemic areas"), or is infected with yellow fever, then the easiest and safest thing to do is to get a yellow fever vaccination and a signed International Certificate of Vaccination.

## YELLOW FEVER VACCINE

Yellow fever vaccination, a one-dose shot, may be administered to adults and children over 9 months of age. This vaccine is only administered at designated yellow fever centers, usually your local health department. If at continued risk, a booster is needed every 10 years.

## MEDICAL REASONS NOT TO RECEIVE THE VACCINE

- **Infants under 4 months** must not be immunized;
- **Persons severely allergic to eggs** should not be given the vaccine. Generally, persons able to eat eggs or egg products can safely receive the vaccine;
- It is prudent on theoretical grounds to **avoid vaccinating pregnant women**, and for non-immunized pregnant women to postpone travel to epidemic areas until after delivery (pregnant women who must travel to high risk areas should be vaccinated);
- Persons **whose immune systems are suppressed** due to HIV infection, or those travelers undergoing treatments for cancers (leukemia, lymphoma, etc.), or receiving corticosteroids, alkylating drugs, antimetabolites, or radiation, in general should not be vaccinated unless traveling to an area of known yellow fever transmission (patients with

suppressed immune systems have a theoretical risk of encephalitis due to the yellow fever vaccine virus).

## YELLOW FEVER CERTIFICATE

After immunization, an International Certificate of Vaccination is issued and is valid 10 days after vaccination to meet entry and exit requirements for all countries. The Certificate is good for 10 years. **You must take the Certificate with you.**

## MEDICAL WAIVER

Travelers who have a medical reason not to receive the yellow fever vaccine should obtain a medical waiver. Most countries will accept a medical waiver for persons with a medical reason not to receive the vaccine (e.g. infants less than 4 months old, pregnant women, persons hypersensitive to eggs, or those with an immunosuppressed condition.) When required, CDC recommends obtaining written waivers from consular or embassy officials before departure. Follow these guidelines:

  •   A physician's letter clearly stating the medical reason not to receive the vaccine might be acceptable to some governments;

  •   It should be written on letterhead stationery and bear the stamp used by a health department or official immunization center to validate the International Certificate of Vaccination;

  •   Check embassies or consulates for specific waiver requirements.

## INSTRUCTIONS FOR THE FOLLOWING GEOGRAPHIC TABLES

Listed next to each country are the yellow fever recommendation and requirement codes, which are explained at the bottom of the pages. The explanations are listed in order of broadest requirements (those that apply to most travelers) to the narrower requirements (fewer people are likely to be in this category).

A dash (-) indicates no vaccination is required or recommended. "REQ." refers to requirement codes. "CON." refers to conditional requirements: readers are alerted to the country's special conditional requirements (see S and E below in the explanation of table codes).

On the next page, we've listed full explanations for the various codes used in the geographic tables listed in the following pages. We've also given a brief version of this summary along with each geographic table.

## CODES USED IN THE FOLLOWING TABLES

√ = *Yellow fever vaccination recommended by CDC for travelers (over 9 months) going outside urban areas.*

*1* = *Vaccination and Certificate required for all travelers. For age requirements, see instructions above.*

*E* = *Vaccination and Certificate required for travelers arriving from a yellow fever "Endemic" country. (See the box titled Yellow Fever "Endemic" countries.)*

*S* = *Special requirements/recommendations, see "Special Requirements/ Recommendations."*

*3* = *Vaccination and Certificate required for travelers arriving from a country any part of which is infected with yellow fever, as listed on the biweekly Summary of Health Information for International Travel, the "Blue Sheet," CDC Fax document 220022.*

*2* = *Vaccination and Certificate required for travelers arriving from infected areas in countries currently infected with yellow fever, as listed on the biweekly Summary of Health Information for International Travel, the "Blue Sheet," CDC Fax document 220022.*

*- = No Vaccination required.*

# CARIBBEAN & WEST INDIES

| COUNTRY | REQ. | CDC | CON. | AGE | |
|---|---|---|---|---|---|
| Antigua & Barbuda | 2 | | | over | 1y |
| Bahamas | 2 | | | over | 1y |
| Barbados | 2 | | | over | 1y |
| Bermuda (UK) | - | | | | |
| Cayman Is. (UK) | - | | | | |
| Cuba | - | | | | |
| Dominica | 2 | | | over | 1y |
| Dominican Republic | - | | | | |
| Grenada | 2 | | | over | 1y |
| Guadeloupe | 2 | | | over | 1y |
| Haiti | 2 | | | over | 0 |
| Jamaica | 2 | | | over | 1y |
| Martinique (France) | 2 | | | over | 1y |
| Montserrat (UK) | - | | | | |
| Netherlands Antilles | 2 | | | over | 6m |
| Puerto Rico (US.) | - | | | | |
| Saint Lucia | 2 | | | over | 1y |
| St Vincent & the Grenadines | 2 | | | over | 1y |
| St Kitts & Nevis | 2 | | | over | 1y |
| Trinidad & Tobago | 2 | √ | | over | 1y |
| Virgin Islands, US | - | | | | |
| Virgin Islands, UK | - | | | | |

**Summary of Codes**
√ = CDC recommended
1 = Required for all travelers
E = Required, arriving from "Endemic" country
S = Special requirements/recommendations
3 = Required, arriving from a infected country
2 = Required, arriving from a infected area
- = No Vaccination required

## CENTRAL AMERICA

| COUNTRY | REQ. | CDC | CON. | AGE | |
|---------|------|-----|------|-----|---|
| Belize | 2 | | | over | 0 |
| Costa Rica | - | | | | |
| El Salvador | 2 | | | over | 6m |
| Guatemala | 3 | | | over | 1y |
| Honduras | 2 | | | over | 0 |
| Mexico | 2 | | | over | 6m |
| Nicaragua | 2 | | | over | 1y |
| Panama | | √ | S | | |

## TEMPERATE SOUTH AMERICA

| COUNTRY | REQ. | CDC | CON. | AGE |
|---------|------|-----|------|-----|
| Argentina | | √ | S | |
| Chile | - | | | |
| Falkland Islands (UK) | - | | | |
| Uruguay | | | | |

## TROPICAL SOUTH AMERICA

| COUNTRY | REQ. | CDC | CON. | AGE | |
|---------|------|-----|------|-----|---|
| Bolivia | 2 | √ | S | over | 0 |
| Brazil | 2 | √ | S | over | 9m |
| Colombia | | √ | S | | |
| Ecuador | 2 | | √ | over | 1y |
| French Guiana | 1 | | √ | over | 1y |
| Guyana | 2 | √ | S,E | over | 0 |
| Paraguay | | √ | S | | |
| Peru | 2 | √ | S | over | 6m |
| Suriname | 2 | √ | | over | 0 |
| Venezuela | | √ | | | |

**Summary of Codes**
√ = CDC recommended
1 = Required for all travelers
E = Required, arriving from "Endemic" country
S = Special requirements/recommendations
3 = Required, arriving from a infected country
2 = Required, arriving from a infected area
- = No Vaccination required

There are also a variety of special requirements and recommendations for these regions; see the next page for details.

# SPECIAL REQUIREMENTS/RECOMMENDATIONS FOR THE AMERICAS

- **Argentina**: Risk in northeastern forest areas only.
- **Bolivia**: Bolivia recommends vaccination for all travelers from non-infected areas who are destined for risk areas such as the Departments of Beni, Chuquisaca, Cochobamba, Pando, Santa Cruz, Tarija and part of La Paz Department.
- **Brazil**: Brazil recommends vaccination for travel to rural areas in Acre, Amazonas, Goiàs, Maranhâo, Mato Grosso, Mato Grossa do Sul, Parà and Rodõnia States and the Territories of Amapà and Roraima.
- **Columbia**: Columbia recommends vaccination for travelers to the middle valley of the Magdalena River, eastern and western foothills of the Cordillera Oriental from the frontier with Ecuador to that with Venezuela, Urabá, foothills of the Sierra Nevada, eastern plains (Orinoquia) and Amozonia.
- **Guyana**: Certificate is also required for travelers from Belize, Guatemala, Honduras, and Nicaragua.
- **Paraguay**: Certificate only required for travelers leaving Paraguay destined to "Endemic" countries.
- **Panama**: Vaccination recommended for travelers who are destined for the province of Darien.
- **Peru**: Peru recommends vaccination for those who intend to visit any rural areas of the country.

## AFRICA

| COUNTRY | REQ. | CDC | CON. | AGE | |
|---|---|---|---|---|---|
| Algeria | 2 | | | over | 1y |
| Angola | 2 | √ | | over | 1y |
| Benin | 1 | √ | | over | 1y |
| Botswana | - | | | | |
| Burkina Faso | 1 | √ | | over | 1y |
| Burundi | 2 | √ | | over | 1y |
| Cameroon | 1 | √ | | over | 1y |
| Canary Islands | - | | | | |
| Cape Verde | | | | | |
| Islands | 3 | | S | over | 1y |
| Central African | | | | | |
| Republic | 1 | √ | | over | 1y |
| Chad | | √ | S | over | 1y |
| Comoros | - | | | | |
| Congo | 1 | √ | | over | 1y |
| Cote d'Ivoire | 1 | √ | | over | 1y |
| Djibouti | 2 | | | over | 1y |
| Egypt | 2 | | S,E | over | 1y |
| Equat. Guinea | 2 | √ | | over | 0 |
| Eritrea | 2 | | | over | 1y |
| Ethiopia | 2 | √ | | over | 1y |
| Gabon | 1 | √ | | over | 1y |
| Gambia | 2 | √ | E | over | 1y |
| Ghana | 1 | √ | | over | 0 |
| Guinea | 2 | √ | | over | 1y |
| Guinea-Bissau | 2 | √ | E | over | 1y |
| Kenya | 2 | √ | S | over | 1y |
| Lesotho | 2 | | | over | 0 |
| Liberia | 1 | √ | | over | 1y |
| Libyan Arab | | | | | |
| Jamahiriya | 2 | | | over | 1y |
| Madagascar | 2 | | S | over | 0 |
| Malawi | 2 | | | over | 0 |
| Mali | 1 | √ | | over | 1y |
| Mauritania | 1 | | S | over | 1y |
| Mauritius | 2 | | E | over | 1y |
| Mayotte | - | | | | |
| Morocco | - | | | | |
| Mozambique | 2 | | | over | 1y |
| Namibia | 2 | | S,E | over | 1y |
| Niger | 1 | √ | S | over | 1y |

# AFRICA

| COUNTRY | REQ. | CDC | CON. | AGE |
|---|---|---|---|---|
| Nigeria | 2 | √ | | over 1y |
| Reunion | 2 | | | over 1y |
| Rwanda | 1 | √ | | over 1y |
| Sao Tome/ | | | | |
| Principe | 1 | | | over 1y |
| Senegal | 2 | √ | E | over 0 |
| Seychelles | 2 | | S | over 1y |
| Sierra Leone | 2 | √ | | over 0 |
| Somalia | 2 | | | over 0 |
| South Africa | 3 | | E | over 0 |
| St. Helena | - | | | |
| Sudan | 2 | √ | S,E | over 1y |
| Swaziland | 2 | | | over 0 |
| Tanzania | 2 | √ | S,E | over 1y |
| Togo | 1 | √ | | over 1y |
| Tunisia | 2 | | | over 1y |
| Uganda | 2 | √ | E | over 1y |
| Zaire | 1 | √ | | over 1y |
| Zambia | - | | | |
| Zimbabwe | 2 | | | over 0 |

**Summary of Codes**
√ = CDC recommended
1 = Required for all travelers
E = Required, arriving from "Endemic" country
S = Special requirements/recommendations
3 = Required, arriving from a infected country
2 = Required, arriving from a infected area
- = No Vaccination required

There are also a variety of special requirements and recommendations for these regions; see the next page for details.

## SPECIAL REQUIREMENTS/RECOMMENDATIONS FOR AFRICA

- **Cape Verde Islands**: Certificate required from travelers coming from countries having reported cases in the last 6 years.
- **Egypt**: Add Botswana and Malawi, plus Belize, Costa Rica, Guatemala, Honduras, Nicaragua, Trinidad, and Tobago to "Endemic" list. Travelers in transit without certificate are detained in airport precincts.
- **Chad**: Chad recommends vaccination for all travelers over 1 yr. of age.
- **Kenya**: CDC currently recommends yellow fever vaccine for all travelers to Kenya.
- **Mauritania**: No certificate required if arriving from non-infected country and staying under two weeks.
- **Madagascar**: Requirement also includes transiting travelers.
- **Namibia**: Required for all unscheduled air flights. A certificate is required also from travelers arriving from countries in the endemic zones. A certificate is required also from travelers on unscheduled flights, who have transited an infected area. Children under one year of age may be subject to surveillance.
- **Niger**: Niger recommends vaccination for travelers leaving the country.
- **Seychelles**: Certificate required from travelers within the preceding 6 days transited through an endemic area.
- **Sudan**: Certificate may be required from travelers leaving Sudan.
- **Tanzania**: Risk in northwestern forest areas only.

## INDIAN SUBCONTINENT

| COUNTRY | REQ. | CDC | CON. | AGE | |
|---------|------|-----|------|-----|---|
| Afghanistan | 2 | | | over | 0 |
| Bangladesh | 3 | | S,E | over | 0 |
| Bhutan | 2 | | | over | 0 |
| India | 3 | | S,E | over | 0 |
| Maldives | 2 | | | over | 0 |
| Nepal | 2 | | | over | 0 |
| Pakistan | 3 | | S,E | over | 0 |
| Sri Lanka | 2 | | | over | 1y |

## MIDDLE EAST

| COUNTRY | REQ. | CDC | CON. | AGE | |
|---------|------|-----|------|-----|---|
| Bahrain | - | | | | |
| Cyprus | - | | | | |
| Iran | - | | | | |
| Iraq | 2 | | | | |
| Israel | - | | | | |
| Jordan | | | E | over | 0 |
| Kuwait | - | | | | |
| Lebanon | 2 | | | over | 0 |
| Oman | 2 | | | over | 0 |
| Qatar | 2 | | | over | 1y |
| Saudi Arabia | 3 | | | over | 0 |
| Syria | 2 | | | over | 0 |
| Turkey | - | | | | |
| UAE | - | | | | |
| Yemen | 2 | | | over | 1y |

## EAST ASIA

| COUNTRY | REQ. | CDC | CON. | AGE |
|---------|------|-----|------|-----|
| China | 2 | | | |
| Hong Kong | - | | | |
| Japan | - | | | |
| South Korea | - | | | |
| North Korea | - | | | |
| Macau | - | | | |
| Mongolia | - | | | |
| Taiwan | 2 | | | |

# SOUTHEAST ASIA

| COUNTRY | REQ. | CDC | CON. | AGE |
|---|---|---|---|---|
| Brunei | 2 | | E | over 1y |
| Cambodia | 2 | | | over 0 |
| Indonesia | 2 | | E | over 0 |
| Laos | 2 | | | over 0 |
| Malaysia | 2 | | E | over 1y |
| Myanmar | 2 | | S | over 0 |
| Philippines | 2 | | | over 1y |
| Singapore | 3 | | E | over 1y |
| Thailand | 2 | | E | over 1y |
| Vietnam | 2 | | | over 1y |

**Summary of Codes**
√  = CDC recommended
1  = Required for all travelers
E  = Required, arriving from "Endemic" country
S  = Special requirements/recommendations
3  = Required, arriving from a infected country
2  = Required, arriving from a infected area
-  = No Vaccination required

Below you'll find a variety of special requirements and recommendations for the regions listed on the previous page and this page:

# SPECIAL REQUIREMENTS/RECOMMENDATIONS FOR INDIAN SUBCONTINENT, MIDDLE EAST, EAST ASIA, & SOUTHEAST ASIA

- **Bangladesh**: Add Belize, Costa Rica, Guatemala, Honduras, Nicaragua, Trinidad, and Tobago to "Endemic" list. Any person (including infants) arriving by air or sea without a certificate within 6 days of departure from or transit through an infected area will be isolated up to 6 days.
- **India**: Add Trinidad and Tobago to "Endemic" list.
- **Jordan**: Endemic zones in Africa.
- **Pakistan**: Certificate is not required of infants less than 6 months of age if the mother's certificate shows she was vaccinated prior to the birth of the child.
- **Myanmar**: Certificate required from nationals and residents of Myanmar departing for infected areas.

# AUSTRALIA & SOUTH PACIFIC ISLANDS

| COUNTRY | REQ. | CDC | CON. | AGE | |
|---|---|---|---|---|---|
| Australia | 3 | | | over | 1y |
| American | | | | | |
| Samoa | 2 | | | over | 1y |
| Christmas | | | | | |
| Island | 3 | | | over | 1y |
| Cook Island | - | | | | |
| Fiji | 2 | | | over | 1y |
| Guam | - | | | | |
| Kiribati | 2 | | | over | 1y |
| Nauru | 2 | | | over | 1y |
| Marshall | | | | | |
| Islands | - | | | | |
| Micronesia | - | | | | |
| New Caledonia | 2 | | | over | 1y |
| New Zealand | - | | | | |
| Niue | 2 | | | over | 1y |
| Northern Mariana | | | | | |
| Islands | - | | | | |
| Papua New | | | | | |
| Guinea | 2 | | | over | 1y |
| Pitcairn | 2 | | | over | 1y |
| Samoa | 2 | | | over | 1y |
| Solomon | | | | | |
| Islands | 2 | | | over | 0 |
| Tokelau | - | | | | |
| Tahiti | 2 | | | over | 0 |
| Tonga | 2 | | | over | 1y |
| Tuvalu | - | | | | |
| US Trust Terr. | | | | | |
| of the Pacific | | | | | |
| Islands | - | | | | |
| Vanuatu | - | | | | |
| Wake Island | - | | | | |

# NORTH AMERICA

| COUNTRY | REQ. | CDC | CON. | AGE |
|---|---|---|---|---|
| Canada | - | | | |
| St. Pierre & Miquelon | - | | | |
| United States | - | | | |

**Summary of Codes**

√ = CDC recommended
1 = Required for all travelers
E = Required, arriving from "Endemic" country
S = Special requirements/recommendations
3 = Required, arriving from a infected country
2 = Required, arriving from a infected area
- = No Vaccination required

# WESTERN EUROPE

| COUNTRY | REQ. | CDC | CON. | AGE |
|---|---|---|---|---|
| Andorra | - | | | |
| Austria | - | | | |
| Azores | 2 | | S | over 1y |
| Belgium | - | | | |
| Denmark | - | | | |
| Faroe Islands | - | | | |
| Finland | - | | | |
| France | - | | | |
| Germany | - | | | |
| Gibraltar | - | | | |
| Greece | 2 | | | over 6m |
| Greenland | - | | | |
| Iceland | - | | | |
| Ireland | - | | | |
| Italy | - | | | |
| Liechtenstein | - | | | |
| Luxembourg | - | | | |
| Madeira | 2 | | S | over 1y |
| Malta | 2 | | S | over 9m |
| Monaco | - | | | |
| Netherlands | - | | | |
| Norway | - | | | |
| Portugal | | | S | over 1y |
| San Marino | - | | | |
| Spain | - | | | |
| Sweden | - | | | |
| Switzerland | - | | | |
| United Kingdom | - | | | |

**Summary of Codes**
√  = CDC recommended
1  = Required for all travelers
E  = Required, arriving from "Endemic" country
S  = Special requirements/recommendations
3  = Required, arriving from a infected country
2  = Required, arriving from a infected area
-  = No Vaccination required

There are also a variety of special requirements and recommendations for this region; see the next page for details.

## SPECIAL REQUIREMENTS/RECOMMENDATIONS FOR WESTERN EUROPE

- **Azores**: Except no certificate required from travelers in transit at Santa Maria.
- **Madeira**: no certificate is required from passengers in transit at Funchal and Porto Santo.
- **Malta**: Children under 9 months of age arriving from an infected area may be subject to isolation or surveillance.
- **Portugal**: Certificate required only for travelers in transit to the Azores and Madeira from an infected county. However, no certificate is required from passengers in transit at Funchal, Porto Santo, and Santa Maria.

# EASTERN EUROPE &
# THE NEW INDEPENDENT STATES OF THE
# FORMER SOVIET UNION (NIS)

| COUNTRY | REQ. | CDC | CON. | AGE |
|---|---|---|---|---|
| Albania | 2 | | | over 1y |
| Armenia | - | | | |
| Azerbaijan | - | | | |
| Belarus | - | | | |
| Bosnia/ | | | | |
| Herzegovina | - | | | |
| Bulgaria | - | | | |
| Croatia | - | | | |
| Czech Rep. | - | | | |
| Estonia | - | | | |
| Georgia | - | | | |
| Hungary | - | | | |
| Kazakhstan | - | | | |
| Kyrgyzstan | - | | | |
| Latvia | - | | | |
| Lithuania | - | | | |
| Moldova | - | | | |
| Poland | - | | | |
| Romania | - | | | |
| Russia | - | | | |
| Serbia/ | | | | |
| Montenegro | - | | | |
| Slovak Rep. | - | | | |
| Slovenia | - | | | |
| Tajikistan | - | | | |
| Turkmenistan | - | | | |
| Ukraine | - | | | |
| Uzbekistan | - | | | |

**Summary of Codes**
√  = CDC recommended
1  = Required for all travelers
E  = Required, arriving from "Endemic" country
S  = Special requirements/recommendations
3  = Required, arriving from a infected country
2  = Required, arriving from a infected area
-  = No Vaccination required

# YELLOW FEVER "ENDEMIC" COUNTRIES
*according to the World Health Organization*

**Countries in Africa**
Angola
Benin
Burkino Faso
Burundi
Cameroon
Central African Republic
Chad
Congo
Cote D'ivoire
Djibouti
Equatorial Guinea
Ethiopia
Gabon
Gambia
Ghana
Guinea
Guinea-bissau
Kenya
Liberia
Mali
Mauritania
Niger
Nigeria
Rwanda
Sao Tome & Principe
Senegal
Sierra Leone
Somalia
Sudan
Tanzania
Togo
Uganda
Zaire
Zambia

**Countries in South America**
Bolivia
Brazil
Colombia
Ecuador
French Guiana
Guyana
Panama
Peru
Suriname
Venezuela

## Appendix 3

# OTHER INSECT DISEASES

## GENERAL RECOMMENDATIONS

The diseases listed in this section are transmitted by insect bites. To reduce mosquito bites, travelers should remain in well-screened areas, use mosquito nets, and wear clothes that cover most of the body. Travelers should also take insect repellent with them to use on any exposed areas of the skin.

The most effective repellent is **DEET**, an ingredient in most insect repellents. However, insect repellents with DEET should always be used according to label directions and sparingly on children. Avoid applying high-concentration (greater than 35%) products to the skin, particularly on children. Rarely, seizures or other problems have developed after contact with DEET. Travelers should also purchase a flying insect-killing spray to use in living and sleeping areas during the evening and night.

For greater protection, clothing and bed-nets can be soaked in or sprayed with **permethrin**, which is an insect repellent licensed for use on clothing. If applied according to the directions, permethrin will repel insects from clothing for several weeks. Portable mosquito bed-nets, repellents repellents with DEET, and permethrin can be purchased in hardware or backpacking stores.

## DISEASES

### Filariasis *(Bancroftian)*

Occurs in **Central and South America, Africa, Indian Subcontinent, Asia**: a parasitic round worm infestation transmitted through the bite of mosquitoes. Once inside a host, the worm lives in the lymph vessels and tissues; blockage may cause marked enlargement of the legs or other extremities (elephantiasis). No vaccine is available.

## Leishmaniasis

Occurs in **Central and South America, Africa, Indian Subcontinent, Europe:** [cutaneous (skin), mucocutaneous (inside the mouth and nose), and visceral (kala-azar)]: Leishmaniasis is caused by a parasitic protozoan transmitted by the bite of sand flies. Symptoms include fever, weakness, swollen spleen (kala-azar), and skin sores (cutaneous leishmaniasis). No vaccine, but treatment is available.

## Onchocerciasis *(River Blindness)*

Occurs in **Central and tropical South America and Africa:** a parasitic worm infestation transmitted by the bite of black flies. Symptoms include lumps under the skin, itchy rash, or eye lesions (potential blindness). No vaccine, but treatment is available.

## American Trypanosomiasis *(CHAGAS Disease)*

Occurs in **South and Central America:** American trypanosomiasis is caused by infection with a protozoal parasite transmitted by contact with the feces of the reduviid bug (also known as cone nose or kissing bug), which infests mud, adobe, and thatch buildings. May cause fever or no symptoms during early stages. In later stages, heart disease and enlarged intestines may develop. Avoiding overnight stays in buildings infested with the reduviid bug eliminates risk. Blood transfusion may transmit this infection in some countries. No vaccine, and treatment is limited.

## African Trypanosomiasis *(Sleeping Sickness)*

Occurs in **West, Central, and East Africa:** African trypanosomiasis is caused by infection with a protozoal parasite transmitted by the bite of an infected tsetse fly. Symptoms include a boil-like sore at the site of the bite several days after the bite. Fever, headaches and severe illness follow. No vaccine is available. The main risk is for the traveler on safari in rural areas.

## Bartonellosis *(Oroya Fever)*

Occurs in **South America:** Bartonellosis is caused by infection with a rickettsia organism (an organism smaller than a bacteria) transmitted by the bite of a sand fly. Symptoms include exhaustion due to anemia, high fever, followed by wart-like eruptions on the skin. No vaccine, but treatment is available.

## Yellow Fever

Occurs in **Tropical South America and Africa**: a viral infection transmitted by mosquitoes. In South America, sporadic infections occur almost exclusively in forestry and agricultural workers who are exposed occupationally in or near forests. Symptoms include fever, jaundice (yellowing of the skin), and hemorrhaging (bleeding). A safe vaccine is available, but no treatment exists.

## Plague

Occurs in **Southeast Asia, Central Asia, South America, and Western North America**: a bacterial infection transmitted by the bite of an infected flea or sometimes through exposure to plague infected animals or their tissue. Plague can be spread from person to person. Epidemic plague is generally associated with domestic rats. Almost all of the cases reported during the decade were rural and occurred among people living in small towns, villages, or agricultural areas rather than in larger, more developed towns and cities. The bacterium may be introduced through flea bites or a cut or break in the skin during exposure to rodents or rabbits. Classic plague symptoms include a very painful, usually swollen, and often hot to the touch lymph node, fever, and extreme exhaustion. A vaccine for prevention and treatment is available.

## Relapsing Fever

Occurs in **South America, Africa, Asia, Western North America**: a bacterial infection transmitted through the bite of either lice or ticks. Symptoms include fever, headaches, vomiting, diarrhea, enlarged liver or spleen, and a rash. If untreated, the fever can recur approximately every other week. No vaccine for prevention, but treatment is available.

## Chikungunya Fever

Occurs in **Africa, Indian Subcontinent, Southeast Asia**: sporadic cases as well as large outbreaks have occurred in these areas. Chikungunya Fever is a viral infection transmitted by mosquitoes. Symptoms include fever, headache, nausea, a rash, and the abrupt onset of pain in one or more joints. Deaths rarely occur from Chikungunya Fever, but residual joint stiffness can last for weeks or months. Treatment is limited and no vaccine is available.

## Oropouche Virus Disease

Occurs in **Brazil, Panama, and Trinidad**: large outbreaks have occurred of this nonfatal viral infection transmitted by gnats or midges found in some urban areas of the Amazon Basin. Symptoms include abrupt high fever, severe headache, muscle and joint pain, nausea, and diarrhea. Treatment is limited and no vaccine is available.

### Ross River Virus *(Epidemic Polyarthritis)*
Occurs in **Australia and a few South Pacific Islands**: Ross River Virus infection is transmitted by mosquito bites. Symptoms include the abrupt onset of low-grade fever, joint pain, and a rash. After infection, a prolonged arthritis can occur, but generally the arthritis will clear up in weeks or months. Treatment is limited and no vaccine is available.

### Congo-Crimean Hemorrhagic Fever
Occurs in **Eastern Europe, Central Asia, Indian Subcontinent, and Africa**: this viral infection is transmitted by the bite of an infected tick. Symptoms include sudden onset of fever, chills, aches and pains, head-ache, and severe pain in the arms or legs. A rash may appear and internal bleeding occurs sometimes. The illness can be severe and deaths have been reported. Treatment is limited and no vaccine is available.

### Lassa Fever, Rift Valley Fever, Ebola, & Marborg Disease
Occurs in **Africa**: these diseases are caused by viruses, and although they can cause severe illness, they are not a significant health problem to most travelers. Lassa Fever transmission is associated with rats, while Rift Valley Fever is transmitted via mosquitoes. In addition, all of these viruses can be transmitted through contact with an infected person or animal. Treatment is limited and no vaccines are available.

# FOOD & WATER, & TRAVELER'S DIARRHEA

Contaminated food and drink are the major sources of stomach or intestinal illness while traveling. Intestinal problems due to poor sanitation are found in far greater numbers outside the United States and other industrialized nations.

## WATER

In areas with poor sanitation, only the following beverages may be safe to drink: boiled water, hot beverages, such as coffee or tea made with boiled water, canned or bottled carbonated beverages, beer, and wine. Ice may be made from unsafe water and should be avoided. It is safer to drink from a can or bottle of beverage than to drink from a container that was not known to be clean and dry.

However, water on the surface of a beverage can or bottle may also be contaminated. Therefore, the area of a can or bottle that will touch the mouth should be wiped clean and dry. Where water is contaminated, travelers should not brush their teeth with tap water.

### Treatment of Water

**Boiling** is the most reliable method to make water safe to drink. Bring water to a vigorous boil, then allow it to cool; do not add ice. At high altitudes allow water to boil vigorously for a few minutes or use chemical disinfectants. Adding a pinch of salt or pouring water from one container to another will improve the taste.

**Chemical disinfection** can be achieved with either iodine or chlorine, with iodine providing greater disinfection in a wider set of circumstances. For disinfection with iodine, use either tincture of iodine or tetraglycine hydroperiodide tablets, such as Globaline, Potable-Aqua and others. These disinfectants can be found in sporting goods stores and pharmacies. Read and follow the manufacturer's instructions. If the water is cloudy, strain it through a clean cloth, and double the number of disinfectant tablets added. If the water is very cold, either warm it or allow increased time for disinfectant to work.

CDC makes no recommendation as to the use of any of the portable filters on the market due to lack of independently verified results of their efficacy.

As a last resort, if no source of safe drinking is available, tap water that is uncomfortably hot to touch may be safer than cold tap water; however, many disease-causing organisms can survive the usual temperature reached by the hot water in overseas hotels, and boiling or proper disinfection is still advised.

## FOOD

Food should be selected with care. Any raw food could be contaminated, particularly in areas of poor sanitation. Foods of particular concern include: salads, uncooked vegetables and fruit, unpasteurized milk and milk products, raw meat, and shellfish. If you peel fruit yourself, it is generally safe. Food that has been cooked and is still hot is generally safe.

For infants less than 6 months of age, breast feed or give powdered commercial formula prepared with boiled water.

Some fish are not guaranteed to be safe, even when cooked, because of the presence of toxins in their flesh. Tropical reef fish, red snapper, amber jack, grouper, and sea bass can occasionally be toxic at unpredictable times if they are caught on tropical reefs rather than open ocean. The barracuda and puffer fish are often toxic, and should generally not be eaten. Highest risk areas include the islands of the West Indies, and the tropical Pacific and Indian Oceans.

## TRAVELER'S DIARRHEA

The typical symptoms of **traveler's diarrhea** (**TD**) are diarrhea, nausea, bloating, urgency and malaise. TD usually lasts from 3 to 7 days. It is rarely life threatening. Areas of high risk include the developing countries of Africa, the Middle East, and Latin America. The risk of infection varies by type of eating establishment the traveler visits – from low risk in private homes, to high risk for food from street vendors.

TD is slightly more common in young adults than in older people, with no difference between males and females. TD is usually acquired through ingestion of fecally contaminated food and water.

The best way to prevent TD is by paying meticulous attention to choice of food and beverage. CDC does not recommend use of antibiotics to prevent TD, because they can cause additional problems themselves. Bismuth subsalicylae, taken as an active ingredient of Pepto-Bismol* (2 oz. 4 times daily, or 2 tablets 4 times daily), appears to be an effective preventative agent for TD, but is not recommended for prevention of TD for periods of more than three weeks. Side effects include temporary blackening of tongue and stools, occasional nausea and constipation, and, rarely, ringing in the ears. Bismuth subsalicylate should be avoided by persons with aspirin-allergy, renal insufficiency, gout, and by those who are taking anticoagulants, probenecid, or methotrexate. It is important for the traveler to consult a physician about the use of bismuth subsalicylate, especially for children, adolescents, and pregnant women.

If you do become ill with traveler's diarrhea, it is usually self-limited and treatment requires only simple replacement of fluids and salts lost in diarrheal stools. This is best achieved by use of an oral rehydration solution such as World Health Organization Oral Rehydration Salts (ORS) solution. ORS packets are available at stores or pharmacies in almost all developing countries. ORS is prepared by adding one packet to boiled or treated water. Packet instructions should be checked carefully to ensure that the salts are added to the correct volume of water. ORS solution should be consumed or discarded within 12 hours if held at room temperature, or 24 hours if held refrigerated.

Iced drinks and noncarbonated bottled fluids made from water of uncertain quality should be avoided. Dairy products can aggravate diarrhea in some people and should be avoided.

Bismuth subsalicylate preparation (1 oz of liquid or two 262.5 mg tablets every 30 minutes for eight doses) decreases the rate of stooling and shortened the duration of illness in several studies.

Treatment was limited to 48 hours at most, with no more than 8 doses in a 24-hour period. There is concern about taking, without supervision, large amounts of bismuth and salicylate, especially in individuals who may be intolerant to salicylates, who have renal insufficiency, or who take salicylates for other reasons. Travelers should consult their physicians before using this or any other medications.

Antidiarrheals, such as Lomotil* or Immodium*, can decrease the number of diarrheal stools, but can cause complication for persons with serious infections. These drugs should not be used by anyone with a high fever or blood in their stools.

Antimicrobial drugs such as doxycycline, trimethoprim/sulfamethoxazole (Bactrim™*, Septra™*), and fluroquinolones (ciprofloxacin and norfloxacin) may shorten the length of illness. Consult your physician for prescriptions and dose schedules.

It is important for the traveler to consult a physician about treatment of diarrhea in children and infants, because some of the drugs mentioned are not recommended for them. The greatest risk for children and especially infants is dehydration. Dehydration is best prevented by use of ORS solution in addition to the infant's usual food. ORS packets are available at stores or pharmacies in almost all developing countries. ORS is prepared by adding one packet to boiled or treated water. The dehydrated child will drink ORS avidly; ORS is given *ad lib* to the child as long as the dehydration persists. The infant who vomits the ORS will usually keep it down if the ORS is offered by spoon in frequent small sips. Packet instructions should be checked carefully to ensure that the salts are added to the correct volume of water. Breast-fed infants should continue nursing on demand. For bottle-fed infants, full-strength lactose-free or lactose-reduced formulas should be administered. Older children receiving semi-solid or solid foods should continue to receive their usual diet during diarrhea.

Immediate medical attention is required for the infant with diarrhea who develops signs of moderate to severe dehydration, bloody diarrhea, fever in excess of 102° F degrees, or persistent vomiting. While medical attention is being obtained, the infant should be offered ORS.

Most episodes of TD resolve in a few days. As with all diseases, it is best to consult a physician rather than attempt self-medication, especially for pregnant women and children. Travelers should seek medical help if diarrhea is severe, bloody, or does not resolve within a few days, or if it is accompanied by fever and chills, or if the traveler is unable to keep fluids intake up and becomes dehydrated.

*The use of trade names is for identification only and does not imply an endorsement by the Public Health Service or the US Department of Health and Human Services.

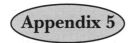

**Appendix 5**

# VACCINE RECOMMENDATIONS

## FOR TRAVELING INFANTS & CHILDREN LESS THAN 2 YEARS OF AGE

The following vaccines should be reviewed with a physician at least 10 weeks before departure to ensure the proper scheduling of the various appropriate vaccines and dosages. Additional immunization recommendations are found in *Appendix 14, Vaccine Recommendations: Health-care Provider Vaccine Information.*

### Diphtheria, Tetanus, & Pertussis Vaccine

Infants and children up to two years of age should have received 3 doses of **DTP Vaccine**. One dose of DTP affords little protection, two doses provide some protection, and three doses 70-80% protection. Parents must note that less than the three recommended doses of DTP puts a child at greater risk of infection. Travelers may wish to receive the remaining doses of the vaccine at the recommended intervals while abroad.

### Measles, Mumps, & Rubella Vaccine

The **MMR vaccine** should be administered to all children 15 months of age or older. For younger children going to areas of high risk, measles vaccine may be given earlier. Infants less than 6 months of age are protected by maternally derived antibodies.

### Polio Vaccine

Three doses of trivalent oral polio vaccine (**OPV**) is normally recommended for all infants and children by two years of age. Enhanced inactivated poliovirus vaccine (**eIPV**) is also available.

## Hepatitis B Vaccine

Hepatitis B vaccine (**HBV**) is a routine vaccination for infants and children under 2 years of age. All infants and children should be vaccinated. Vaccination normally begins at birth or age 2 months, with three doses of vaccine recommended by age 2.

## Hib Vaccine

By age 2 years, four doses of Haemophilus Influenza B (**HbCV**) vaccine are normally recommended for infants and children.

## Immune globulin

Immune globulin for protection against hepatitis A is recommended for infants and children under 2 years of age traveling to areas of the world with intermediate or high rates of hepatitis A. The new hepatitis A vaccines are not licensed for use by children less than 2 years of age.

## Typhoid Fever Vaccine

For typhoid fever, breast feeding is likely to protect infants. Careful preparation of formula and food from boiled or chlorinated water can help protect non-breast-fed infants and children up to two years of age. The old injectable killed typhoid fever vaccine is licensed for use in children as young as 6 months of age. The new injectable **ViCPS** typhoid vaccine is recommended for children 2 years of age and older when traveling to areas where there is questionable sanitation.

## Meningococcal Vaccine

For Meningococcal vaccine, effectiveness of the vaccine in children is dependent upon the child's age when the vaccine is administered. Protection may not be completely effective in children vaccinated between 3 months and 2 years, especially for vaccination before 3 months of age. The vaccine may be safely given to infants, but it may be less effective than in adults.

## Yellow Fever Vaccine

Yellow Fever vaccine should not be administered to any infant under 4 months of age, and children 4-6 months old should be considered only under very unusual circumstances. Infants 6-9 months old can receive the vaccine if they cannot avoid traveling to areas of risk and when a high level of protection against mosquito bites is not possible. Infants 9 months or older should be vaccinated as required or recommended for travel to South America or Africa.

## Cholera Vaccine

One cholera vaccine, administered parenterally with a 2-dose primary series, is currently licensed in the United States. The risk of cholera to US travelers of any age is so low that it is questionable whether vaccination is of benefit. No data are available concerning the efficacy or side effects of cholera vaccine in children less than 6 months of age. Cholera vaccine is not recommended for children less than 6 months of age. Breast-feeding is protective against cholera; careful preparation of formula and food using safe water and foodstuffs should protect non-breast-fed infants. If a child less than 6 months of age is to travel to areas requiring cholera immunization, a medical waiver should be obtained before travel. For older infants and children traveling to areas that require vaccination, a single-dose of vaccine is sufficient to satisfy local requirements.

## FOR TRAVELERS 2 YEARS OF AGE & OLDER

The following vaccines should be reviewed with a physician at least 10 weeks before departure to ensure the proper scheduling of the various appropriate vaccines and dosages.

## PRIMARY VACCINE SERIES

For travelers over 2 years of age, the following immunizations normally given during childhood should be up to date:

| Diseases | Vaccines |
|---|---|
| Measles, Mumps, and Rubella | MMR Vaccine |
| Diphtheria, Tetanus, and Pertussis | DTP or DTaP Vaccine until age 7; Td Vaccine after age 7 |
| Polio | OPV Vaccine |
| Haemophilus Influenza B | HbCV Vaccine |
| Hepatitis B | HB Vaccine |

Children over 2 should be "on schedule" with each vaccine's primary-series schedule, while adults should have completed the primary series. If you are unsure about your vaccine history, consult with your physician.

In addition, adult travelers may want to consider:
   • **Influenza (Flu) Vaccine**: recommended for adults 65 years or older, or other high risk individuals.
   • **Pneumococcal Vaccine**: recommended for adults 65 years or older, or other high risk individuals.

## BOOSTER OR ADDITIONAL DOSES

### Tetanus& Diphtheria

A booster dose of adult Tetanus-diphtheria (Td) is recommended every 10 years.

### Polio

An additional single-dose of vaccine should be received by adult travelers going to the developing countries of Africa, Asia, the Middle East, and the Indian Subcontinent, and the majority of the New Independent States of the former Soviet Union. This additional dose of polio vaccine should be received only once during the adult years. Enhanced Inactivated Polio Vaccine (**eIPV**) is recommended for this dose.

### Measles

Persons born in or after 1957 should consider a second dose of measles vaccine before traveling abroad.

### Yellow Fever Vaccine

Recommended for travel to certain parts of Africa and South America.

### Hepatitis B Vaccine

Recommended for those who will live 6 months or more in areas of developing countries where there are high rates of hepatitis B (Southeast Asia, Africa, the Middle East, the islands of the South and Western Pacific, and the Amazon region of South America), and who will have frequent close contact with the local population. Moreover, children who have not received hepatitis B vaccine by age 11-12 should receive the vaccine.

### Hepatitis A Vaccine and/or Immune Globulin (IG)

Recommended for all areas **except** Japan, Australia, New Zealand, Northern and Western Europe and North America (excluding Mexico).

### Typhoid Vaccine

Recommended for travelers spending 6 weeks or more in areas where food and water precautions are recommended – many parts of the world, especially developing countries.

### Meningococcal Vaccine

Recommended for travelers to sub-Saharan Africa, especially if close contact with the locals is anticipated, or if travel occurs during the dry season from December through June.

## Japanese Encephalitis or Tick-borne Encephalitis Vaccine
These vaccines should be considered for long-term travelers to geographic areas of risk.

## Cholera
The risk of cholera to US travelers is so low that it is questionable whether cholera vaccine is of benefit.

## SIMULTANEOUS ADMINISTRATION OF THE DIFFERENT VACCINES
Many vaccines can be safely administered simultaneously without any decrease in effectiveness. Immune Globulin – IG – may be simultaneously administered at different body locations with an inactivated vaccine such as DTP, eIPV, hepatitis A vaccine, etc. However, IG diminishes the effectiveness of certain live virus vaccines, such as MMR, if IG is given simultaneously. IG does not interfere with either OPV or yellow fever vaccine when given simultaneously. For additional information on simultaneous administration of vaccines, see *Appendix 14, Vaccine Information.*

## PREGNANCY & IMMUNIZATIONS
Women who are pregnant or who are likely to become pregnant within 3 months should not receive **MMR vaccine. Yellow fever** or **polio (OPV)** should be given to pregnant women only if there is a substantial risk of exposure. If given during pregnancy, waiting until the second or third trimester minimizes theoretical concerns over possible birth defects. For polio, **OPV** is recommended over **eIPV** when immediate protection is needed.

No convincing evidence for risk to the unborn baby from inactivated viral or bacterial vaccines or toxoids administered to pregnant women has been documented. These vaccines include: hepatitis A, hepatitis B, rabies, injectable typhoid, meningococcal, pneumococcal, Tetanus-diphtheria toxoid (Td - adult formulated), and injectable polio (eIPV). Immune globulin can be given to pregnant women. Specific information is not available on the safety of cholera vaccine during pregnancy; therefore, it is prudent on theoretical grounds to avoid vaccinating pregnant women.

All vaccines may be administered safely to children of pregnant women and to breast-feeding mothers.

## Appendix 6

# SAUDI ARABIA HAJJ REQUIREMENTS

This appendix is reprinted from the World Health Organization's *Weekly Epidemiologic Record*.

Although Saudi Arabia updates its specific requirements yearly, the following information generally applies year-after-year.

## SAUDI ARABIA
The requirements for the forthcoming Hajj season are as follows:

### Yellow Fever Vaccination
All travelers arriving from a country, any part of which is infected by yellow fever, are required to produce a valid yellow fever vaccination certificate, in accordance with the country's normal requirements. Travelers arriving in Saudi Arabia without the required certificate will be vaccinated on arrival and placed under strict surveillance for 6 days from the day of vaccination, but freedom of movement will be permitted.

### Meningococcal Vaccination
Pilgrims and "Umra" visitors are required to produce a certificate of vaccination against meningococcal meningitis issued not more than 3 years and not less than 10 days before arrival in Saudi Arabia. Pilgrims coming from countries with diseases subject to the International Health Regulations and countries where meningitis is endemic shall be examined. Suspect cases shall be isolated and contacts put under observation.

## Restrictions on Food

Foodstuffs carried by travelers, including pilgrims, shall not be allowed into the country, except for small quantities for the use of road travelers during their journey, provided they are placed in easy-to-open-and-inspect containers.

# HUMAN IMMUNODEFICIENCY VIRUS (HIV) INFECTION & ACQUIRED IMMUNODEFICIENCY SYNDROME (AIDS)

## INTERNATIONAL TRAVELERS HEALTH INFORMATION
### Background Information

Acquired Immunodeficiency Syndrome (**AIDS**) is a severe, often life-threatening, illness caused by the human immunodeficiency virus (**HIV**). The incubation period for AIDS is very long and variable, ranging from a few months to many years. Some individuals infected with HIV have remained without symptoms for more than a decade. Currently, there is no vaccine to protect against infection with HIV. Although there is no cure for AIDS, treatments for HIV infection and prevention for several opportunistic diseases that characterize AIDS are available as a result of intense international research efforts.

HIV infection and AIDS have been reported worldwide. Comprehensive surveillance systems are lacking in many countries, so that the true number of cases is likely to be far greater than the numbers officially reported from some, particularly the non-industrialized nations. The number of persons infected with HIV is estimated by the World Health Organization (WHO) to be in the range of 13-14 million worldwide. Because HIV infection and AIDS are globally distributed, the risk to international travelers is determined less by their geographic destination than by their individual behavior.

## Transmission & Prevention Information

The global epidemic of HIV infection and AIDS has raised several issues regarding HIV infection and international travel. The first is the international traveler's need for information regarding HIV transmission and how HIV infection can be prevented.

HIV infection is preventable. HIV is transmitted through sexual intercourse, needle-sharing, by medical use of blood or blood components, and during pregnancy or at birth from an infected woman. HIV is not transmitted through casual contact; air, food, or water routes; contact with inanimate objects; or through mosquitoes or other arthropod vectors. The use of any public conveyance (e.g., airplane, automobile, boat, bus, train) by persons with AIDS or HIV infection does not pose a risk of infection for the crew or other passengers.

Travelers are at risk if they:
   • have sexual intercourse (heterosexual or homosexual) with an infected person;
   • use or allow the use of contaminated, unsterilized syringes or needles for any injections or other skin-piercing procedures including acupuncture, use of illicit drugs, steroid injections, medical/dental procedures, ear piercing, or tattooing;
   • use infected blood, blood components, or clotting factor concentrates. HIV infection by this route is a rare occurrence in those countries or cities where donated blood/plasma is screened for HIV antibody.

Travelers should avoid sexual encounters with a person who is infected with HIV or whose HIV-infection status is unknown. This includes avoiding sexual activity with intravenous drug users and persons with multiple sexual partners, such as male or female prostitutes. Condoms decrease, but do not entirely eliminate, the risk of transmission of HIV. Persons who engage in vaginal, anal, or oral-genital intercourse with anyone who is infected with HIV or whose infection status is unknown should use latex condoms. Use of spermicides with condoms may provide additional protection.

In many countries, needle sharing by IV drug users is a major source of HIV transmission and other infections such as hepatitis B. Do not use drugs intravenously or share needles for any purpose.

## Safety of Blood, Blood Products, & Needles

In the United States, Australia, New Zealand, Canada, Japan, and Western European countries, the risk of infection of transfusion-associated HIV infection has been virtually eliminated through required testing of all donated blood for antibodies to HIV.

If produced in the United States according to procedures approved by the Food and Drug Administration, immune globulin preparations (such as those used for the prevention of hepatitis A and B) and hepatitis B virus vaccine undergo processes that are known to inactivate HIV and, therefore, these products should be used as indicated.

In less developed nations, there may not be a formal program for testing blood or biological products for antibody to HIV. In these countries, use of unscreened blood clotting factor concentrates or those of uncertain purity should be avoided (when medically prudent). If transfusion is necessary, the blood should be tested, if at all possible, for HIV antibodies by appropriately-trained laboratory technicians using a reliable test.

Needles used to draw blood or administer injections should be sterile, preferably of the single-use disposable type, and prepackaged in a sealed container. Insulin-dependent diabetics, hemophiliacs, or other persons who require routine or frequent injections should carry a supply of syringes, needles, and disinfectant swabs (e.g., alcohol wipes) sufficient to last their entire stay abroad.

## HIV Testing by Countries

International travelers should be aware that some countries serologically screen incoming travelers (primarily those with extended visits, such as for work or study) and deny entry to persons with AIDS and those whose test results indicate infection with HIV. Persons who are intending to visit a country for a substantial period or to work or study abroad should be informed of the policies and requirements of the particular country. This information is usually available from consular officials of individual nations.

Appendix 8

# CHOLERA INFORMATION

**Cholera** has been very rare in industrialized nations for the last 100 years; however, the disease is still common today in other parts of the world, including the Indian Subcontinent and sub-Saharan Africa. In 1991, epidemic cholera appeared in Peru and quickly spread to many countries in South and Central America. Cases have occurred in the United States among persons who traveled to cholera-affected countries or who ate contaminated food brought back by travelers.

Although cholera can be life-threatening, it is easily prevented and treated. In the United States, because of advanced water and sanitation systems, cholera is not a major threat; however, everyone, especially travelers, should be aware of how the disease is transmitted and what can be done to prevent it.

## What is Cholera?
Cholera is an acute, diarrheal illness caused by infection of the intestine with the bacterium *Vibrio cholerae*. The infection is often mild or without symptoms, but sometimes it can be severe. Approximately one in 20 infected persons has severe disease characterized by profuse watery diarrhea and vomiting, often with leg cramps. In these persons, rapid loss of body fluids leads to dehydration and shock. Without treatment, death can occur within hours.

## How Does a Person Get Cholera?
A person may get cholera by drinking water or eating food contaminated with the cholera bacterium. In an epidemic, the source of the contamination is usually the feces of an infected person. The disease can spread rapidly in areas with inadequate treatment of sewage and drinking water.

The cholera bacterium may also live in the environment in brackish rivers and coastal waters. Shellfish eaten raw or undercooked have been a source of cholera, and a few persons in the United States have contracted cholera after eating raw or undercooked shellfish from the Gulf of Mexico.

The disease is not likely to spread directly from one person to another; therefore, casual contact with an infected person is not a risk for becoming ill.

## What is the Risk for Cholera in the United States?

In the United States, cholera was prevalent in the 1800s, but has been virtually eliminated by modern sewage and water treatment systems. However, as a result of improved transportation, more persons from the United States travel to parts of Latin America, Africa, or Asia where epidemic cholera is occurring. US travelers to areas with epidemic cholera may be exposed to the cholera bacterium. In addition, travelers may bring contaminated food back to the United States; food-borne outbreaks have been caused by contaminated food, especially seafood, brought into this country by travelers.

## What Should Travelers Do to Avoid Getting Cholera?

The risk for cholera is very low for US travelers visiting areas with epidemic cholera. When simple precautions are observed, contracting the disease is unlikely.

All travelers to areas affected by cholera should observe the following recommendations:

- Drink only water that you have boiled or treated with chlorine or iodine. Other safe beverages include tea and coffee made with boiled water and carbonated, bottled beverages with no ice.
- Eat only foods that have been thoroughly cooked and are still hot.
- Eat only fruit or vegetables that you have peeled yourself.
- Avoid undercooked or raw fish or shellfish, including ceviche.
- Make sure all vegetables are cooked — avoid salads.
- Avoid foods and beverages from street vendors.
- Do not bring perishable seafood back to the United States.

**A simple rule of thumb is: "Boil it, cook it, peel it, or forget it."**

## Is a Vaccine Available to Prevent Cholera?

One cholera vaccine, administered with two injections, is currently licensed in the United States. However, it confers only brief and incomplete immunity and is not routinely recommended for travelers. There are no cholera vaccination requirements for entry or exit in any country or the United States.

## Can Cholera Be Treated?

Cholera can be simply and successfully treated by immediate replacement of the fluid and salts lost through diarrhea. Patients can be treated with oral rehydration solution, a prepackaged mixture of sugar and salts to be mixed with bottled or boiled water and drunk in large amounts. This solution is used throughout the world to treat diarrhea. Severe cases also require intravenous fluid replacement. With prompt rehydration, fewer than 1% of cholera patients die.

Antibiotics shorten the course and diminish the severity of the illness, but they are not as important as rehydration. Persons who develop severe diarrhea and vomiting in countries affected by cholera should seek medical attention promptly.

## How Long Will the Epidemic in Latin America Last?

Predicting how long the epidemic in Latin America will last is difficult. The cholera epidemic in Africa has lasted more than 20 years. In areas with inadequate sanitation, a cholera epidemic cannot be stopped immediately, and there are no signs that the epidemic in the Americas will end soon. Latin American countries that have not yet reported cases are still at risk for cholera in the coming months and years. Major improvements in sewage and water treatment systems are needed in many of these countries to prevent future epidemic cholera.

## What is the US Government Doing to Combat Cholera?

US and international public health authorities are working to enhance surveillance for cholera, investigate cholera outbreaks, and design and implement preventive measures. The **Centers for Disease Control and Prevention (CDC)** is investigating epidemic cholera wherever it occurs and is training laboratory workers in proper techniques for identification of *V. cholerae*. In addition, CDC is providing information on diagnosis, treatment, and prevention of cholera to public health officials and is educating the public about effective preventive measures.

The **Agency for International Development (AID)**, the US government agency responsible for foreign aid programs, is sponsoring some of the international government activities and is providing medical supplies to affected countries.

The **Environmental Protection Agency (EPA)** is working with water and sewage treatment operators in the United States to prevent contamination of water with the cholera bacterium.

The **Food and Drug Administration (FDA)** is testing imported and domestic shellfish for *V. cholerae* and monitoring the safety of US shellfish beds through the shellfish sanitation program.

With cooperation at the local, state, national, and international levels, assistance will be provided to countries where cholera is present, and the risk to US residents will remain small.

## Where Can a Traveler Get More Information About Cholera?

The global picture of cholera changes periodically, so travelers should seek updated information on countries of interest. Twice a month the CDC updates the list of cholera affected countries in the Fax Document: *Biweekly HIIT Summary (Blue Sheet), document number 221120*. In addition, any changes in cholera disease situation will be reflected in both the Regional Health Information and Outbreak Bulletin areas of CDC's Travel VIS/FAX Service.

## Appendix 9

# HEPATITIS A VACCINE & IMMUNE GLOBULIN (IG)

### DISEASE & VACCINE INFORMATION
### Mode of Transmission

Hepatitis A is a viral disease transmitted orally by eating or drinking contaminated food or water. This form of transmission is termed "enteric." Hepatitis A infection rates are low in developed countries in Northern and Western Europe, Australia, New Zealand, Japan and North America. However, in developing countries in Africa, Latin America, Eastern Europe, the Middle East, and most of Asia, hepatitis A infection is widespread.

In developing countries, **hepatitis A virus (HAV)** is usually acquired during childhood, most frequently without symptoms or as a mild infection. Transmission may occur by direct person-to-person contact, from contaminated water, ice, or shellfish harvested from sewage-contaminated water; or from fruits, vegetables or other foods which are eaten uncooked, but which may become contaminated during handling. Hepatitis A virus is inactivated by boiling or cooking to 185°F (85°C) for 1 minute; cooked foods may serve as vehicles for disease if they are contaminated after cooking. Adequate chlorination of water as recommended in the US will inactivate HAV.

## Risk

The risk of hepatitis A for US citizens traveling abroad varies with living conditions, length of stay, and the rate of occurrence of HAV infection in areas visited. In general, travelers to northern and western Europe, Japan, Australia, New Zealand and North America (except Mexico) are at no greater risk of infection than they would be in the US. Areas of the world with intermediate or high rates of hepatitis A do pose an increased risk for travelers.

For travelers to developing countries, risk of infection increases with duration of travel and is highest for those who live in or visit rural areas, trek in back country, or frequently eat or drink in settings of poor sanitation. Recent studies have shown that many cases of travel-related hepatitis A occur in travelers with "standard" tourist itineraries, accommodations, and food and beverage consumption behaviors. In developing countries, travelers should minimize their exposure to hepatitis A and other food and water-borne diseases by avoiding potentially contaminated water or food. Travelers should avoid drinking water (or beverages with ice) of unknown purity and eating uncooked shellfish or uncooked fruits or vegetables that are not peeled or prepared by the traveler.

## Recommendations

**Hepatitis A vaccine** or **immune globulin (IG)** is recommended for all susceptible travelers to or for persons working in countries with intermediate or high rates of HAV infection.

• Vaccination with hepatitis A vaccine is preferred for persons who plan to travel repeatedly or reside for long periods in intermediate or high risk geographic areas. For these travelers, vaccination with the age-appropriate does is recommended for children 2 years of age and older, adolescents, and adults.

• For persons of all ages desiring only short-term protection (less than three months), Immune globulin is recommended.

• Immune globulin is recommended for traveling children less than 2 years of age.

## Dosing Information

### Vaccine

There are two hepatitis A vaccines currently licensed in the United States: **HAVRIX®** (manufactured by SmithKline Beecham Biologicals), and **VAQTA®** (manufactured by Merck Co., Inc.). Both are inactivated vaccines, adsorbed to aluminum hydroxide as an adjuvant. HAVRIX® contains 2-phenoxyethanol as a preservative. The vaccines are licensed in adult and pediatric formulations, with different dosages and administration schedules, and should be administered by intramuscular injection into the deltoid muscle.

## HAVRIX®

Adults (over 18 years) should be given two doses, with the second dose administered 6 to 12 months after the first dose.

For children and adolescents (2 to 18 years), there are two dosage schedules:
   • 3 dose series: 360 EL.U. is given in a 3 dose series; the second dose 1 month after the first dose and the third dose 6-12 months after the first dose.
   • 2 dose series: 720 EL.U. is given with the second dose administered 6 to 12 months after the first dose.

Note: EL.U. refers to the amount of vaccine to be administered.

## VAQTA®

Adults (over 17 years) should be given two 50 unit (U) doses, with the second dose administered 6 months later.

The schedule for children and adolescents (ages 2 to 17) includes two doses of VAQTA®, with the second dose administered 6 to 18 months after the first dose.

Travelers can be considered to be protected four weeks after receiving the initial vaccine dose. (Author's note: Although the vaccine manufacturer specifies immunity after two weeks, CDC believes that, based on available data, four weeks are required to develop protective immunity.) Individuals who will travel to intermediate or high risk areas less than 4 weeks after the initial dose of vaccine should also be given IG (0.02 ml/kg of body weight), but at a different injection site. The vaccine series must be completed for long-term protection. Estimates derived from modeling techniques suggest that the vaccine may provide protective antibody against hepatitis A for at least 20 years.

### *Immune Globulin*
Travelers who are allergic to a vaccine component or otherwise elect not to receive vaccine should receive a single-dose of **IG** (0.02ml/kg of body weight) if travel is for less than 3 months. For prolonged travel or

residence in developing countries, a higher dosage of IG should be used (0.06 ml/kg of body weight) and should be repeated every 5 months.

## Pre-vaccination Testing

Pre-vaccination testing is not necessary for children because of their expected low prevalence of prior infection. For some adult travelers who are likely to have had hepatitis A in the past, (i.e., persons older than 40 years of age, persons born in parts of the world with intermediate or high levels of hepatitis A, or persons with clotting disorders) screening for HAV antibodies through laboratory tests before travel may be useful to determine immunity and eliminate unnecessary vaccination or IG preventive treatment.

Factors to consider before doing pre-vaccination testing include: 1) the cost of vaccination compared with the cost of laboratory testing, including the cost of an additional visit, and 2) the likelihood that pre-vaccination testing will not interfere with completion of the vaccine series.

## Safety

### Immune Globulin

IG for intramuscular administration, prepared by the **Cohn-Oncley procedure** (the standard procedure in the US) is safe from transmission of infectious agents, such as hepatitis B virus or HIV. IG produced in developing countries may not meet the standards for purity required in most developed countries. Persons in need of repeat doses in other countries should use products that meet US license requirements.

### Hepatitis A Vaccine

Experience to date indicates that hepatitis A vaccine has an excellent safety profile. CDC reports that:

"Approximately 50,000 persons have received HAVRIX® in clinical studies. No serious adverse events have been observed which could be attributed definitively to hepatitis A vaccine. In combined clinical trials, 16,252 doses of VAQTA® were given to 9,191 healthy children, adolescents, and adults. No serious vaccine-related adverse experiences were observed during clinical trials. For both vaccines, the most common side effects are mild problems that usually disappear within 1 to 2 days. These may include soreness or swelling at the site of injection, headache, tiredness and/or loss of appetite. As with any medication, there are very small risks of serious problems such as severe allergic reaction and even death that could occur after getting the vaccine. Most people who have received hepatitis A vaccine have no problems from it."

## Who Should Not Be Immunized?
*Immune Globulin*
Pregnancy is not a reason to avoid the use of IG. Serious adverse events from IG are rare.

*Hepatitis A vaccine*
Hepatitis A vaccine should not be administered to persons with a history of hypersensitivity reactions to components in the vaccine (i.e., alum or the preservative 2-phenoxyethanol). If a previously immune person receives the vaccine accidentally, the risk of adverse events are not increased. Because the vaccine is inactivated, no special precautions need to be taken in vaccination of immunocompromised persons.

Concerning women and pregnancy, CDC also states that: "The theoretical risk to the developing fetus is expected to be low when vaccine is administered to pregnant women. No animal or human data exist from which to determine the safety of hepatitis A vaccination during pregnancy. The theoretical risk of vaccination should be weighed against the risk of hepatitis A in women who may be at high risk of exposure to HAV."

314

# SUMMARY OF HEALTH INFORMATION FOR INTERNATIONAL TRAVEL

*(CDC Blue Sheet)*

## CHOLERA "INFECTED" COUNTRIES
### AFRICA
Angola
Benin
Burkina Faso
Burundi
Cameroon
Chad
Cote d'Ivoire
Djibouti
Ghana
Guinea
Guinea-Bissau
Kenya
Liberia
Malawi
Mali
Mauritania
Mozambique
Niger
Nigeria

Rwanda
Sao Tome & Principe
Sierra Leone
Somalia
Swaziland
Tanzania
Togo
Uganda
Zaire
Zambia

## SOUTHEAST ASIA
Cambodia
China
Indonesia
Laos
Myanmar
Philippines
Vietnam

## SOUTH AMERICA
Argentina
Bolivia
Brazil
Colombia
Ecuador
French Guiana
Guyana
Peru
Suriname
Venezuela

## EASTERN EUROPE
Republic of Moldova
Romania
Russian Federation
Ukraine

## CENTRAL AMERICA
Belize
Costa Rica
El Salvador

Guatemala
Honduras
Mexico
Nicaragua
Panama

## INDIAN SUBCONTINENT
Afghanistan
Bhutan
India
Iraq
Nepal

## YELLOW FEVER "INFECTED" COUNTRIES
### AFRICA
Angola: Provinces – Bengo & Luanda
Cameroon: Northern Province
Gabon: Ogooue'-Ivindo Province
Gambia: Upper River Division
Ghana: Upper West Region, Jiripa Dist.
Guinea: Siguiri Region
Mali: Kayes Region, Koulikoro Region
Nigeria: States – Anambra, Bauchi, Bendel, Benue, Cross River, Imo, Kaduna, Kwara, Lagos, Niger, Ogun, Ondo, Oyo, and Plateau.
Sudan: South of 12° North Latitidue
Zaire: North of 10° South Latitidue

### SOUTH AMERICA
Bolivia: Departments – Beni, Cochabamba, La Paz, and Santa Cruz.
Brazil: Territories – Amapa States: Amazonas, Maranhao, Para
Colombia: Departments – Antioquia, Boyaca, Cesar, Choco, Cundinamarca, Norte de Santander, Santander, and Vichada; Intendencias: Arauca, Caqueta, Casanare, Cucuta, Guaviare, Meta, and Putumayo.
Ecuador: Provinces – Morona-Santiago, Napo, Pastaza, Sucumbios, and Zamora Chinchipe.
Peru: Departments – Amazonas, Ancash, Ayacucho, Cusco, Huanuco, Junin, Loreto, Madre de Dios, Pasco, Puno, San Martin, and Ucayali.

## PLAGUE "INFECTED" COUNTRIES
Vietnam

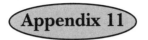

Appendix 11

# RABIES

## INTERNATIONAL TRAVELER RABIES IMMUNIZATION RECOMMENDATIONS

Rabies vaccination is not a requirement for entry into any country; however, travelers to rabies endemic countries should be warned about the risk of acquiring rabies outside the United States. Rabies is almost always transmitted by bites that introduce the virus into wounds. Dogs are the main reservoir of the disease in many developing countries, but other mammals may be involved. All animal bites should be evaluated by a medical professional.

Any animal bite or scratch should be thoroughly cleansed with a lot of soap and water. This treatment significantly reduces the risk of rabies. Also, local health authorities should be notified immediately; you may need rabies post-exposure treatment. Upon returning to the United States, contact your physician or state health department.

Pre-exposure vaccination is recommended for persons living in or visiting countries with endemic dog rabies and whose activities may place them at higher risk of rabies exposure. These include most countries in Central and South America, the Indian Subcontinent, Southeast Asia, and most of Africa. Most island countries in the Caribbean and Oceania are free of rabies. Pre-exposure vaccination greatly simplifies, but does not eliminate, the need for post-exposure treatment.

For international travelers, three 0.1 ml **intradermal (ID)** *or* three 1.0 ml **intramuscular (IM)** vaccinations are given over a 21 day period. If the intradermal (ID) dose/route is chosen, the vaccinations should be initiated early enough to allow all three does to be completed before departure. Persons who will also be taking mefloquine or chloroquine for malaria prevention should complete their three-dose ID rabies vaccinations **before** these medications are begun, as they may interfere with the antibody response to rabies vaccine. Otherwise, the intramuscular (IM) dose/route should be used. This dose/route provides a sufficient margin of safety for persons taking antimalarial drugs.

## Appendix 12

# DENGUE FEVER

**Dengue** is a mosquito-transmitted viral disease occurring chiefly in tropical and subtropical areas of the world. Epidemic transmission is usually seasonal, during and shortly after the rainy season. There are no travel restrictions for any country with regard to dengue; however many cases have been reported in travelers returning from the areas listed below.

## Risk

Generally, there is a low risk of acquiring dengue during travel to tropical areas except during periods of epidemic transmission. Dengue outbreaks have occurred with increasing frequency in recent years in most countries of the Tropics.

The risk is greatest in the Indian Subcontinent, Southeast Asia, southern China, Central and South America (except Chile, Paraguay, and Argentina), the Caribbean (except Cuba and the Cayman Islands), Mexico and Africa. There is a somewhat lower risk for travelers to Taiwan and the Pacific Islands. The Middle East and Northern Australia have a still lower risk of dengue transmission. New Zealand is free of dengue fever.

## Transmission

Dengue viruses are transmitted by *Aedes* mosquitoes, which are most active during the day. Mosquitoes that transmit dengue usually are found near human dwellings and often are present indoors. Dengue is predominant in urban centers, but may be found in rural areas; it is rarely found at elevations above 4,000 feet.

## Prevention

There is no vaccine for dengue fever; therefore, the traveler should avoid mosquito bites by using insect repellents on skin and clothing and remaining in well screened or air-conditioned areas. Travelers are advised to use aerosol insecticides indoors and use bed-nets if sleeping quarters are not screened or air-conditioned.

## Symptoms

Dengue fever is characterized by sudden onset, high fever, severe headaches, joint and muscle pain, nausea, vomiting and rash. The rash appears 3-4 days after the onset of fever. Infection is diagnosed by a special laboratory test of blood that detects the presence of the virus or antibodies. The illness may last up to 10 days, but complete recovery can take 2 to 4 weeks. Dengue is commonly confused with other infectious illnesses such as influenza, measles, malaria, typhoid, and scarlet fever. The symptoms of dengue can be treated with bed rest, fluids, and medications to reduce fever, such as acetaminophen. Aspirin should be avoided.

More severe forms of the disease – "dengue hemorrhagic fever" or "dengue shock syndrome" – are very rare among travelers. Symptoms initially are indistinguishable from dengue fever, but the illness progresses to faintness, shock, and generalized bleeding. Dengue does not produce long-term complications. See your physician if you become sick within a month of returning from travel in a tropical area. Be prepared to give your complete travel itinerary, so that the physician can evaluate the possibility that your symptoms were caused by a dengue infection.

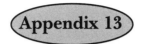

# JAPANESE ENCEPHALITIS

## DISEASE DESCRIPTION

**Japanese Encephalitis** is a mosquito-borne viral disease that occurs throughout Asia. In all areas, Japanese Encephalitis is primarily a **rural** disease.

Transmission is usually seasonal, following the prevalence of mosquitoes. In China, Korea, and other temperate areas, the transmission season extends through the summer and fall. In other subtropical and tropical regions, risk is associated with the rainy season, which varies in each country. For instance, recent epidemics have occurred in northern India, Nepal, and Sri Lanka, from October to December. However, in tropical areas, sporadic cases may occur at any time of the year.

The chance that a traveler to Asia will develop Japanese Encephalitis is probably very small. Only 12 cases among Americans traveling or working in Asia are known to have occurred since 1981. Only certain mosquito species are capable of transmitting Japanese Encephalitis. In areas infested with mosquitoes, usually only a small portion of the mosquitoes are actually infected with Japanese Encephalitis virus. Among persons who are infected by a mosquito bite, only 1 in 50 to 1 in 1,000 persons will develop an illness. The majority of infected persons develop mild symptoms or no symptoms at all. However, among persons who develop encephalitis, the consequences of the illness may be grave.

Japanese Encephalitis begins clinically as a flu-like illness with headache, fever, and often gastrointestinal symptoms. Confusion and disturbances in behavior also may occur at an early stage. The illness may progress to a serious infection of the brain (i.e., encephalitis), and in one-third of cases the illness may be fatal. Another one-third of cases survive with serious neurologic after-effects, such as paralysis or other forms of brain damage, and the remaining one-third of cases recover without further problems. After the onset of the infection, and until the illness has run its course, only supportive treatment is available. Infection in pregnant women during the first and second trimester has been associated with miscarriages.

## JAPANESE ENCEPHALITIS VACCINE

The vaccine for Japanese Encephalitis (**JE vaccine**) is currently available in the United States through most traveler's clinics. Vaccination is not recommended for all travelers to Asia. CDC recommends the vaccine only to those who work or have extensive visits during the transmission season to rural areas. The vaccine is recommended only for persons who will travel in rural areas for four weeks or more, except under special circumstances such as a known outbreak of Japanese Encephalitis.

Risk of acquiring Japanese Encephalitis is proportional to exposure to the mosquitos that breed chiefly in rural rice-growing and pig-farming regions. Therefore, risk is low among the vast majority of persons whose itineraries are limited to cities or who will travel to the countryside only for short periods. These travelers do not require the vaccine. Older persons (over 55 years old) may be at higher risk for disease after infection and should be carefully considered for vaccination if they travel in areas of risk.

The vaccine is given in three doses on days 0, 7, and 30 and protection can be expected 10 days following the last dose. A short course of vaccine can be given on days 0, 7, and 14, but this vaccination schedule is less effective than the longer course. Serious allergic side effects from the vaccine have been reported from up to 0.1% of vaccinees. These side effects can be delayed for several days after vaccination and consist of hives and dangerous swelling of the throat and mouth. Persons who have multiple allergies, especially to bee stings and various drugs, appear to be at higher risk for side effects and probably should not be vaccinated except under strict medical supervision.

Close medical supervision should be available for persons receiving the vaccine for at least 48 hours after vaccination. Fever and local reactions such as redness, swelling, and pain are reported in about 10% of those vaccinated. There is no information on the safety of this vaccine in children under age 1. The vaccine appears to be over 90% protective against the illness. A booster dose may be required three years after the primary vaccination if the traveler is still at risk for infection.

The vaccine is also available in many Asian countries and travelers needing the JE vaccine abroad are advised to contact the local US Embassy or consulate for a list of reputable clinics that may have the vaccine. In China, the vaccine may be obtained at the US Embassy and consulates in major cities, but only by citizens who will live in China for an extended period.

Because of the potential for other mosquito-borne diseases in Asia, all travelers are advised to use precautions to avoid mosquito bites. The mosquitoes that transmit Japanese Encephalitis feed chiefly outdoors during the cooler hours at dusk and at dawn. Travelers are advised to minimize outdoor exposure at these times, to wear mosquito repellents containing **DEET** as an active ingredient, and to stay in air-conditioned or well-screened rooms. Repellents containing high concentrations of DEET should be used with care on children, because of the potential for neurological side effects. Travelers to rural areas should bring a portable bed-net, which can be obtained at backpacking and army-navy surplus stores, and aerosol room insecticides to kill indoor mosquitoes. **Permethrin**, a mosquito repellent/insecticide, can be applied to clothing.

## Who Should Not Be Vaccinated?

Some people should **generally** not receive the vaccine. The CDC recommends that the vaccine **not** be administered to the following persons **unless the benefit of the vaccine clearly outweighs the risk**:

· Persons with a history of multiple allergies or hypersensitivity to components of the vaccine.

· Pregnant women, unless there is a high risk of Japanese Encephalitis during the woman's stay in Asia.

## Appendix 14

# VACCINE RECOMMENDATIONS FOR TRAVELERS

Note: This appendix is more technical than the other appendices, and is intended primarily as information for health care providers.

## DIPHTHERIA, TETANUS, PERTUSSIS (DTP) VACCINE
### PRIMARY VACCINATION
### Children 6 Weeks Through 6 Years Old
### (up to the seventh birthday)

One dose of DTP should be given IM (intramuscular) on four occasions - the first three doses at 4 to 8 week intervals, beginning when the infant is approximately 6 weeks to 2 months old; customarily, doses of vaccine are given at 2, 4, and 6 months of age. Individual circumstances may warrant giving the first three doses at 6, 10, and 14 weeks of age to provide protection as early as possible, especially during pertussis outbreaks. The fourth dose is given approximately 6-12 months after the third dose to maintain adequate immunity during the preschool years. This dose is an integral part of the primary vaccinating course. DTP containing whole cell pertussis vaccine should be used for the first three doses. For the fourth dose, a product containing **acellular pertussis vaccine (DTaP)** may be used. If a contraindication to pertussis vaccination exists, DT should be substituted for DTP.

### Children Greater Than Or Equal To 7 Years Of Age & Adults

For primary vaccination, a series of three doses of Td (Tetanus-diphtheria vaccine) should be given IM; the second dose is given 4-8 weeks after the first, and the third dose 6-12 months after the second. Td rather than DT is the preparation of choice for vaccination of all persons greater than or equal to 7 years of age because side effects from higher doses of diphtheria toxoid are more common than they are among younger children.

## Interruption Of Primary Vaccination Schedule

Interrupting the recommended schedule or delaying subsequent doses does not lead to a reduction in the level of immunity reached on completion of the primary series. Therefore, there is no need to restart a series if more than the recommended time between doses has elapsed.

## BOOSTER VACCINATION
### Children 4-6 Years Old (up to the seventh birthday)

Those who received all four primary vaccination doses before their fourth birthday should receive a fifth dose of either DTP or DTaP before entering kindergarten or elementary school. This booster dose is not necessary if the fourth dose in the primary series was given on or after the fourth birthday.

### Children Greater Than Or Equal To 7 Years Of Age & Adults

Tetanus toxoid should be given with diphtheria toxoid as Td every 10 years. If a dose is given sooner as part of wound management, the next booster is not needed until 10 years thereafter. More frequent boosters are not indicated and can result in an increased occurrence and severity of adverse reactions. One means of ensuring that persons receive boosters every 10 years is to vaccinate them routinely at mid-decade ages, i.e., 15 years old, 25 years old, 35 years old, etc.

## MEASLES, MUMPS, & RUBELLA (MMR) VACCINE
### Measles

All travelers are strongly urged to be immune to measles. The protection of young adults who have escaped measles disease and have not been vaccinated is especially important. Consideration should be given to providing one dose of measles vaccine to persons born in or after 1957, who travel abroad, who have not previously received two doses of measles vaccine, and who do not have other evidence of measles immunity, unless there is a contraindication. In general, persons can be considered immune to measles if they 1) were born before 1957, 2) have documentation of physician-diagnosed measles, 3) have laboratory evidence of measles immunity, or 4) have proof of receipt of two doses of live measles vaccine on or after the first birthday.

The age at vaccination should be lowered for those children traveling to areas where measles is endemic or epidemic. Children 12-14 months of age may receive MMR before their departure, without need for an additional dose until school entry. Children 6-11 months of age should receive a dose of monovalent measles vaccine before departure, although MMR may be used if monovalent measles vaccine is not available. Children who receive monovalent measles vaccine or MMR before their first birthday must be revaccinated with two doses of MMR vaccine at later ages. Whereas the optimal age for the first revaccination is 15 months, the age for revaccination may be as low as 12 months if the child remains in a high-risk area. The second revaccination dose would normally be given when a child enters school or according to local policy.

Because virtually all infants less than 6 months of age will be protected by maternally derived antibodies, no additional protection against measles is necessary in this age group.

## Mumps
Mumps is still endemic throughout most of the world. While vaccination against mumps is not a requirement for entry into any country, susceptible children, adolescents, and adults would benefit by being vaccinated with a single-dose of vaccine (usually as MMR), unless contraindicated, before beginning travel. Because of concern about inadequate seroconversion due to persisting maternal antibodies and because the risk of serious disease from mumps infection is relatively low, persons less than 12 months of age need not be given mumps vaccine before travel.

## Rubella
Persons without evidence of rubella immunity who travel abroad should be vaccinated against rubella because rubella is endemic and even epidemic in many countries throughout the world. No immunization or record of immunization is required for entry into the United States. However, international travelers should have immunity to rubella (i.e., laboratory evidence of rubella antibodies or verified rubella vaccination on or after the first birthday). Protection is especially important for susceptible women of child-bearing age, particularly those planning to remain out of the country for a prolonged period.

## HAEMOPHILUS INFLUENZAE TYPE B (HIB) VACCINE

The Advisory Committee on Immunization Practices (ACIP) recommends that all children receive one of the conjugate vaccines licensed for infant use – **HbOC** or **PRP-OMP** – beginning routinely at 2 months of age. Administration of the vaccine series may be initiated as early as age 6 weeks.

If HbOC is to be used, previously unvaccinated infants 2-6 months of age should receive three doses given at least two months apart. Unvaccinated infants 7-11 months of age should receive two doses of HbOC, given at least two months apart, before they are 15 months old. Unvaccinated children 12-14 months of age should receive a single-dose of vaccine before they are 15 months of age. An additional dose of HbOC should be given to all children at 15 months of age, or as soon as possible thereafter, at an interval not less than two months after the previous dose. The other two conjugate vaccines licensed for use at 15 months of age may be used for this dose, but there are no data demonstrating that a booster response will occur. An interval as short as one month between doses is acceptable, but not optimal.

If PRP-OMP is to be used, previously unvaccinated infants 2-6 months of age should receive two doses two months apart and a booster dose at 12 months of age. Children 7-11 months of age not previously vaccinated should receive two doses two months apart and a booster dose at 15 months of age (or as soon as possible thereafter), not less than two months after the previous dose. Children 12-14 months of age not previously vaccinated should receive a single-dose and a booster dose at 15 months of age (or as soon as possible thereafter), not less than two months after the previous dose. The other two conjugate vaccines licensed for use at 15 months of age may be used for this dose, but there are no data demonstrating that a booster response will occur. An interval as short as one month between doses is acceptable but not optimal.

Unvaccinated children 15-59 months of age may be given any one of the three conjugate vaccines licensed for this age group.

Ideally, the same conjugate vaccine should be used throughout the entire vaccination series. No data exist regarding the interchangeability of different conjugate vaccines with respect to safety, immunogenicity, or efficacy. However, situations will arise in which the vaccine provider does not know which type of Hib conjugate vaccine the child to be vaccinated had previously received. Under these circumstances, it is prudent for vaccine providers to ensure that at a minimum an infant 2-6 months of age receives a primary series of three doses of conjugate vaccine. These recommendations may change as data become available regarding the response to different conjugate vaccines in a primary series.

Hib Conjugate vaccines may be given simultaneously with diphtheria and tetanus toxoids and pertussis vaccine adsorbed (DTP); combined measles, mumps, rubella vaccine (MMR); oral poliovirus vaccine (OPV); or inactivated poliovirus vaccine (IPV). Any of the vaccines may be injected in the thigh, and two injections may be given in the same deltoid. All licensed conjugate vaccines should be administered by the intramuscular route. There are no known contraindications to simultaneous administration of any Hib conjugate vaccine with either pneumococcal or meningococcal vaccine.

## HEPATITIS A
### Pre-exposure Prophylaxis
The major group for whom pre-exposure prophylaxis is recommended is international travelers. The risk of hepatitis A for US citizens traveling abroad varies according to living conditions, length of stay, and the incidence of **hepatitis A virus (HAV)** infection in areas visited.

In general, travelers to Northern and Western Europe, Japan, Australia, New Zealand and North America (except Mexico) are at no greater risk of HAV infection than they would be in the US. Other areas of the world with intermediate or high rates of hepatitis A pose an increased risk for travelers. In developing countries, risk of HAV infection increases with duration of travel and is highest for those who live in or visit rural areas, trek in backcountry, or frequently eat or drink in settings of poor sanitation. Recent studies have shown that many cases of travel-related hepatitis A occur in travelers with "standard" tourist itineraries, accommodations, and food and beverage consumption behaviors. In developing countries, travelers should minimize their exposure to hepatitis A and other enteric diseases by avoiding potentially contaminated water or food. Travelers should avoid drinking water (or beverages with ice) of unknown purity and eating uncooked shellfish or uncooked fruits or vegetables they did not personally peel or prepare.

**Hepatitis A vaccine** or **immune globulin (IG)** is recommended for all susceptible persons traveling to or working in countries with intermediate or high rates of HAV infection. Vaccination of children 2 years of age and older, adolescents, and adults at the age-appropriate dose is preferred for those who plan to travel repeatedly or reside for long periods in intermediate or high risk areas. Immune globulin is recommended for travelers under 2 years of age. Immune globulin is recommended for persons 2 years of age and older who desire only short term protection.

Two hepatitis A vaccines are licensed in the United States: **HAVRIX®** (manufactured by SmithKline Beecham Biologicals) and **VAQTA®** (manufactured by Merck Co., Inc.). Both are inactivated vaccines. The vaccine should be administered by intramuscular injection into the deltoid muscle. It is licensed in adult and pediatric formulations, with different dosages and administration schedules. Travelers can be considered to be protected four weeks after receiving the initial vaccine dose. Persons who travel to intermediate or high risk areas less than 4 weeks after the initial dose of vaccine should also be given IG (0.02 ml/kg of body weight), but at a different injection site. The vaccine series must be completed for long-term protection. Estimates derived by modeling techniques suggest that vaccine may provide protective antibody against hepatitis A for at least 20 years.

For travelers who plan to use IG, a single-dose of IG (0.02 ml/kg of body weight) is recommended if travel is for less than 3 months. For prolonged travel or residence in developing countries a higher dosage of IG should be used (0.06 ml/kg of body weight) and should be repeated every 5 months. Immune globulin produced in developing countries may not meet the standards for purity required in most developed countries. Persons needing repeat doses overseas should use products that meet US license requirements.

## Pre-Vaccination Testing

Pre-vaccination testing is not indicated for children because of their expected low prevalence of prior HAV infection. For some adult travelers who are likely to have had hepatitis A in the past (i.e., persons older than 40 years of age, persons born in parts of the world with intermediate or high levels of hepatitis A, and persons with clotting disorders), screening for HAV antibodies before travel may be useful to determine susceptibility and eliminate unnecessary vaccination or IG prophylaxis. Factors to consider before doing pre-vaccination testing include: 1) the cost of vaccination compared with the cost of serologic testing, including the cost of an additional visit, and 2) the likelihood that pre-vaccination testing will not interfere with completion of the vaccine series.

## HEPATITIS B

Hepatitis B vaccine is a routine vaccination for infants and children under 2 years of age. All infants and children should be vaccinated. If a child reaches 11-12 years of age and has not received hepatitis B vaccine, vaccine should be given. For other age groups, vaccination should be considered for persons who plan to reside for more than 6 months in areas with high levels of endemic **hepatitis B virus (HBV)** infection (such as Southeast Asia, Africa, the Middle East, the islands of the South and Western Pacific, and the Amazon region of South America), and who will have close contact with the local population. Vaccination should also be considered for short-term travelers who are likely to have contact with blood from or sexual contact with residents of areas with high levels of endemic disease.

Ideally, hepatitis B vaccination of travelers should begin at least 6 months before travel to allow for completion of the full vaccine series. An alternative four-dose schedule may provide better protection during travel if the first three doses can be delivered before travel.

## POLIOMYELITIS OPV & EIPV VACCINES

Travelers to countries where **poliomyelitis** is epidemic or endemic are considered to be at increased risk of poliomyelitis and should be fully immunized. In general, travelers to developing countries should be considered to be at increased risk of exposure to wild polio virus. A primary series consists of either three doses of trivalent **oral polio vaccine (OPV)** or **enhanced potency inactivated polio vaccine (eIPV)**. Unvaccinated or partially vaccinated travelers should complete a primary series with the vaccine that is appropriate to their age and previous immunization status. Persons who have previously received a primary series may need additional doses of a polio vaccine before traveling to areas with an increased risk of exposure to wild polio virus.

## CHILDREN & ADOLESCENTS

Trivalent oral polio vaccine (OPV) is the vaccine of choice for all infants, children, and adolescents (up to 18th birthday) if there are no contraindications to vaccination with OPV. Inactivated polio vaccine (eIPV) also is available. Those who have not completed a primary series should do so. If time is a limiting factor, at least one dose of OPV or eIPV should be given. Those who have completed a primary series of OPV (or a primary series and a supplementary dose administered between 4 and 6 years of age) should be given, **once**, a single additional dose of OPV. Likewise, those who have completed a primary series of IPV (or a primary series and a supplementary dose administered between 4 and 6 years of age) should be given a dose of eIPV or OPV. The need for further supplementary doses of OPV or eIPV has not been established.

When time permits, children traveling to endemic areas should receive at least three doses of OPV at intervals of at least 6-8 weeks. Children who have received three prior doses of OPV should receive a fourth dose if at least 6 weeks have elapsed since the third dose. In the United States, the Advisory Committee on Immunization Practices (ACIP) recommends that a primary series of three doses of oral polio virus vaccine (OPV) be given beginning preferably at 6 weeks of age and at intervals of at least 6 weeks (the third dose typically is given several months after the second). However, in polio endemic areas, the Expanded Programme on Immunization of the World Health Organization recommends that a dose of OPV be given in the newborn period, e.g., at birth or before 6 weeks of age, with three additional doses (the primary series) given subsequently at 6, 10, and 14 weeks of age.

While ideally the ACIP recommendations on age and intervals between doses of OPV should be followed, if travel to an endemic country will occur before a child is 6 weeks of age, a dose of OPV should be given prior to travel. A dose of vaccine administered before 6 weeks of age should not be counted as part of the standard 3-dose primary series. If the child remains in an endemic country, the child should receive the first dose of the standard 3-dose primary series no sooner than 4 weeks after the newborn period dose and the remaining two doses of the primary series at 4-week intervals. If the child has left the endemic area, the first dose of the primary series should be given 6 weeks after the newborn period dose, the second dose 6 weeks after the first dose, and the third dose of the primary series 8-12 months after the second as is generally the practice in the United States.

Children traveling to an endemic country who have received a first or second dose of the primary series of OPV, but lack sufficient time to complete the primary series schedule as generally practiced in the United States, should receive their second and/or third doses of OPV four weeks after their prior dose(s). Children with less than a primary series at the time of departure to an endemic area and who remain in an endemic area should complete the 3-dose primary series within the endemic area with doses at 4-week intervals.

No data or recommendations are available for the use of eIPV prior to 6 weeks of age. Otherwise, a primary series of eIPV consists of three doses that can be given at the same intervals as are recommended for OPV.

## ADULTS
### Unvaccinated Or Unknown Immunization Status
For unvaccinated adults and adults whose immunization status is unknown who are traveling to countries in which the risk of exposure to wild polio virus is increased, primary immunization with eIPV is recommended whenever this is feasible; eIPV is preferred because the risk of vaccine-associated paralysis following OPV is slightly higher in adults than in children.

Three doses of eIPV should be given before departure using the normal schedule. In circumstances where time does not permit this to be done, the following alternatives are recommended:
  • If less than 3 months, but more than 2 months are available before protection is needed, three doses of eIPV should be given at least 4 weeks apart.
  • If less than 8 weeks, but more than 4 weeks are available before protection is needed, two doses of eIPV should be given at least one month apart.
  • If less than 4 weeks are available before protection is needed, a single-dose of OPV or eIPV is recommended.

In the latter two recommendations above, the remaining doses of vaccine should be given later, at the recommended intervals, if the person remains at increased risk.

### Previously Received Less Than Full Primary Series
### Of OPV Or Any Type IPV
Adults who are at increased risk of exposure to poliomyelitis and who have previously received less than a primary series of OPV and/or IPV should be given the remaining required doses with either OPV or eIPV vaccine, regardless of the interval since the last dose and of the type of vaccine previously received.

### Previously Received Complete Series With Any One
### Or Combination Polio Vaccines
Adults who are at increased risk of exposure to poliomyelitis and who have previously completed a primary series with any one or combination of polio vaccines can be given, **once**, a dose of OPV or eIPV. The need for further doses of either vaccine has not been established.

## TYPHOID FEVER

Typhoid fever is an acute bacterial disease caused by *Salmonella* typhi. The onset of typhoid fever is normally gradual, with fever, malaise, chills, headache, and generalized aches in the muscles and joints. The spleen is usually enlarged, there is generally a decrease in the number of white blood cells, and small, discrete, rose-colored spots may appear on the trunk. Diarrhea is infrequent, and vomiting, which may occur toward the end of the first week, is not usually severe. Abdominal distention and tenderness are common. Diagnosis comes from isolation of *Salmonella* typhi from the blood or stool of an infected person.

*Salmonella* typhi is transmitted by contaminated food and water and is prevalent in many developing countries of Latin America, Africa, and Asia. It became rare in the United States and other industrialized countries with the development of protected water supplies, pasteurization of milk, and improved sewage systems. The best protection is to avoid consuming food or water that may be contaminated. Travelers to developing countries can lower their risk of infection by drinking only bottled or boiled beverages and eating only cooked food. In addition, vaccines are available that afford significant protection.

Quinolones or third generation cephalosporins are the most effective drugs for treatment of acute typhoid fever when antibiotic sensitivities of the organism are not known. Trimethoprim-sulfamethoxazole, ampicillin, amoxicillin, and chloramphenicol are effective alternatives for suspect organisms.

Eliminating the bacteria from carriers is difficult. A 6-week course of ampicillin with probenecid has been successful for treating chronic carriers with normal gallbladders and without evidence of gallstones. A prolonged course of amoxicillin has been reported to be effective even in patients with gallstones or non-functioning gallbladders. Other effective treatments include trimethoprim-sulfamethoxazole and fluoroquinolones.

Removal of the gallbladder is also useful in eradicating the carrier state and may be necessary for patients whose illnesses relapse after therapy or who cannot tolerate antimicrobial therapy.

The incidence of typhoid fever in the United States fell from 1 case per 100,000 population in 1955 to 0.2 cases per 100,000 in 1966 and has since remained fairly stable. Between 1985 and 1994, 72% of cases in the United States were imported, in contrast to 33% between 1967 and 1972. The major sources of imported cases between 1985 and 1994 were people coming from Mexico and the Indian Subcontinent. The case fatality rate during this time was 0.5%.

## Typhoid Vaccines

Currently, available vaccines have been shown to protect 70%–90% of recipients. Therefore, even vaccinated travelers should be cautious in selecting their food and water.

The **oral vaccine** consists of four capsules containing live attenuated bacteria. They are taken every other day for 7 days. The entire four doses should be repeated every 5 years if the person is at continued risk. Reactions are rare and include nausea, vomiting, abdominal cramps, and skin rash.

The new injectable **ViCPS vaccine** consists of one shot. A booster dose given every two years provides continued protection for repeated exposure. Reactions are rarer than with the old, killed injectable typhoid vaccine, and include discomfort at the site of injection for 1-2 days, fever, and headache.

Either of these vaccines may be given simultaneously with other vaccines.

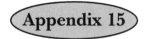

# HEPATITIS B

Note: This appendix is more technical than the other appendices, and is intended primarily as information for health care providers.

## HEPATITIS B VACCINE

Two companies have a **hepatitis B vaccine** licensed for use in the United States and both are produced by recombinant DNA technology. Three doses of vaccine are required to achieve effective immunization and will induce adequate antibody in 80–95% of persons who get three doses. The vaccination schedule most often used is three intramuscular (IM) injections, with the second and third doses administered at 1 and 6 months after the first.

Adults and older children should receive the injections in the deltoid. Infants should receive the injections in the thigh. Buttock injection should never be used.

When interchanging different hepatitis B vaccines, the immune response remains the same.

The administration of hepatitis B vaccine does not interfere with the simultaneous administration of other vaccines. Intradermal vaccination results in lower seroconversion rates and lower final titers of protective antibody and should only be used under a research protocol.

The recommended doses vary by product, recipient's age, and, for infants, by the hepatitis B surface antigen status of the mother.

## BOOSTER DOSES

Adults and children who develop adequate antibody after vaccination are completely protected against clinical infection and the carrier state for at least 10 years. Although some people may lose antibody over time, immunologic memory still persists for at least ten years and confers protection against chronic hepatitis B virus infection. Therefore, for children and adults whose immune status is normal, booster doses of vaccine are not recommended.

## INTERRUPTED SCHEDULES

If the vaccination series is interrupted after the first dose, the second dose should be administered as soon as possible. The second and third doses should be separated by an interval of at least two months.

## HCW SAFETY OF IG & VAX

Immune globulin, hepatitis B immune globulin, and hepatitis B vaccine are safe when administered to infants, children, and adults. No instance of transmission of human immunodeficiency virus, the virus that causes AIDS, or other viruses has been observed with any of these products.

All of these products can be administered during pregnancy and lactation. Only limited data are available on the safety of hepatitis B vaccine for the developing fetus. However, because the vaccine contains non-infectious hepatitis B surface antigen particles, there should be no risk to the fetus. In contrast, hepatitis B virus infection in a pregnant woman may result in severe disease for the mother and chronic infection in the newborn.

# PRESCRIPTION DRUGS FOR MALARIA

Note: This appendix is more technical than the other appendices, and is intended primarily as information for health care providers.

All travelers to areas of the world where malaria is present are advised to use the appropriate drug regimen and personal protection measures to prevent malaria. The regional chapter information provided in this book specifies both the appropriate drug regimen and personal protection measures for geographical regions and countries. The following information describes the various drugs used to prevent malaria, or in the case of Fansidar, to treat an attack of malaria when medical help is not available.

## PREVENTION
### DRUGS USED IN CHLOROQUINE-RESISTANT AREAS
**Mefloquine**

This drug is marketed in the United States under the name **Lariam**®. The adult dosage is 250 mg (one tablet) once a week. Mefloquine should be taken one week before leaving, weekly while in the malarious area, and weekly for 4 weeks after leaving the malarious area.

Minor side effects one may experience while taking mefloquine include gastrointestinal disturbances and dizziness, which tend to be mild and temporary. More serious side effects at the recommended dosage have rarely occurred.

Mefloquine should **not** be used by travelers with a:
- history of epilepsy or psychiatric disorder,
- known hypersensitivity to mefloquine.

In consultation with a physician, mefloquine may be used by pregnant women and children less than 30 pounds, when travel to an area with chloroquine-resistant malaria is unavoidable.

## Doxycycline

Travelers who cannot take mefloquine should take **doxycycline** to prevent malaria if they are traveling in a malarious area. This drug is taken every day at an adult dose of 100 mg, to begin on the day before entering the malarious area, while there, and continued for 4 weeks after leaving. If doxycycline is used, there is no need to take other preventive drugs, such as chloroquine.

Possible side effects include skin photosensitivity that may result in an exaggerated sunburn reaction. This risk can be minimized by wearing a hat and using sun block. Women who take doxycycline may develop vaginal yeast infections and should discuss this with their doctor before using doxycycline.

Doxycycline should **not** be used by:
- pregnant women during their entire pregnancy,
- children under 8 years of age, or
- travelers with a known hypersensitivity to doxycycline

## Chloroquine & Proguanil

**Chloroquine** is used to prevent malaria for travelers who cannot take mefloquine or doxycycline. Chloroquine is often marketed in the United States under the brand name **Aralen®**. The adult dosage is 500 mg (salt) once a week. This drug should be taken one week before entering a malarious area, weekly while there, and weekly for 4 weeks after leaving the malarious area.

Travelers to sub-Saharan Africa who use chloroquine should, if possible, also consider taking simultaneously, **proguanil**. The adult dose of proguanil is 200 mg/day. Proguanil is not available in the United States, but can be purchased in Canada, Europe, and many African countries.

Rare side effects to chloroquine include upset stomach, headache, dizziness, blurred vision, and itching. Generally these effects do not require the drug to be discontinued.

## DRUGS USED IN CHLOROQUINE-SENSITIVE AREAS
### Chloroquine

The drug **chloroquine** alone is used to prevent malaria for travelers going to specific geographical regions such as North Africa, the Caribbean, Temperate South America, most of Central America, and part of the Middle East. In these regions chloroquine is still effective in preventing malaria. Chloroquine is often marketed in the United States under the brand name **Aralen®**. The adult dosage is 500 mg (salt) once a week. This drug should be taken one week before entering a malarious area, weekly while there, and weekly for 4 weeks after leaving the malarious area. Rare side effects to chloroquine include upset stomach, headache, dizziness, blurred vision, and itching. Generally these effects do not require the drug to be discontinued.

## SUMMARY OF PRESCRIPTION DRUGS FOR MALARIA

| Drug | Usage | Adult Dosage | Child Dosage |
|---|---|---|---|
| Mefloquine (Lariam®) | In areas where Chloroquine-resistant malaria has been reported. | 228 mg base (250 mg salt), orally, once/week | under 15 kg: 3.6 mg/kg base (4 mg/kg salt); 15-19 kg: 1/4 tab/week; 20-30 kg: 1/2 tab/week; 31-45 kg: 3/4 tab/week; over 45 kg: 1 tablet/week |
| Doxycycline | An alternative to mefloquine. | 100 mg orally, once/day | over 8 years of age: 2 mg/kg, orally/day, maximum dose of 100 mg/day |
| Chloroquine (Aralen®) | In areas where Chloroquine-resistant malaria has not been reported. | 300 mg base (500 mg salt) orally, once/week | 5 mg/kg base (8.3 mg/kg salt) orally, once/week, maximum dose of 300 mg base |
| Proguanil (Paludrine®) (Not available in the United States) | Used simultaneously with Chloroouine as an alternative to mefloquine or Doxycycline. | 200 mg, orally, once/day, in combination with chloroquine once a week | under 2 years: 50 mg/day; 2-6 years: 100 mg/day; 7-10 years: 150 mg/day; over 10 years: 200 mg/day |
| Primaquine | Traveler must be tested before use. Post-exposure prevention for "relapsing" malaria. | 15 mg base (26.3 mg salt), orally, once/day for 14 days | 0.3 mg/kg base (0.5 mg/kg salt), orally, once/day for 14 days |

## DRUGS USED FOR TEMPORARY SELF-TREATMENT
Fansidar™

Chloroquine may not prevent malaria (in areas where there is chloroquine-resistant malaria) and travelers who use chloroquine must take additional measures. In addition to stringent personal protection measures, they should also take with them one or more treatment doses of **Fansidar™**.

*No one with a history of Sulfa allergy whould take Fansidar™.*

Each treatment dose for an adult consists of three tablets. These three tablets should be taken as a single-dose to treat any fever during the travel if professional medical care is not available within 24 hours. *Such presumptive self-treatment of a possible malaria infection is only a temporary measure*; the traveler should seek medical care as soon as possible. Travelers should continue taking the weekly dose of chloroquine after treatment with Fansidar™.

### PRESCRIPTION DRUG FOR SELF-TREATMENT OF MALARIA

| Drug | Usage | Adult Dosage | Child Dosage |
|---|---|---|---|
| Pyrimethamine-sulfadoxine (Fansidar®) | For treatment only. If using Chloroquine in a Chloroquine-resistant area, a self-dose of Fansidar™ should be carried during travel. | 3 tablets (75 mg pyrimethamine and 1,500 mg sulfadoxine), orally, as a single-dose. | 5-10 kg: 1/2 tablet 11-20 kg: 1 tablet 21-30 kg: 1 1/2 tablets 31-45 kg: 2 tablets over 45 kg: 3 tablets |

**NOTE**: An overdosage of antimalarial drugs can be fatal. The medicine should be stored in childproof containers and placed out of the reach of children.

## PREVENTING MOSQUITO BITES
In addition to taking drugs to prevent malaria, travelers also need to take measures to reduce exposure to malaria-carrying mosquitoes, which bite during the evening and night. To reduce mosquito bites, travelers should remain in well-screened areas, use mosquito nets, and wear clothes that cover most of the body. Travelers should also take insect repellent with them to use on any exposed areas of the skin.

The most effective repellent is **DEET** (N,N-diethyl meta-toluamide), an ingredient in most insect repellents. Insect repellents containing DEET should always be used according to label directions and sparingly on children. Adults should use 30-35% DEET on exposed areas of the skin. Avoid applying higher-concentration (greater than 35%) products to the skin. Pediatric insect repellents with 6-10% DEET are available.

Rarely, toxic reactions or other problems have developed after contact with DEET. Travelers should also purchase a flying insect-killing spray to use in living and sleeping areas during the evening and night. For greater protection, clothing and bed-nets can be soaked in or sprayed with **permethrin**, which is an insect repellent licensed for use on clothing. If applied according to directions, permethrin will repel insects from clothing for several weeks. Portable mosquito bed-nets, repellents with DEET, and permethrin can be purchased in hardware, back-packing, or military surplus stores.

# INDEX

## CDC PHONE NUMBERS

*CDC now operates two services for travelers interested in obtaining up-to-the-minute worldwide health information. These phone and fax numbers are current as of press time, but may be subject to change. The numbers are:*
- *Voice Information Line, Tel. 404/332-4555*
- *Fax Information Line, Tel. 404/332-4564*

**TRAVEL NOTES**

# TRAVEL NOTES

## TRAVEL NOTES

# TRAVEL NOTES

## TRAVEL NOTES

# OPEN ROAD PUBLISHING

*Your Passport to Great Travel!*

Our books have been praised by *Travel & Leisure, Booklist, US News & World Report, Endless Vacation, L.A. Times,* and many other magazines and newspapers! Don't leave home without an Open Road travel guide to one of these great destinations:

**Austria Guide,** $15.95
**Czech & Slovak Republics Guide,** $16.95
**France Guide,** $16.95
**Holland Guide,** $15.95
**Ireland Guide,** $16.95
**Italy Guide,** $17.95
**London Guide,** $13.95
**Paris Guide,** $12.95
**Portugal Guide,** $16.95
**Rome Guide,** $13.95
**Spain Guide,** $17.95

**Bahamas Guide,** $13.95
**Belize Guide,** $14.95
**Bermuda Guide,** $14.95
**Central America Guide,** $17.95
**Costa Rica Guide,** $16.95
**Guatemala Guide,** $17.95
**Honduras & Bay Islands Guide,** $15.95
**Southern Mexico & Yucatan Guide,** $14.95
**China Guide,** $18.95
**Hong Kong & Macau Guide,** $13.95
**Vietnam Guide,** $14.95
**Israel Guide,** $16.95

**America's Most Charming Towns & Villages,** $16.95
**California Wine Country Guide,** $11.95
**Disney World & Orlando Theme Parks,** $13.95
**Florida Golf Guide,** $19.95
**Las Vegas Guide,** $12.95
**San Francisco Guide,** $14.95
**New Mexico Guide,** $14.95

*And look for our forthcoming travel guides*: Caribbean, Greek Islands, Turkey, Moscow, Prague, Japan, Philippines, Thailand, Tahiti & French Polynesia, Kenya, Egypt, Hawaii, Arizona, Texas, Boston, and America's Grand Hotels.

**PLEASE USE ORDER FORM ON NEXT PAGE**

# ORDER FORM

Name and Address: _____

_____

_____

_____ Zip Code: _____

| Quantity | Title | Price |
|----------|-------|-------|
|          |       |       |
|          |       |       |
|          |       |       |
|          |       |       |
|          |       |       |
|          |       |       |
|          |       |       |

Total Before Shipping _____

Shipping/Handling _____

**TOTAL** _____

**Orders must include price of book <u>plus</u> shipping and handling**. For shipping and handling, please add $3.00 for the first book, and $1.00 for each book thereafter.

Ask about our discounts for special order bulk purchases.

*ORDER FROM:* **OPEN ROAD PUBLISHING**
*P.O. Box 20226, Columbus Circle Station, New York, NY 10023*